Lecture Notes in Economics and Mathematical Systems

Managing Editors: M. Beckmann and H. P. Künzi

Mathematical Economics

168

Convex Analysis and Mathematical Economics

Proceedings of a Symposium, Held at the University of Tilburg, February 20, 1978

Edited by Jacobus Kriens

Springer-Verlag
Berlin Heidelberg New York 1979

Editor
Prof. J. Kriens
University of Tilburg
Department of Econometrics
Hogeschoollaan 225
5037 GC Tilburg/The Netherlands

AMS Subject Classifications (1970): 90A15

ISBN 3-540-09247-1 Springer-Verlag Berlin Heidelberg New York
ISBN 0-387-09247-1 Springer-Verlag New York Heidelberg Berlin

Printing and binding: Beltz Offsetdruck, Hemsbach/Bergstr.
2142/3140-543210

PREFACE

On February 20, 1978, the Department of Econometrics of the University of Tilburg organized a symposium on Convex Analysis and Mathematical Economics to commemorate the 50th anniversary of the University. The general theme of the anniversary celebration was "innovation" and since an important part of the departments' theoretical work is concentrated on mathematical economics, the above mentioned theme was chosen.

The scientific part of the Symposium consisted of four lectures, three of them are included in an adapted form in this volume; the fourth lecture was a mathematical one with the title "On the development of the application of convexity".

The three papers included concern recent developments in the relations between convex analysis and mathematical economics.

Dr. P.H.M. Ruys and Dr. H.N. Weddepohl (University of Tilburg) study in their paper "Economic theory and duality", the relations between optimality and equilibrium concepts in economic theory and various duality concepts in convex analysis. The models are introduced with an individual facing a decision in an optimization problem. Next, an n-person decision problem is analyzed, and the following concepts are defined: optimum, relative optimum, Nash-equilibrium, and Pareto-optimum. These concepts are shown to be closely related. Various duality operations are defined and used to give better insight into the structure, and to be applied in different economic situations. Applications are given (e.g. the theory of public goods), and generalizations are developed. The results are, finally, used and adapted for decision problems over (discrete and finite) time periods.

The title of Dr. J.J.M. Evers' (University of Technology, Twente) paper runs "The dynamics of concave input-output processes". Representing economic activities by a set $S \subset R_+^m \times R^n$ of feasible input/output combinations, and associating with each pair $(x,y) \in S$ a utility value $\mu(x;y)$, $\mu: S \to R^1$ is called an input/output process if a free disposal condition on the inputs is satisfied and, in addition, the hypograph is closed and convex. A specific property of the concept is, that, combining any number of I/O-processes in any sensible way, the logical structure is preserved. Moreover, a duality transformation is introduced, resulting into dual systems with again the same structure. Special attention is given to dynamic I/O-processes, invariant dynamic optimality and the existence of optimal trajectories.

The third paper is by Prof. Dr. R.T. Rockafellar (University of Washington, Seattle) and has a title "Convex processes and Hamiltonian dynamical systems in economics". The state x(t) of an economic model in continuous time is constrained by $\dot{x}(t) \in A(x(t))$, where A is a set-valued mapping which represents the underlying technology. If the graph of A is a convex cone, A is called a convex process. The "efficient" state trajectories x(t) can then be characterized in terms of the system $(-\dot{p}(t), \dot{x}(t)) \in \partial H(x(t), p(t))$, where H is a concave-convex function called the Hamiltonian associated with A, and p(t) is a price vector. Much can be learned by studying the behavior of this system around a relative saddlepoint of H.

Finally, I want to express may sincere thanks to all who contributed to make the symposium a success and to Mrs. Ella Broks for doing a difficult typing job excellently.

J. Kriens, editor
Tilburg University
The Netherlands

February 1979.

CONTENTS

I. ECONOMIC THEORY AND DUALITY

P.H.M. Ruys and H.N. Weddepohl

UNIVERSITY OF TILBURG, NETHERLANDS.

1. Introduction.

Convex analysis plays an important role in mathematical economics, particularly in relation to the notions of optimum and equilibrium. Also, most equilibrium definitions in economics are closely related to the (game theoretical) concept of Nash-equilibrium (see Debren [3]).

The definitions of an optimum (including Pareto optimum), and a Nash-equilibrium will be applied to concepts defined in a finite euclidean space. In this case they can be associated with convex sets separated by a hyperplane.

The vectors in the dual space which define the separating hyperplanes may be interpreted as prices in economic theory. It is the theory of duality which analyses the relation between sets, functions or correspondences, and their dual characteristics in terms of prices.

A characterization of a model or a concept in the dual space gives usually a better insight in the problem and its solution. There are, however, also direct applications of duality theory.

A classical application of duality to economics is the so called indirect utility function (see e.g. [5, p. 120]. Shephard [22] has applied duality in production theory; a survey is given by Diewert [5]. The authors have worked on duality in relation to equilibrium and other economic concepts for several years ([16], [17], [18], [19], [24], [25], [26], [27]). Some of their earlier results are included in this paper and some new applications are introduced.
A summary of results on duality is given in Appendix A.1. In Appendix A.2 the relation between this concept of duality and the one in mathematical programming, is considered.

In section 2 we introduce four optimality concepts: optimum, relative optimum, Nash-equilibrium and Pareto-optimum. The claim that these concepts are closely related is proven in section 5. These proofs are based upon the introduction of one or more fictitious agents, and upon duality operations. Both techniques will appear also in proofs of theorems in other sections.

Section 3 is devoted to duality operations on economic notions, which are used in the next sections.

Three models are given which can be considered as applications of the optimality theory outlined in section 1 or as concrete interpretations of the abstract economies defined: an economy with public goods (section 4), a competitive economy (section 5) and an intertemporal economy (section 7).

2. Abstract economies.

An abstract economy is defined by four primitive concepts: a set of agents H, a set of actions X_i, for each $i \in H$, a preference correspondence P_i, for each $i \in H$, and a constraint set $\bar{C}_i$ or a constraint correspondence C_i for each $i \in H$.

2.1. Optimum.

We first consider an abstract economy with a single agent that has a constraint set $\bar{C}$, and denote it by $\mathcal{E}_0$:

$$\mathcal{E}_0 := (X,\ P:X \rightrightarrows X,\ \bar{C}).$$

The set of actions X is a subset of the finite euclidean space R^n. It can be interpreted as a consumption set if the agent is a consumer who considers all conceivable consumption bundles. The preference correspondence $P:X \rightrightarrows X$ represents a strong preference relation on X. The set $P(x)$ consists of all actions in X that are better than x. For a strong preference relation it is assumed that $x \notin P(x)$, i.e. P is irreflexive. If preferences are given by a weak correspondence R (which is also reflexive), a strong preference correspondence P can be derived from it by defining $P(x) := R(x) \setminus R^{-1}(x)$ which is the set of elements in $R(x)$ that are not a member of $R^{-1}(x)$. The constraint set $\bar{C} \subset R^n$ represents a feasibility constraint on actions: in choosing an action from X, the agent is constrained to remain in $\bar{C} \cap X$. It may be noticed that in the definition of $\mathcal{E}_0$, $\bar{C}$ may without loss of generality be replaced by $\bar{C} \cap X$. In the applications below it is however more convenient to allow for constraints that are not a-priori in X.

<u>Definition 2.1.</u> Given the abstract economy $\mathcal{E}_0$, an action x is called an <u>optimum</u> if it is:

(i) feasible : $x \in X \cap \bar{C}$;
(ii) maximal : $P(x) \cap \bar{C} = \emptyset$.

A simple example of an abstract economy $\mathcal{E}_0$ is given by the following Linear Programming problem:

maximize $a.x$
subject to: $b_k.x \leqq c_k$, $k=1,\dots,m$; $x \geqq 0$.

Then $\mathcal{E}_0$ is defined by:

$$X := R^n_+;$$

$$P(x) := \{y \in X \mid a.y > a.x\};$$

$$\bar{C} := \{x \in R^n \mid b_k.x \leqq c_k,\ k=1,\dots,m\}.$$

An optimal action $\hat{x}$ in $\mathcal{E}_0$ is evidently a solution of the L.P.-problem.

Necessary conditions for the existence of an optimum in $\mathcal{E}_0$ are given by the following theorem, due to Ky Fan [6]:

<u>Theorem 2.2:</u> Let $\mathcal{E}_0 := (X,\ P: X \rightrightarrows X,\ \bar{C})$ be such that:
(i) $X \cap \bar{C}$ is compact, convex and nonempty;
(ii) P han an open graph in $X \times X$, and $x \notin \text{Conv } P(x)$;
then there exists an optimum $\hat{x}$.
If also:
(iii) $x \in \text{Cl } P(x)$, for all $x \in X \cap \bar{C}$,
then $\hat{x} \in \text{Bnd } \bar{C}$.

<u>Proof:</u>
Define $\mathring{P}(x) := \text{Conv } P(x)$. Then $\mathring{P}$ also has an open graph, and $x \notin \mathring{P}(x)$. Clearly, $\mathring{P}(x) \cap \bar{C} = \emptyset$ implies $P(x) \cap \bar{C} = \emptyset$. Suppose that there does not exist an optimum with respect to $\mathring{P}$, then $F(x) := \mathring{P}(x) \cap \bar{C}$ is non-empty for all $x \in X \cap \bar{C}$. Since F is lower hemi continuous in $X \cap \bar{C}$, and convex-valued, there exists a continuous selection $f: (X \cap \bar{C}) \to (X \cap \bar{C})$ in

$F:(X \cap \bar{C}) \rightrightarrows (X \cap \bar{C})$, according to Micheal [11]. Brouwer's fixed-point theorem then implies that there exists an action $x=f(x) \in F(x)$. This contradicts $x \notin \mathring{P}(x)$.
Suppose further that $\hat{x} \in \text{Cl } P(\hat{x})$ and $\hat{x} \in \text{Int } \bar{C}$. Then $P(\hat{x}) \cap \bar{C} \neq \emptyset$, and $\hat{x}$ cannot be an optimum. □

Condition (ii) above requires that the graph of the correspondence P, i.e. $\{(x,y) \in X \times X | y \in P(x)\}$, is open relative to $X \times X$, and that the convex hull of P(x) does not contain x. Condition (iii) is called local non-satiation; it requires that any neighbourhood of x contains a better element and it implies that the restrictions given by the constraint set are actually active (or binding) at an optimum $\hat{x}$. In this case, $\hat{x} \in \text{Cl } P(\hat{x}) \cap \bar{C}$, (and $P(\hat{x}) \cap \bar{C} = \emptyset$).
From condition (ii) it follows that $\text{Conv } P(\hat{x}) \cap \bar{Y} = \emptyset$, which is necessary and sufficient for the existence of a hyperplane

$$H(p,\alpha) := \{y \in R^n | p.y = \alpha\}$$

separating the sets $P(\hat{x})$ and $\bar{C}$, and containing the optimum $\hat{x}$. The theory of duality (which is further studied in section 3 and the Appendix A.1) is based on this property of an optimum.

2.2. Relative optimum.

Next we consider the abstract economy with a single agent that faces a constraint correspondence instead of a constraint set, and denote this economy by $\mathcal{E}_R$:

$$\mathcal{E}_R := \{X, P: X \rightrightarrows X, C: X \rightrightarrows R^n\}.$$

The constraint correspondence $C: X \rightrightarrows R^n$ determines the constraint set C(x) which the agent faces if he is considering the action $x \in X$. Clearly the considered action x is feasible if and only if $x \in C(x) \cap X$. C(x) may depend on x.

Definition 2.3: Given the abstract economy $\mathcal{E}_R$, an action x is said to be a relative optimum[1)] in $\mathcal{E}_R$, if it is:

(i) feasible: $x \in X \cap C(x)$;

(ii) maximal : $P(x) \cap C(x) = \emptyset$.

---

1) See Borglin and Keiding [2] where such an action is called an equilibrium choice.

An example of an abstract economy $\mathcal{E}_R$ will be given in section 7.4., where a dynamic economy with consumption is defined. In the example the constraint set (i.e. the set of current consumption possibilities) is dependent on current consumption via future consumption and investment programs.
Another example of a relative optimum is a local optimum, in which case the constraint correspondence is defined by $C(x) := N(x) \cap \bar{C}$, with $N(x)$ being some closed neighbourhood of x and $\bar{C}$ being a constraint set.

It is evident that a relative optimum is a more general and weaker concept than an optimum, since an optimum in $\mathcal{E}_0$ is always a relative optimum in $\mathcal{E}_R$, with $C(x) = \bar{C}$. Conversely, a relative optimum in $\mathcal{E}_R$ is not necessarily an optimum in $\mathcal{E}_0$, with $\bar{C}$ defined by $\bar{C} := \{x \mid x \in C(x)\}$. Necessary conditions for the existence of a relative optimum can be deduced from theorem 2, which deals with a more general economy.

2.3. Nash-equilibrium.

Consider the abstract economy with a finite set of agents, $H := \{1,...,h\}$. Each agent $i \in H$ has its own action set X_i in R^{n_i}. The collective action set X is defined by:

$$X := X_1 \times X_2 \times \ldots \times X_h \subset R^n, \text{ with } n := \Sigma n_i.$$

Each agent $i \in H$ has a preference correspondence $P_i\colon X \rightrightarrows X_i$, associating with some $x =: (x_i,x_{-i}) \in X$, a set of actions $P_i(x_i,x_{-i}) := P_i(x) \subset X_i$, which the agent considers to be better than action x_i, given the actions x_{-i} of the other agents, i.e. $x_{-i} := (x_1,x_2,\ldots,x_{i-1},x_{i+1},\ldots,x_h)$. Further each agent $i \in H$ has a constraint correspondence $C_i : X \rightrightarrows R^{n_i}$, associating with some $x =: (x_i,x_{-i}) \in X$, a set of actions $C_i(x) \subset R^{n_i}$ that are feasible for agent i, given the actions (x_i,x_{-i}) of all agents (and notably of course the actions x_{-i} of other agents). This economy is called an abstract economy with h agents and constraint correspondences, and denoted by $\mathcal{E}_N$:

$$\mathcal{E}_N := \{H, X_i, P_i : X \rightrightarrows X_i, C_i\colon X \rightrightarrows R^{n_i}\}$$

Definition 2.4. Given the abstract economy $\mathcal{E}_N$ with h agents, an action $x \in R^n$ is said to be a Nash-equilibrium in $\mathcal{E}_N$, if it is:

(i) feasible for all agents: $x_i \in C_i(x) \cap X_i$, $\forall\, i \in H$;

(ii) maximal for all agents: $P_i(x) \cap C_i(x) = \emptyset$, $\forall\, i \in H$.

A Nash-equilibrium is a concept from game theory, describing the situation in which no agent can improve upon an individual action, given the actions of the other agents.

Obviously a Nash-equilibrium coincides with a relative optimum if $\mathcal{E}_N$ is an abstract economy with a single agent.

The following theorem gives necessary conditions for the existence of a Nash-equilibrium. We first give the following definitions.

Given X and $C_i: X \rightrightarrows R^{n_i}$, then $B_i: X \rightrightarrows X_i$ and $A_i \subset X_i$ are defined by:

$$B_i(x) := C_i(x) \cap X_i,$$

(2.5)

$$A_i := \{x_i \in X_i \mid \exists\, y \in X : x_i \in B_i(y)\}$$

<u>Theorem 2.6.</u> (Sonnenschein and Shafer): Let $\mathcal{E}_N := \{H, X_i, P_i: X \rightrightarrows X_i, C_i : X \rightrightarrows R^{n_i}\}$, be such that:

(i) A_i is compact and non-empty for each i;

(ii) $B_i(x)$ is compact, convex and non-empty for all $x \in X$ and all $i \in H$

(iii) B_i is a continuous correspondence for all i;

(iv) $x_i \notin \text{Conv}\, P_i(x)$, for all $i \in H$ and $x \in X$;

(v) P_i has an open graph, for all $i \in H$;

then there exists a Nash-equilibrium $\hat{x}$ in $\mathcal{E}_N$.

If also:

(vi) $x_i \in \text{Cl}\, P_i(x)$, for all $i \in H$ and $x \in X$,

then $\hat{x}$ is on the boundary of $C_i(\hat{x})$: $\hat{x}_i \in \text{Bnd}\, C_i(\hat{x})$, for all i.

<u>Proof:</u>[1)]

Let $\mathring{A}_i := \text{Conv}\, A_i$, $\mathring{A} := \Pi \mathring{A}_i$ and $\mathring{P}(x) := \text{Conv}\, P_i(x)$. Define a correspondence $F_i: \mathring{A} \rightrightarrows \mathring{A}_i$ by:

$$F_i(x) := \mathring{P}_i(x) \cap B_i(x).$$

Let $Z_i := \{x \in \mathring{A} \mid F_i(x) \neq \emptyset\}$. Since $\mathring{P}_i$ and B_i are l.h.c., Z_i is an open set. The correspondence $F_i: Z_i \rightrightarrows \mathring{A}_i$ is l.h.c. and therefore contains a continuous selection $f_i: Z_i \rightarrow \mathring{A}_i$ with $f_i(x) \in F_i(x)$. Define $G_i: \mathring{A} \rightrightarrows \mathring{A}_i$ by:

---

1) Shafer and Sonnenschein [21] give another proof. The idea of this proof has been borrowed from Gale and Mas Collel [8] . A generalization of the theorem is given by J. Greenberg [9] .

$$G_i(x) := \begin{cases} f_i(x) & \text{if } x \in Z_i \\ B_i(x) & \text{if } x \notin Z_i. \end{cases}$$

$G := \prod_I G_i$, is an uhc correspondence from $\mathring{A}$ into itself and satisfies Kakutani's conditions for the existence of a fixed point, $x \in G(x)$. This point is a Nash-equilibrium, because by definition is $x_i \in B_i(x)$ and $x \notin Z_i$. For, if $x \in Z_i$, then $x_i \in F_i(x) = \mathring{P}_i(x) \cap B_i(x)$, which contradicts the irreflexivity of $\mathring{P}_i$.
Finally, suppose $x \in \text{Cl } P_i(x)$ and $x \in \text{Int } B_i(x)$, then $\mathring{P}_i(x) \cap B_i(x) \neq \emptyset$, contradicting condition (ii) of definition 2.4. □

By definition 2.4 it is true that in a Nash-equilibrium $\text{Conv } P_i(x) \cap B_i(x) = \emptyset$. This implies that both sets can be separated by a hyperplane $H(p_i,\alpha_i)$ for some $p_i \in R^{n_i}$ and $\alpha_i \in R$.

2.4. Pareto-optimum.

Consider an abstract economy with a finite set of agents H. Now, unlike the situation in the preceding section, all agents have the same action set $X \subset R^n$ and they will have to make a collective decision on the choice of a collective action from X. Each agent has his own preference correspondence P_i on X. There is a collective constraint set $\bar{C} \subset R^n$. Denote this economy by $\&_P$, where:

$$\&_P := \{H, X, P_i: X \rightrightarrows X, \bar{C}\}$$

Definition 2.7. Given the abstract economy $\&_P$ an action $x \in X$ is a (strong) Pareto optimum if:
(i) $x \in \bar{C} \cap X$;
(ii) there exists no $y \in \bar{C}$, such that $y \in P_i(x)$, for all $i \in H$.

A strong Pareto optimum in $\&_P$ is thus an action $x \in X$, which is
(i) feasible: $x \in \bar{C} \cap X$;
(ii) maximal : $\bigcap_i P_i(x) \cap \bar{C} = \emptyset$.

A Pareto optimum in $\&_P$ is also an optimum in the economy $\&_0 := \{X, P: X \rightrightarrows X, \bar{C}\}$ with a single agent, as considered in section 2.1, where the preference correspondence P is defined by:

$$P(x) := \bigcap_i P_i(x).$$

Hence sufficient conditions for existence may be derived from theorem 2.2.

It may be noticed that a <u>weak Pareto optimum</u> in $\mathcal{E}_P$ is said to be an action $x \in \bar{C} \cap X$ such that no $y \in \bar{C} \cap X$ exists, satisfying $y \notin P_i^{-1}(x)$ for all i and $y \in P_i(x)$, for at least one i.

2.5. Relative Pareto optimum.

Consider an abstract economy with a finite set of agents H, with a collective action set $X \subset R^n$ and with preference correspondences $P_i: X \twoheadrightarrow X$, as in section 2.4, but where there is a (collective) constraint correspondence $C: X \twoheadrightarrow R^n$. This economy is denoted by

$$\mathcal{E}_{RP} := \{H, X, P_i: X \twoheadrightarrow X, C: X \twoheadrightarrow X\}.$$

<u>Definition 2.8:</u> A <u>relative Pareto optimum</u> in $\mathcal{E}_{RP}$ is an action $x \in X$, such that it is:

(i) feasible: $x \in C(x) \cap X$;

(ii) maximal : $\cap P_i(x) \cap C(x) = \emptyset$.

(ii) requires that no $y \in C(x) \cap X$ exists such that $y \in P_i(x)$ for all i, similar to the condition for a Pareto optimum.

Clearly a relative Pareto optimum in $\mathcal{E}_{RP}$ is a relative optimum in an economy $\mathcal{E}_R$, derived from $\mathcal{E}_{RP}$, where:

$$\mathcal{E}_R = \{X, P: X \twoheadrightarrow X, C: X \twoheadrightarrow X\}$$

and

$$P(x) := \cap P_i(x).$$

So sufficient conditions for existence may be derived from theorem 2.6.

2.6. Comparison of optimum- and equilibrium-concepts.

We now consider an abstract economy, where the features of the abstract economies introduced in sections 2.3., 2.4. and 2.5. are combined, so that Nash-equilibria, Pareto optima and relative Pareto optima can be defined.

The abstract economy $\mathcal{E}$ consists of the finite set H of agents. Each agent has an action set $X_i \subset R^{n_i}$ with $X := \Pi X_i \subset R^n (n = \Sigma n_i)$, a preference correspondence $P_i: X \twoheadrightarrow X$ and a constraint correspondence $C_i: X \twoheadrightarrow R^{n_i}$, hence:

$$\mathcal{E} := \{H,\ X_i,\ P_i: X \rightrightarrows X,\ C_i: X \rightrightarrows R^{n_i}\}.$$

From $\mathcal{E}$ three economies $\mathcal{E}_N$, $\mathcal{E}_P$ and $\mathcal{E}_{RP}$ may be derived. Define:

$$\hat{P}_i(x) := \{y_i \in X_i \mid (y_i, x_{-i}) \in P_i(x)\},$$

$$C(x) := \prod_i C_i(x),$$

$$\bar{C} := \{x \in R^n \mid x \in C(x)\} = \{x \in R^n \mid \forall i: x_i \in C_i(x)\}$$

Then:

$$\mathcal{E}_N := \{H,\ X_i,\ \hat{P}_i: X \rightrightarrows X_i,\ C_i: X \rightrightarrows R^{n_i}\},$$

$$\mathcal{E}_{RP} := \{H,\ X,\ P_i: X \rightrightarrows X,\ C: \hat{X} \rightrightarrows R^n,$$

$$\mathcal{E}_P := \{H,\ X,\ P_i: X \rightrightarrows X,\ \bar{C}\}.$$

A <u>Nash-equilibrium</u> in $\mathcal{E}$ is a Nash-equilibrium in the derived economy $\mathcal{E}_N$, i.e. an action x such that:

(i) $\forall i: x_i \in C_i(x) \cap X_i$

(ii) $\forall i: \hat{P}_i(x) \cap C_i(x) = \emptyset$.

A <u>Pareto optimum</u> in $\mathcal{E}$ is a Pareto optimum in $\mathcal{E}_P$, i.e. an action x, such that:

(i) $\forall i: x_i \in C_i(x) \cap X_i$

(ii) $\cap P_i(x) \cap \bar{C} \neq \emptyset$.

A <u>relative Pareto optimum</u> in $\mathcal{E}$ is a relative Pareto optimum in $\mathcal{E}_{RP}$, i.e. an action x such that:

(i) $\forall : x_i \in C_i(x) \cap X_i$

(ii) $\cap P_i(x) \cap C(x) \neq \emptyset$.

In general Nash equilibria, Pareto optima and relative Pareto optima do not coïncide.

<u>Example.</u>
An example of an "economy" in which these solution concepts do not coïncide is given by the "prisoners dilemma":

$$\mathcal{E} := \{\{1,2\},\ X,\ P_i: X \rightrightarrows X,\ C_i: X \rightrightarrows X_i\},$$

where the action space X contains the four combinations of confessing or denying, $X := \{(c,c),(c,d),(d,c),(d,d)\}$, the constraint correspondence $C_i(.) := \{c,d\}$, for both agents. Given P_1 and P_2 in the table below, the corresponding $\hat{P}_1$, $\hat{P}_2$ and P can be derived:

	P_1	P_2	$\hat{P}_1$	$\hat{P}_2$	P
(d,d)	{(c,d)}	{(d,c)}	{c}	{c}	∅
(d,c)	{(c,d),(d,d),(c,c)}	∅	{c}	∅	∅
(c,d)	∅	{(d,c),(d,d),(c,c)}	∅	{c}	∅
(c,c)	{(c,d),(d,d)}	{(d,c),(d,d)}	∅	∅	{(d,d)}

Then the action (c,c) is a Nash-equilibrium, because

$$c \in X_i \cap C_i \text{ and } \hat{P}_i(c,c) \cap C_i = \emptyset \quad , \quad i = 1,2.$$

The actions {(d,d),(c,d),(d,c)} are Pareto optima, because they all belong to $X \cap \bar{C}$ and have no better alternatives. These actions also constitute the set of relative Pareto optima, as $C(x) = \bar{C}$. □

In economic theory preferences are often assumed to be independent or separable. Preferences are said to be <u>independent</u>, when there are no external effects, which means that an action of agent j does not affect agent i with respect to his preferences (possibly it does through the constraint). Then the following condition holds:

For $(x_i,x_{-i}),(x_i,v_{-i}),(y_i,y_{-i}),(y_i,z_{-i})$ in X:

$$(y_i,y_{-i}) \in P_i(x_i,x_{-i}) \Rightarrow (y_i,z_{-i}) \in P_i(x_i,v_{-i}).$$

In this case preferences are sufficiently determined by $\tilde{P}_i: X_i \rightrightarrows X_i$ and $\hat{P}_i$ and P_i may be derived by:

$$\hat{P}_i(x) := \tilde{P}_i(x_i),$$

$$P_i(x) := \tilde{P}_i(x_i) \times X_{-i}, \text{ (for } X_{-i} = \prod_{j \neq i} X_j\text{)}.$$

<u>Separability</u> of preferences is weaker; it is defined by the following condition:

For $(x_i,x_{-i}),(y_i,x_{-i}),(x_i,x_{-i}),(y_i,y_{-i})$ in X,

$$(y_i,x_{-i}) \in P_i(x_i,x_{-i}) \Rightarrow (y_i,y_{-i}) \in P_i(x_i,y_{-i})$$

Notice that it is not required that: $(y_i,x_{-i}) \in P_i(x_i,y_{-i})$, which is implies by independence. In the case of separability we have:

$$P_i(x) = \hat{P}_i(x) \times X_{-i}$$

Remark: If preferences are defined by a utility function u_i: $X \rightarrow R$ and $P_i(x) := \{y \in X | u(y) > u(x)\}$, then
independence means: $u_i(x) = u_i(x_i)$ and
separability means that functions f,g and h exist such that: $u_i(x) = f(g(x_i),h(x_{-i}))$.

3. Introduction to duality.

A survey of duality theory will be given in the appendix. In this section we give a short introduction to dual sets and correspondences and consider some applications to optima, preferences and equilibria in abstract economies.

3.1. Duality operations.

Actions and sets of actions in the space R^n, as introduced in the preceding section, can under certain conditions be represented by points and sets in the dual space R^{n*}. R^{n*} is the space of all real-valued linear functions on R^n, and is again a finite Euclidean space, isomorphic to R^n; it is also called price space, because the points in R^{n*} can usually be interpreted as (shadow) prices or "valuations" in economics.

Representation of sets of actions by sets of prices is based on the unique relation between a hyperplane in R^n and a point in R^{n*}. Given some value $\alpha \in R$, and $p \in R^{n*}$, define:

$$H(p,\alpha) := \{x \in R^n \mid p.x = \alpha\}.$$

Such a hyperplane separates R^n into two half spaces. If the value of α is normalized to 1, then we define:

$$H(p) := H(p,1),$$

and the halfspaces

$$H_-(p) := \{x \in R^n \mid p.x \leqq 1\},$$

$$H_+(p) := \{x \in R^n \mid p.x \geqq 1\},$$

called resp. lower-, and upper-closed halfspace.

Given a set X in R^n, the dual set of X (see Def. A.1) consists of all linear functions in R^{n*} which correspond with either lower, or upper halfspaces that all contain X. Thus the lower dual set of X is defined by:

$$X_-^* := \{p \in R^{n*} \mid X \subset H_-(p)\}$$

$$= \{p \in R^{n*} \mid \forall x \in X : p.x \leqq 1\},$$

the upper dual set of X:

$$X_+^* := \{p \in R^{n*} \mid X \subset H_+(p)\}$$

$$= \{p \in R^{n*} \mid \forall x \in X : p.x \geqq 1\}.$$

These dual sets may be empty, and do not necessarily represent the primal set X completely, i.e. without loss of information. However, if X is a closed, convex and aureoled set (see Def. A.2) not containing zero, then: $X = (X_+^*)_+^*$ (see prop. A.8). Further, if X is a closed, convex set containing zero, then $X = (X_-^*)_-^*$. In these cases the duality operation on sets gives a complete characterization of the original set.

This principle can also be applied to define dual correspondences or multifunctions. Two types of dual correspondences are introduced in A.1.2 In order to relate them with economic concepts, their definitions are recalled here.

Let $F:X \rightrightarrows Y$ be a correspondence with $X \subset R^m$ and $Y \subset R^n$.

The point-dual correspondence (see Definition A.11) is a correspondence from the original set X into the dual space, $F^*:X \rightrightarrows R^{n*}$. It is obtained by taking the dual of each image F(x), i.e. $F_+^*(x) := [F(x)]_+^*$ and $F_-^*(x) := [F(x)]_-^*$.

The graph-dual correspondence (see Def. A.12) is a correspondence of a subset of R^{m*} into a subset of R^{n*}. It is obtained by taking the dual of the graph of F and then deriving the dual multifunction from this dual set:

$$F_+^{\otimes}(p) := \{q \in R^{n*} \mid (p,-q) \in [\text{Graph } (F)]_-^{*}\},$$

$$F_-^{\otimes}(p) := \{q \in R^{n*} \mid (-p,q) \in [\text{Graph } (F)]_-^{*}\}.$$

The inverse of a graph-dual correspondence is called an adjoint (see A.1.2).

3.2. Duality with respect to an optimum.

If an abstract economy as considered in section 2.1 satisfies certain assumptions, the sets and correspondences by which it is defined, can be represented in the dual space. Then also optimum and equilibrium concepts have a dual characterization.

Particulary, let in the economy $\mathcal{E}_0 := \{X, P: X \rightrightarrows X, \bar{C}\}$ of section 2.1 the following assumptions hold:

Assumptions 3.1:

(a) X is closed and convex and $0 \notin X$;

(b.1) P has an open graph, is point convex and $x \notin P(x)$, for all x;

(b.2) $0 \in \bar{C}$ and $X \cap \bar{C}$ is compact.

Then, by theorem 2.2, an optimum $\hat{x}$ exists (where $\hat{x} \in X \cap \bar{C}$ and $P(\hat{x}) \cap \bar{C} = \emptyset$). Therefore, there exists a hyperplane $H(\hat{p})$ which contains $\hat{x}$ and separates $\bar{C}$ and $P(\hat{x})$.

From property A.9 it follows that the price $\hat{p}$ which generates the separating hyperplane $H(\hat{p})$ belongs to the dual sets $P^*(\hat{x}) := [P(\hat{x})]_+^*$ and $\bar{C}^* := \bar{C}_-^*$, whereas the hyperplane $H(\hat{x}) := \{p \in R^{n*} \mid p.\hat{x} = 1\}$ separates $P^*(\hat{x})$ and $\bar{C}^*$ and contains $\hat{p}$. (See fig. 3.a). So, the hyperplane characterizing an optimum $\hat{x}$ in $\mathcal{E}_0$, is generated by a price $\hat{p}$ which itself has a position in the dual space which is similar to the position of $\hat{x}$ the action space. Therefore the economy $\mathcal{E}_0$ can also be represented by the triple:

$$(X, P^*: X \rightrightarrows R^{n*}, \bar{C}^*).$$

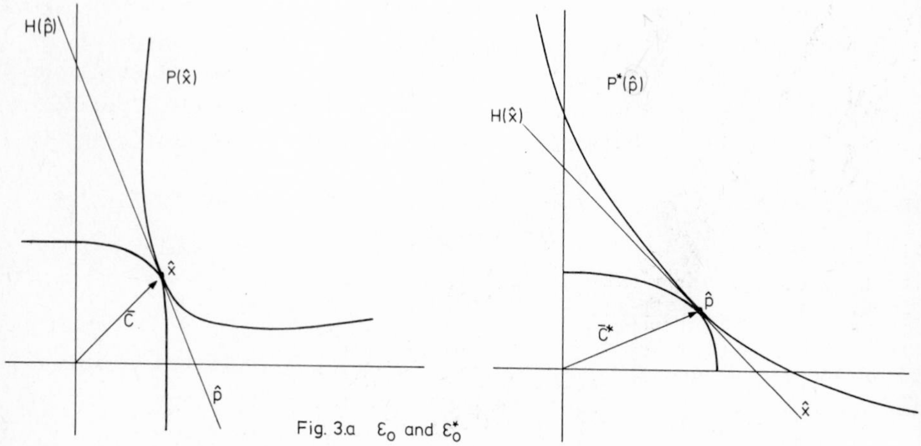

Fig. 3.a $\mathcal{E}_0$ and $\mathcal{E}_0^*$

An optimum corresponds to $(\hat{x},\hat{p})$, such that:

(i) $\hat{p} \in P^*(\hat{x}) \cap \bar{C}^*$;

(ii) $\text{Int } P^*(\hat{x}) \cap \bar{C}^* = \emptyset$.

($P^*(\hat{x})$ being a closed set!).

The capacity of duality operations to give characterizations of concepts is based on mapping boundary elements (actions) into boundary elements (prices), using a common constraint (the function value α). These boundary elements have economic significance: always in terms of efficiency, sometimes also in terms of optimality or equilibrium.

The price generating a separating hyperplane through the optimum is called a <u>characteristic price</u>, and the individual prices generating in a similar way seperating hyperplanes with respect to a Nash-equilibrium, are called <u>Nash-equilibrium prices.</u>

In the next section we consider a representation of $\mathcal{E}_0$ completely in the dual space.

3.3. Dual preferences.

Preferences are given by the correspondence P from X into itself. Under certain assumptions a dual preference correspondence P^* of some set $V^* \subset R^{n*}$ into itself can be defined. Then $P^*(p)$ is a set of prices which are "worse" or "less favourable" then p (see [24]) or have, particulary in the interpretation of section 4, "higher valuations" than p (see also [18]).

Assumptions 3.2:

(A) X is closed, convex and aureoled and $0 \notin X$.

(B) $P: X \rightrightarrows X$ satisfies:

(1) if $y \notin P(x) \cup P^{-1}(x)$, then $P(x) = P(y)$ and $P^{-1}(x) = P^{-1}(y)$ (completeness);

(2) for all $x,y \in X: P(x) \subset P(y)$ or $P(x) \supset P(y)$ (transitivity);

(3) for all $x \in X$: $P(x)$ is convex and aureoled and $x \notin P(x)$;

(4) there exists a closed convex set $V \subset X$, such that $P(x) = \emptyset$ if $x \in V$ and $x \in \mathrm{Cl}\, P(x)$ if $x \notin V$;

(5) P has an open graph in $X \times X$.

If $R: X \rightrightarrows X$ is a correspondence defined by:

$$R(x) := X \setminus P^{-1}(x), \tag{3.3}$$

then, by (B1) and (B2), R represents a complete transitive preference relation. "$y \in R(x)$" can be interpreted as "y is at least as good as x". Under (B4) we have for $x \notin V$:

$$R(x) = \mathrm{Cl}\, P(x).$$

It can also be shown that R has a closed graph.

(B3) ensures that $P^{**}(x) = \mathrm{Cl}\, P(x)$ if $x \notin V$ (see property A.8).

By (B4) the agent is satiated in V, since there exist no actions better than any action in V. It follows from (B1) and (B2) that $R(x) = V$ if $x \in V$, since $R(x) = X \setminus P^{-1}(x)$. The agent is locally non satiated by (B4) in any $x \notin V$.

Remark:

If (B4) does not hold, but instead $x \in \mathrm{Cl}\, P(x)$ for all $x \in X$, then we can artificially construct a satiation set V, and redefine P, such that (B4) becomes true. This is done as follows.

Let x_0 be any point of the interior of X and define

$$V := \text{Cl } P(x_0) = R(x_0).$$

Clearly we have for $x \in V : X \supset V \supset P(x)$. The set V should be chosen in such a way that points of V are not of interest in the problem at hand, particularly because they cannot be feasible and could therefore not be an optimum or be a component of a Nash equilibrium. The set V will be handled as if the agent is satiated in V and the preference is adapted: $\tilde{P}: X \rightrightarrows X$ is defined by: $\tilde{P}(x) := P(x)$ if $x \notin V$ and $\tilde{P}(x) := \emptyset$ if $x \in V$. Now $\tilde{P}$ satisfies (B4).

At prices $p \in V^*$, no interior point of the "artificial satiation set" V is obtainable, i.e. $p.x > 1$ for $x \in \text{Int } V$. Since no bundle can be or will be chosen from V anyway, nothing is lost by restricting our attention to prices in V^* and excluding all prices in $R^{n*} \setminus V^*$. Thus $x \in V$ may be compared with $p \notin V^*$.
On the other hand, $x \notin X$ is interpreted as a bundle below the level of subsistence. These bundles cannot be achieved by prices $p \in X^*$, and are in that sense equally "totally dissatisfactory". X^* may be considered a "starvation set" of prices. Hence X^*, resp. V^* play similar roles in the price space, as V, resp. X play in the action space. (See fig. 3.b).

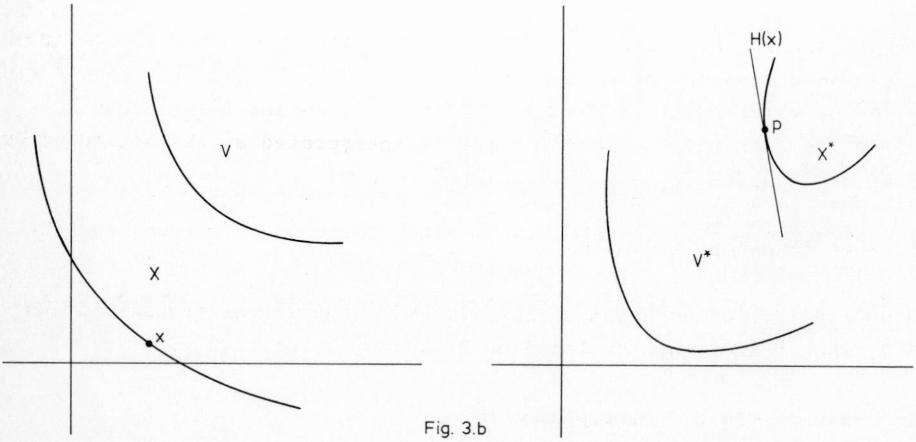

Fig. 3.b

Define $M: V^* \rightrightarrows R^n$ by

(3.4) $$M(p) := \{x \in R^n | p.x < 1\}.$$

M has an open graph. Now define

(3.5) $$Q(p) := \{x \in X | P(x) \cap M(p) = \emptyset\}.$$

For all $p \in V^*$, $V \subset Q(p) \subset X$ and for $p \in X^*$, $Q(p) = X$. Q has a <u>closed</u> graph since the graph of its complement, $\{(x,p) | P(x) \cap M(p) \neq \emptyset\}$, is open.

If $\hat{x}$ is an optimum according to definition 2.1 in the constraint set $\bar{C} = \text{Cl } M(p)$, then $Q(p) = \text{Cl } P(\hat{x}) = R(\hat{x})$, provided that $\hat{x} \in \text{Int } X$. Therefore Q(p) contains all actions that are preferred to any action obtainable at p (i.e. such that $p.x \leqq 1$) and particularly to an optimum $\hat{x}$, if it exists.

Now define $P^*: V^* \rightrightarrows V^*$ (see def. A.10) by

(3.6) $$P^*(p) := \begin{cases} \text{Int } [Q(p)]^*_+, & \text{if } p \notin X^* \\ \emptyset & \text{, if } p \in X^* \end{cases}$$

This definition of P^* is logically equivalent to

(3.7) $$P^*(p) = \text{Int } \{q \in V^* | \forall x \in X: [\forall y \in X: y \in P(x) \Rightarrow p.y \geqq 1] \Rightarrow q.x \geqq 1\}.$$

$P^*(p)$ contains all prices at which all actions, preferred to any action obtainable at p cannot be obtained. If $q \in P^*(p)$ and if for some x and y, $P^*(p) = \text{Int } P^*(x) := \text{Int } [P(x)]^*_+$ and $P^*(q) = \text{Int } P^*(y)$, then $y \in P^{-1}(x)$. In this sense $P^*(p)$ may be interpreted as the set of prices that are "worse" or "less favourable" than p.

Further it can be shown that:

<u>Property 3.8:</u> Under assumptions 3.2, $P^*(p)$ and V^* satisfy assumtions 3.2, when X and P are replaced by V^* and P^* respectively.

Let assumptions 3.2 be replaced by:

Assumptions 3.9:

(A') X is a closed convex cone;

(B1), (B2), (B3), (B5) as in Assumption 3.2;

(B4') $\forall x \in X$: $P(x) \neq \emptyset$ and $P(x) = P(x) + X$.

So, X is a cone (containing 0), P(x) is monotone in the directions of the cone and there is no satiation set. Clearly $X^* = \emptyset$.

Now instead of defining an artificial satiation set, as considered in the remark above, we may define:

$$(3.10) \qquad V^* := X_+^0$$

(X_+^0 being the upper dual cone of X; see definition A.1).
Now $P^*: V^* \rightrightarrows V^*$ is defined by:

$$(3.11) \qquad P^*(p) := \text{Int}\,[Q(p)]^*, \text{ for all } p \in V^* = X_+^0,$$

which is equivalent to (3.6), since $X^* = \emptyset$.

Note that the symmetry between the dual and the original representation is retained, since both X^* and V^{**} are empty. Property 3.8 also holds under assumptions 3.9.

Consider again the economy $\mathcal{E}_0 := \{X, P: X \rightrightarrows X, \bar{C}\}$ of section 3.2. Let the assumptions 3.9 of the present section hold, let $\bar{C} \cap \text{Int}\, X \neq \emptyset$ and $\bar{C} \cap V = \emptyset$.

We may define a dual economy:

$$\mathcal{E}_0^* := \{V^*, P^*: V^* \rightrightarrows V^*, \bar{C}^*\}.$$

Let $\hat{p}$ be an optimum in $\mathcal{E}_0^*$, i.e.:

$$P^*(\hat{p}) \cap \bar{C}^* = \emptyset,$$

$$\hat{p} \in \bar{C}^* \cap V^*.$$

Then there exists a hyperplane $H(\hat{x})$ separating $P^*(\hat{p})$ and $\bar{C}^*$. Now $\hat{x}$ is an optimum in $\mathcal{E}_0^*$. Conversely, if $\hat{x}$ is an optimum in $\mathcal{E}_0$, $H(\hat{p})$ separates $P(x)$ and $\bar{C}$. Then $\hat{p}$ is an optimum in $\mathcal{E}_0^*$ (see Property A.9). (For an application to linear optimization, see section A.2).

4. An economy with public goods (only).

A first application of the concepts derived above is given for an economy in which agents have to decide collectively about the provision of a bundle of commodities which they all enjoy simultaneously. An economic good which can be shared in use by all agents, such that the consumption of it by some agents has no external effects upon other agents, is called a (pure) public good.
Since preferences are assumed to be independent of consumption by other agents, they can be defined by a correspondence $P_i : X_i \rightrightarrows X_i$, for each agent $i \in H$.

It is assumed that the economy contains only public goods (e.g. a community council that, given the budget constraint, has to decide upon various expenditure categories). The choice must be constrained to a production set (which may be the budget set just mentioned).

Two economies will be introduced: one in which no allocation mechanism is defined, and the other in which some mechanism (not necessarily realistic) is implied by the introduction of weights given to the agents. It will be shown that a (Pareto optimal) solution to the first economy determines implicitly weights that are given explicitly in the second economy.

4.1. Pareto optima in E_1.

Consider the economy with H agents, each having a consumption set X_i in R^n, the space of public goods in the economy. A strong preference correspondence $P_i : X_i \rightrightarrows X_i$ is defined, as well as a production set Y in R^n where Y is the set of all possible output bundles of public goods. Denote the economy by:

$$E_1 := \{H, X_i, P_i : X_i \rightrightarrows X_i, Y\}.$$

Since the commodities are public goods, one may apply the operation of intersection on the consumption sets to obtain $X := \cap X_i$, the set of public goods feasible for all consumers simultaneously. Each preference correspondence P_i is thus also defined from X to X. (Notice that the symbol X has a different meaning as at some places of section 2, where X denoted the cartesian product of action sets). Let $\bar{C} := Y$.

The economy E_1 can be trivially translated into the abstract economy $\mathcal{E}_p := \{H, X, P_i\colon X \rightrightarrows X, \bar{C}\}$. Now $\hat{x}$ is a Pareto-optimum if $\hat{x} \in \bar{C} \cap X$, and $\cap P_i(\hat{x}) \cap \bar{C} = \emptyset$. Such a Pareto-optimum is also an optimum in the abstract economy $\mathcal{E}_0 := \{X, P_I\colon X \rightrightarrows X, \bar{C}\}$, for $P_I(x) := \cap P_i(x)$.

From theorem 2.2 it follows that a Pareto optimum exists if $X \cap Y$ is compact, convex and nonempty, and if P has an open graph, is point-compact, and $x \notin P(x)$. Clearly, the conditions on P are fulfilled if they hold for all P_i. If also $x \in \mathrm{Cl}\, P_i(x)$ for all i and x, then $P(x) \neq \emptyset$ implies $x \in \mathrm{Cl}\, P(x)$.
Let all the above conditions be satisfied. Assume also a common direction of local non-satiation, i.e. for all i and all x, there exists a $\lambda > 1$ such that $\lambda x \in P_i(x)$; then $P(x) \neq \emptyset$ for all $x \in X$.
Finally, assume that $0 \in \mathrm{Int}\, Y$ and that $0 \notin X$.
It follows that a Pareto-optimum $\hat{x}$ exists, and with it a characteristic price $\hat{p}$ that generates a hyperplane $H(\hat{p})$ separating $P(\hat{x})$ and Y. Hence (see section 3.2), $\hat{p} \in P^*(\hat{x}) \cap Y^*$, and $H(\hat{p})$ separates $P^*(\hat{x})$ and Y^* (see fig. 4.a). Note that $P^*(\hat{x})$ is a <u>closed</u> set. By property A.5 (7):

$$P^*(\hat{x}) = \mathrm{Conv} \bigcup_i P_i^*(\hat{x}).$$

Therefore $H(\hat{x})$ also separates Y^* and each $P_i^*(x)$, $i \in H$. By definition, $H(\hat{x})$ supports any $P_i^*(\hat{x})$.

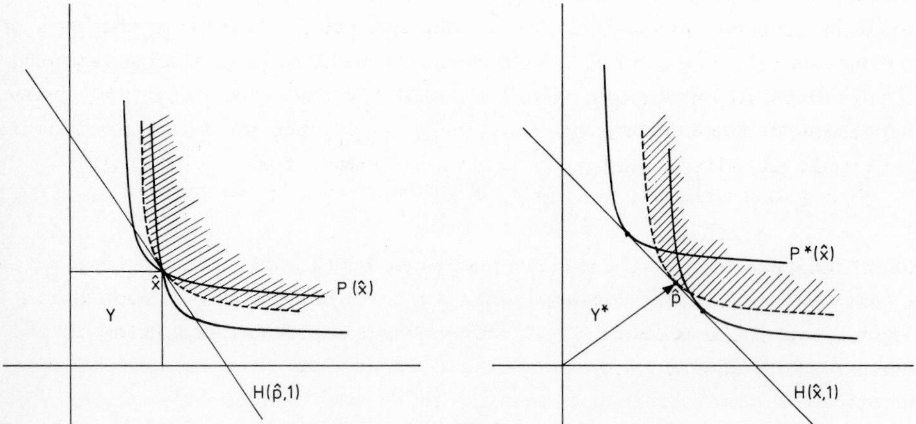

Fig. 4.a

This implies that there exists $\hat{p}_i \in P_i^*(\hat{x})$ and $\alpha_i > 0$ with $\Sigma\alpha_i = 1$, such that:

$$\hat{p} = \Sigma\alpha_i\hat{p}_i.$$

Therefore, with any Pareto optimum $\hat{x}$ in E_1, a characteristic price $\hat{p}$ can be associated, a set of individual "shadow" prices $\hat{p}_i$, and a set of weights α_i. The individual shadow prices generate hyperplanes $H(\hat{p}_i)$ separating $P_i(\hat{x})$ and $\{\hat{x}\}$ (but not necessarily Y), for all i.
The characteristic price $\hat{p}$ generates a hyperplane $H(\hat{p})$ separating $P(\hat{x}) := \cap P_i(\hat{x})$ and Y. This price $\hat{p}$ is a convex combination or a weighted mean of the individual shadow prices $\hat{p}_i$, with weight α_i.

4.2. A Lindahl or public equilibrium in E_2.

The weights implicitly determined by a Pareto-optimum, and the individual prices $\hat{p}_i$ corresponding to a Pareto-optimum $\hat{x}$ can be interpreted in terms of an allocation mechanism, e.g.:

(a) Each consumer spends an amount 1 and pays his own individual shadow price $\hat{p}_i$; the Pareto-optimum $\hat{x}$ in E_1 is then also an optimum for each consumer in his decision problem $E_i := \{X_i, P_i: X \rightrightarrows X, \{x \mid \hat{p}_i.x \leqq 1\}\}$; the characteristic price $\hat{p}$ is a weighted mean of $\hat{p}_i$, with weights α_i.

(b) Each consumer spends the (implicitly given) amount α_i and pays the price $\hat{q}_i := \alpha_i\hat{p}_i$; again, $\hat{x}$ is an optimum in each $(X_i, P_i, \{x|\hat{q}_i.x \leqq \alpha_i\})$, and $\hat{p}$ is the sum of $\hat{q}_i$. (This interpretation is used in the definition of a Lindahl equilibrium).

(c) Each consumer evaluates the Pareto optimal public-goods bundle $\hat{x}$ on a voting paper with possibilities $\{p_i|p_i.\hat{x} \leqq 1\}$; the individual price $\hat{p}_i$ is an optimum in $E_i^* := \{V_i^*, P_i^*, \{p_i|p_i.x \leqq 1\}\}$; the characteristic price $\hat{p}$ is a weighted mean of $\hat{p}_i$, the weights α_i being the (implicit) distribution of political power, for V_i such that $V_i \cap Y = \emptyset$, for all i.

Which interpretation is preferred depends on the institutional situation and on the allocation mechanism one has in mind. But given such an interpretation, the weights (α_i) can be fixed a priori, resulting in the economy (with public goods only):

$$E_2 := \{X_i, P_i, \alpha_i, Y\}.$$

The economy E_2 can be translated in an abstract economy $\mathcal{E}_0 :=$ $\{X, P_0: X \rightrightarrows X, \bar{C}\}$ by means of the following operations:

$$X := \bigcap_i X_i;$$

$$P_0(x) := \bigcup_L \bigcap_i (\lambda_i/\alpha_i) P_i(x) := \mathring{\bigcap_i} \alpha_i^{-1} P_i(x),$$

$$\text{with } L := \{\lambda \in R^h \mid \lambda_i \geqq 0 \text{ and } \Sigma \lambda_i = 1\};$$

$$\bar{C} := Y.$$

The collective or social preference correspondence is thus determined by the operation called dual summation or convex intersection (see A.4) on the individual correspondences. Notice that (see fig. 4.a):

$$\cup P_i(x) \supset P_0(x) \supset \cap P_i(x) := P_I(x).$$

In section 4.1 it has been shown that an optimum in $\mathcal{E}_0$ exists if the following conditions in E_2 hold:

(i) $X \cap Y$ is compact, convex and nonempty;

(ii) for all i, P_i has an open graph, is point-compact, and for all x $x \notin P_i(x)$, $x \in \mathrm{Cl}\, P_i(x)$, and $\exists\, \lambda > 1$: $\lambda x \in P_i(x)$.
For the existence of dual concepts, it is also assumed that:

(iii) $0 \notin X$, $0 \in \mathrm{Int}\, Y$, and P_i is transitive, for all i.

The optimum $\hat{x}$ in $\mathcal{E}_0$ is then defined by:

$$\hat{x} \in Y \text{ and } P_0(\hat{x}) \cap Y = \emptyset,$$

and has a characteristic price $\hat{p}$, such that

$$\hat{p} \in Y^* \text{ and } P_0^*(\hat{x}) \cap Y^* = \emptyset.$$

From property A.5.8 and the definition of P_0 it follows that:

$$P_0^*(\hat{x}) = \sum_i \alpha_i P_i^*(\hat{x}).$$

Hence, there exist individual prices $\hat{p}_i \in P_i^*(\hat{x})$ such that $\hat{p} = \Sigma \alpha_i \hat{p}_i$. These individual prices $\hat{p}_i$ generate hyperplanes $H(\hat{p}_i)$ separating and supporting $\{\hat{x}\}$ and $P_i(\hat{x})$, whereas $H(\hat{p})$ separates and supports Y and $P_0(\hat{x})$. The triple $\{\hat{x},\hat{p},(\hat{p}_i)\}$, resp. $\{\hat{x},\hat{p},(\hat{q}_i)\}$ is defined to be an

equilibrium in the economy E_2.
In the interpretation (b) above, it is called a <u>Lindahl equilibrium</u>, and in the interpretation (c) it is called a <u>public equilibrium.</u> (see [12] and [16]).
A Lindahl equilibrium is usually defined in an economy with both private and public goods. In our economy E_2, it is defined by the triple $\{\hat{x},\hat{p},(\hat{q}_i)\}$ such that:

(i) for all i, $\hat{x}$ is best in $\{x \mid \hat{q}_i.x \leqq \alpha_i\}$ for P_i;

(ii) $\hat{p} = \Sigma \hat{q}_i$;

(iii) $\hat{p}.\hat{x} = \max\{\hat{p}.x \mid x \in Y\}$.

In this case, α_i is interpreted as income in terms of the numéraire or money. The problem with this interpretation is, of course, the fact that the individuals must determine their own prices. This being done correctly is quite improbable.

On the other hand, a public equilibrium in E_2 is defined by the triple $\{\hat{x},\hat{p},(\hat{p}_i)\}$ such that:

(i) for all i, $\hat{p}_i$ is best in $\{p_i \mid p_i.\hat{x} \leqq 1\}$ for P_i^*;

(ii) $\hat{p} = \Sigma \alpha_i p_i$;

(iii) $\hat{p}.\hat{x} = \max\ \{p.\hat{x} \mid p \in Y^*\}$.

The individual shadow prices $\hat{p}_i$ are not expressed any more in terms of money, but these still remain problems with correct revelation.

The definition of a public equilibrium is formally identical to the definition of a competitive equilibrium (see section 6), but defined in the dual economy E_2^*:

$$E_2^* := \{V_i^*, P_i^*, \alpha_i, Y^*\}.$$

Thus $\{\hat{x},\hat{p},(\hat{p}_i)\}$ is such that:

(i) $\hat{p} \in \mathrm{Cl}\ [\Sigma \alpha_i\ P_i^*(\hat{p}_i)] \cap Y^* \cap H(\hat{x})$, and

(ii) $[\Sigma \alpha_i\ P_i^*(\hat{p}_i)] \cap Y^* = \emptyset$.

This will be considered in section 6.

5. Optimality and Nash-equilibrium.

5.1. An optimum formulated as a Nash-equilibrium.

The abstract economy $\mathcal{E}_0 := \{X, P: X \rightrightarrows X, \bar{C}\}$ with a single agent can be reformulated as an economy $\mathcal{E}_N$ with three resp. two agents. Under certain conditions, the optimum in $\mathcal{E}$, in which the characteristic price vector remains implicit, corresponds to a Nash-equilibrium in $\mathcal{E}_N$ or $\mathcal{E}'_N$, where the characteristic price appears explicitly.

(1) Three agents:[1)]

$\mathcal{E}_N := \{X_i, P_i\colon X_i \rightrightarrows X_i,\ C_i\}$ for $i = 1,2,3$, where the action space becomes $R^{3n} = R^{2n} \times R^{n*}$, a typical element being (x,y,p):

agent 1: ("consumer")

$$X_1 := X$$
$$P_1(x,y,p) := P(x)$$
$$C_1(x,y,p) := \{z \in R^n \mid p.z \leqq p.y\}$$

agent 2: ("producer")

$$X_2 := R^n$$
$$P_2(x,y,p) := \{z \in X_2 \mid p.z > p.y\}$$
$$C_2(x,y,p) := \bar{C} =: \bar{C}_2$$

agent 3: ("market")

$$X_3 := R^{n*}$$
$$P_3(x,y,p) := \{p \in X_3 \mid p.(x-y) > 0\}$$
$$C_3(x,y,p) := \{q \in R^{n*} \mid |q| \leq 1\} =: \bar{C}_3$$

Thus the single agent is split up into two agents, the first choosing a maximal element from $B_1(x,y,p) := C_1(x,y,p) \cap X_1$, which will be called his budget set, the second choose from $\bar{C}_2$ an element which maximizes the value at price p. A third agent, the "market agent", is added who chooses a price which maximizes the value of the difference between x and y.

Theorem 5.1: Let $\mathcal{E}_0$ and $\mathcal{E}_N$ be economies in which X and $\bar{C}$ are closed and convex, P has an open graph and is point-convex, $x \notin P(x)$ and $x \in \mathrm{Cl}\ P(x)$ then:

(a) if x is an optimum in $\mathcal{E}_0$, with $x \in \mathrm{Int}\ X$ and $p \neq 0$ an optimum price, then $(x,y,p/|p|)$ is a Nash-equilibrium in $\mathcal{E}_N$ with $x = y$;

(b) if (x,y,p) is a Nash-equilibrium in $\mathcal{E}_N$, then x is an optimum in $\mathcal{E}_0$ and $x = y$.

---

1) A similar formulation for a different but related problem is given in Debreu [3], see section 7.1.

Proof:

(a) $H(p,px)$ separates $\bar{C}$ and $P(x)$ and also $H(p,px)$ and $P(x)$.
Hence $P_1(x,y,p/|p|) \cap B_1(x,y,p/|p|) = \emptyset$ and $x \in B_1(x,x,p/|p|)$.
Also $P_2(x,y,p/|p|) \cap \bar{C}_2 = \emptyset$. Since $(x-y) = 0$, $P_3(x,y,p) \cap \bar{C}_3 = \emptyset$, $p/|p| \in \bar{C}_3$.

(b) By local non-satiation, $px = py$. If $(x-y) \neq 0$, then for $q = \frac{x-y}{|x-y|}$, $q \in P_3(x,y,p) \cap \bar{C}_3$, which is impossible; hence $x-y = 0$.
Since $P_1(x,y,p) \cap C_1(x,y,p) = \emptyset$ and $P_2(x,y,p) \cap \bar{C}_2 = \emptyset$, whereas $C_1(x,y,p) \supset \bar{C}_2 = Y$, $P(x) \cap Y = \emptyset$. □

(2) Two agents:

A simpler way to reformulate the optimum, is obtained by using duality;
We have to assume now that:

$$0 \notin X, \text{ and } 0 \in \text{Int } \bar{C}.$$

$\mathcal{E}'_N := \{X_i, P_i: X \rightrightarrows X_i \; C_i\}$, for $i = 1,2$, where the action space becomes $R^n \times R^{n*}$, a typical element being (x,p).

agent 1: $X_1 := X$
$P_1(x,p) := P(x)$
$C_1(x,p) := \{z \in R^n | p.z \leqq \sup p.\bar{C}\}$

agent 2: $X_2 := R^{n*}$
$P_1(x,p) := \{q \in X_2 | q.x > p.x\}$
$C_2(x,p) := \bar{C}^*_- = \bar{C}_2$.

Thus the first agent chooses a maximal element from his budget set which now is based in maximization of the value on $\bar{C}$ and agent 2 chooses a value maximizing price.

Theorem 5.2: Given the assumptions of theorem 5.1:

(a) if x is an optimum in $\mathcal{E}_0$, with $x \in$ Int X and p an optimum price, then $(x,p/p.x)$ is a Nash-equilibrium in $\mathcal{E}'_N$,

(b) if (x,p) is a Nash-equilibrium in $\mathcal{E}'_N$, then x is an optimum with optimum price p in $\mathcal{E}_0$.

Proof:

(a) $H(p,p.x)$ separates $P(x)$ and Y and $x \in$ Bnd $\bar{C}$.
Since $x \in$ Int X, $P(x) \cap H(p,p.x) = \emptyset$.

Hence also $P_1(x) \cap C_1(x,p/p.x) = \emptyset$. Since $H(p/p.x)$ supports Y in x, $H(x)$ supports Y^* in $p/p.x$. Hence $P_2(x,p/p.x) \cap \bar{C}_2 = \emptyset$.

(b) Since $P_1(x,p) \cap C_1(x,p) = \emptyset$ and $C_1(x,p) \supset \bar{C}, P(x) \cap \bar{C} = \emptyset$. Since $H(x)$ supports Y^* in p, $x \in \bar{C}$. □

5.2. A Nash-equilibrium reduced to a relative optimum.

An abstract economy $\mathcal{E}_N := \{H, X_i, P_i: X \rightrightarrows X_i, C_i\}$ with n agents, can under certain conditions, be reformulated as an economy with a single agent $\mathcal{E}_R$. (A similar result but with a different "aggregation of preferences" is given in Borglin and Keiding, [2]. A related model was considered in Ruys [18].)

Assume $0 \notin X_i$ and $0 \in C_i(x)$, for all i and x. (This can always be achieved by means of change of the origin.) The action set and the constraint correspondence are simply $X := \Pi X_i$ and $C(x) := \Pi C_i(x)$. The preferences $P_i: X \rightrightarrows X_i$ are aggregated as follows into a single preference $P: X \rightrightarrows X$, by means of dual summation (see definition A.4). Let

(5.3) $$\tilde{P}_i(x) := P_i(x) \times \prod_{j \neq i} X_j$$

and

(5.4) $$L := \{\lambda \in R^n \mid \Sigma \lambda_i = 1 \text{ and } \lambda \geqq 0\};$$

then:

(5.5) $$P(x) := \bigcup_L \bigcap_i \lambda_i n \tilde{P}_i(x).$$

So: $$\mathcal{E}_R := \{X, P: X \rightrightarrows X, C: X \rightrightarrows X\}.$$

Theorem 5.6: Let $\mathcal{E}_N$ and $\mathcal{E}_R$ be as defined above and assume:

(1) $0 \notin X_i$ for all i;

(2) for all i and x: $C_i(x)$ is closed and convex and $0 \in C_i(x)$;

(3) for all i and x: $P_i(x) \neq \emptyset$, $x_i \in \mathrm{Cl}\, P_i(x)$ and $x_i \notin \mathrm{Conv}\, P_i(x)$;

(4) P_i has an open graph for all i;

then the following statements are equivalent:

(a) x is a Nash-equilibrium in $\mathcal{E}_N$;

(b) x is a relative optimum in $\mathcal{E}_R$.

Proof:

(a) Let x be a Nash-equilibrium in $\mathcal{E}_N$, hence $x \in C(x)$. Suppose $z \in P(x) \cap C(x)$, hence for all $i: z_i \in C_i(x)$. Since x is a Nash-equilibrium, for all $i: z_i \notin P_i(x) \cap C_i(x)$, hence for all $i: z \notin \tilde{P}_i(x)$. Let $0 < \mu < 1$, then for all $i: \mu z_i \notin P_i(x)$; for, if $\mu z_i \in P_i(x)$, then by assumption (2) $\mu z_i \in P_i(x) \cap C_i(x)$ and that is a contradiction; it follows that for all $i: \mu z \notin \tilde{P}_i(x)$. There must exist $\lambda \in L$, such that for all i: $z \in \lambda_i n\tilde{P}_i(x)$, but this is impossible, since for all least one $j \in H$: $\lambda_j n \geqq 1$, hence $z \notin \lambda_j n \tilde{P}_j(x)$, so $z \notin P(x)$.

(b) Let x be a relative optimum in $\mathcal{E}_R$, hence $x \in C(x)$ and $P(x) \cap B(x) = \emptyset$. Suppose for some $j \in H: P_j(x) \cap C_j(x) \neq \emptyset$, then for some $\lambda_j > \frac{1}{n}$, $\lambda_j n > 1$ and $\lambda_j n\ P_j(x) \cap C_j(x) \neq \emptyset$ (taking into account assumption (2) and (4). Let $z_j \in \lambda_j n\ P_j(x) \cap C_j(x)$.

By local satiation, for all i : $x_i \in Cl\ P_i(x)$. Choose for $i \neq j$

$$\lambda_i = \frac{1-\lambda_j n}{n-1}$$

hence $\lambda_i n < 1$ and by assumptions (2), (3) and (4) for $i \neq j$, there exist z_i such that $z_i \in \lambda_i nP_i(x) \cap C_i(x)$. Hence $z = (z_j, z_{-j}) \cap C(x)$ and $z \in \lambda_i n\tilde{P}_i(x)$ for all i. So $z \in P(x)$ and that is a contradiction.□

6. Competitive equilibrium.

The model of a competitive economy is a basic model in mathematical economics (see e.g. Debreu [4], Arrow and Hahn [1]). We consider an economy with only private goods. There are n commodities; R^n is the commodity space and a point $x \in R^n$ is a bundle of commodities. There is a finite set $H = \{1,2,\ldots,h\}$ of consumers and a single producer (or aggregate production sector). Each consumer $i \in H$ has a consumption set $X_i \subset R^n$; a point $x_i \in X_i$ is a consumption bundle of i and the consumption of all agents is $x = (x_1, x_2, \ldots, x_n) \in X = \Pi X_i$. Total consumption of all agents is ΣX_i. Each agent's preferences are given by a correspondence $P_i: X_i \rightrightarrows X_i$, and preferences are assumed to be independent of the consumption of other consumers. (i.e. $P_i(x) = P_i(x_i)$, see section 2.6). Each consumer has a bundle of resources $w_i \in R^n$. The producer has a production set $Y \subset R^n$; $0 \in Y$; for $y \in Y$, negative components are inputs and positive components are outputs, so Y is the set of possible input-output combinations. There is a price $p \in R^{n*}$ at which consumers and the producer exchange commodities. The profit of the producer equals $p.y$ if p is the price and $y \in Y$. The profit is distributed among consumers according to <u>profit shares</u> θ_i, for $0 \leq \theta_i \leq 1$ and $\Sigma\theta_i = 1$.

The economy is given by

$$E_C := \{H, X_i, P_i: X_i \nrightarrow X_i, w_i, \theta_i, Y\}.$$

It is assumed that the producer maximizes profits and chooses $y \in Y$, such that

$$\pi(p) := p.y = \sup p.Y.$$

The amount that each consumer can spend is:

$$\varphi_i(p) := p.w_i + \theta_i \sup p.Y.$$

The budget set of agent i is:

$$B_i(p) := \{x \in X_i | p.x \leq \varphi_i(p)\},$$

and he is assumed to choose a maximal element from this set.

An equilibrium in E_C is an (h+2)-tuple $((x_i),y,p)$ such that:

(1) $\forall_i : P_i(x_i) \cap B_i(p) = \emptyset$, and $x_i \in B_i(p)$;

(2) $p.y = \sup p.Y$;

(3) $y + \Sigma w_i = \Sigma x_i$.

Since preferences are assumed to be independent (section 2.6), $\bar{P}(x) := P_i(x_i)$ and therefore (1) is equivalent to:

(1') $\forall_i: \bar{P}_i(x) \cap B_i(p) = \emptyset$ and $x_i \in B_i(p)$.

So the equilibrium is a Nash-equilibrium for consumers, at well chosen values of y and p.

6.1. <u>An equilibrium in an economy formulated as a Nash-equilibrium.</u>

As was shown by Debreu [3], an equilibrium in E_C can completely be formulated as a Nash-equilibrium in an abstract economy $\mathcal{E}_N$ derived from E_C in a way, similar to the method followed in section 5. (See also Sonnenschein-Shafer [21]. This can be done in two ways.

(I) By formulating the behaviour of the producer and by adding a market agent (similar to (1) in section 5), in such a way that they both have a preference and a constraint set.
Define the abstract economy $\mathcal{E}_N := \{\hat{H}, \hat{X}_i, \hat{P}_i : \hat{X} \rightrightarrows \hat{X}, \hat{C}_i\}$. The action space becomes $R^{n(h+1)} \times R^{n*}$, with as a typical element (x,y,p), and $\hat{H} := \{H, (h+1), (h+2)\}$ and for

agents $i \in H$:

$$\hat{X}_i := X_i \subset R^n$$

$$\hat{P}_i(x,y,p) := P_i(x_i)$$

$$\hat{C}_i(x,y,p) := \{x \in R^n | p.z \leqq \varphi_i(p)\}$$

agent h+1:

$$\hat{X}_{h+1} := R^n$$

$$\hat{P}_{h+1}(x,y,p) := \{z \in X_{h+1} | p.z > p.y\}$$

$$\hat{C}_{h+1}(x,y,p) := Y$$

agent h+2:

$$\hat{X}_{h+2} := R^{n*}$$

$$\hat{P}_{h+2}(x,y,p) := \{p \in X_{h+2} | p.(\Sigma x_i - y) > 0\}$$

$$\hat{C}_{h+2}(x,y,p) := \{p \in R^{n*} | p \geqq 0 \text{ and } |p| \leqq 1\}.$$

Consumers are optimizing over their budget sets as required in (1) of the definition of an equilibrium. The producer maximizes profits and the (h+2)-nd agent, the market manager, maximizes the value of the difference between consumption and production.
It can be shown that under suitable assumptions, the equilibrium in E_C corresponds to a Nash-equilibrium in the abstract economy $\mathcal{E}_N$ (See [3] and [21]). Note that we have in the Nash-equilibrium for $i \in H$: $H(p,\varphi_i)$ separates $\hat{P}_i(x,y,p)$ and $\hat{C}_i(x,y,p)$; $H(p,p.y)$ separates $P_{h+1}(x,y,p)$ and $C_{h+1}(x,y,p)$, whereas $P_{h+2}(x,y,p) = \emptyset$.

(II) By formalizing the producer as a price maker (as in (2) of section 5) in the abstract economy $\mathcal{E}'_N := \{\hat{H}, \hat{X}_i, \hat{P}_i: \hat{X} \nrightarrow \hat{X}, \hat{C}_i\}$.

The action space is $R^{mn} \times R^{n*}$, with a typical element (x,p) $\hat{H} := \{H, h+1\}$ and for

<u>agents</u> $i \in H$:

$$\hat{X}_i := X_i$$

$$\hat{P}_i(x,p) := P_i(x_i)$$

$$\hat{C}_i(x,p) := \{z \in R^n | p.z_i \leq \varphi_i(p)\}$$

<u>agent</u> h+1:

$$\hat{X}_{h+1} := R^{n*}$$

$$\hat{P}_{h+1}(x,p) := \{q \in \hat{X}_{h+1} | q.\Sigma x_i > p.\Sigma x_i\}$$

$$\hat{C}_{h+1}(x,p) := (Y + \Sigma w_i)^*_-$$

Again under suitable assumptions a Nash-equilibrium in the abstract economy $\mathcal{E}'_N$ corresponds to an equilibrium in E_C.

6.2. <u>An equilibrium characterized by an optimum price.</u>

If the preferences in the economy E_C are given by a complete preordering, as considered in section 3, then we can characterize the equilibrium by an equilibrium price with which the equilibrium allocation can be associated. The equilibrium price can be formulated as an optimum in the sense of definition 2.1.
Assume that X_i and $P_i : X_i \nrightarrow X_i$ fulfill the assumptions 3.2. Assume also that $\text{Conv} \bigcup_i X_i \not\ni 0$. Let $Z := Y + \Sigma w_i$ be starred (see def. A.2), closed and convex, and $\Sigma V_i \cap Z = \emptyset$.

Note first that an equilibrium in E_C is an (n+2)-tuple (x,y,p), such that:

(1) $\Sigma P_i(x_i) \cap Z = \emptyset, \ \Sigma x_i \in Z$

(2) $\forall_i : P_i(x_i) \cap B_i(p, \varphi_i(p)) = \emptyset, \ x_i \in B_i(p, \varphi_i(p))$,

for $B_i(p) := \{x \in X_i | p.x \leqq \varphi_i(p)\}$ and $y = \Sigma x_i - \Sigma w_i$.
We define an economy

$$\mathcal{E}_0^* := \{V^*, \hat{P}^*: V^* \rightrightarrows V^*, \bar{C}^*\}$$

in the price space. Let $V^* := (\Sigma V_i)^* = \bigcup_L \bigcap_i \lambda_i V_i^*$. By assumption $V^* \cap Z^* \neq \emptyset$. Let $\hat{P}_i^* : V_i^* \rightrightarrows V_i^*$ be as defined by (3.6). We define an aggregate preference in terms of prices, $\hat{P}^* : V^* \rightrightarrows V^*$.
Given $p \in V^*$, $\varphi_i(p)$ is i's income; hence $\frac{p}{\varphi_i(p)}$ is i's "personal" price, i.e. the price such that he may spend 1. $\hat{P}_i^*(\frac{p}{\varphi_i(p)})$ are the prices that are worse for i then $\frac{p}{\varphi_i(p)}$ $\hat{P}^*$ is the dual sum (see def. A.4) of the individual preferences:

$$\hat{P}^*(p) = \bigcup_L \bigcap_i \lambda_i P_i^*(\frac{p}{\varphi_i(p)}).$$

For $\hat{P}^*$ we have (under the Assumptions 3.2) by properties A.5 and A.9:

(1) $\hat{P}^*(p)$ is convex, aureoled, for all $p \in V^*$

(2) $\hat{P}^*$ has an open graph

(3) $p \notin \hat{P}^*(p)$ and $p \in \text{Cl}\, \hat{P}^*(p)$, for all $p \in V^*$.

The last property can be seen as follows:
for all i, $\frac{1}{\varphi_i(p)}$ p is on the lower boundary of $\hat{P}_i^*(\frac{1}{\varphi_i(p)} p)$; if we choose $\lambda_i = \varphi_i(p)$, then for all i:

$$p \in \text{Bnd}\, \lambda_i \hat{P}_i^* \left(\frac{1}{\varphi_i(p)} p\right);$$

if $\lambda_i \neq \varphi_i(p)$, for some i, then for some j: $\lambda_j > \varphi_j(p)$.
Then $\frac{\lambda_j}{\varphi_j(p)} p \in \text{Bnd}\, \lambda_j \hat{P}_j^* \left(\frac{1}{\varphi_j(p)} p\right)$, but since $\frac{\lambda_i}{\varphi_i(p)} > 1$, $p \notin \lambda_j \hat{P}_j^*(\frac{1}{\varphi_j(p)} p)$.
This proves (3) above.
Finally the constraint set is defined by

$$C^* := Z_-^* = (Y + \{\Sigma w_i\})_-^*.$$

Let p be an <u>optimum</u> in $\mathcal{E}_0^*$, i.e.

$$p \in Z^{*} \text{ and } \hat{P}^{*}(p) \cap Z^{*} = \emptyset.$$

Then $H(z)$ separates $\hat{P}^{*}(p)$ and Z^{*} and z is a "characteristic action" at p in $\mathcal{E}_0^{*}$. From property 4.9:

$$\text{Rint } \hat{P}^{**}(p) \cap Z = \emptyset \text{ and } x \in Z.$$

From property 4.5 (8):

$$\hat{P}^{**}(p) = \Sigma\, \hat{P}_i^{**}\left(\frac{1}{\varphi_i(p)}\, p\right)$$

Hence there exist $x_i \in \text{Bnd } \hat{P}_i^{**}\left(\frac{1}{\varphi_i(p)}\, p\right)$, such that $\Sigma x_i = x$.

We have $\frac{1}{\varphi_i(p)}\, p\, x_i = 1$, and $x_i' \in \hat{P}_i^{**}\left(\frac{1}{\varphi_i(p)}\, p\right)$ implies $\frac{1}{\varphi_i(p)}\, p \cdot x_i' > 1$.

Hence $p \cdot x_i = \varphi_i(p)$ and x_i is best in the budgetset.

So $((x_i),p)$ is an equilibrium in E_C. □

For a proof of existence along these lines, see [25] and [26].

6.3. Pareto optimum in E_C.

Above we considered equilibria that took into account the a-priori distribution of wealth among consumers by resources w_i and the profit shares θ_i. If we ignore these, we can define Pareto optima in E_C. For that purpose we define an abstract economy (see sections 2.4 and 2.6):

$$\mathcal{E}_P := \{X_i,\ \hat{P}_i : X \twoheadrightarrow X_i,\ \bar{C}\},$$

where

$$\hat{P}_i(x) := P_i(x_i) \times \Pi\, X_j,$$

$$\bar{C} := \{x \in R^n \mid \Sigma x_i \in Z\}.$$

By definition 2.7 a Pareto optimum in $\mathcal{E}_P$ is a solution x, such that:

$$\text{(i)} \quad \cap\, \hat{P}_i(x) \cap \bar{C} = \emptyset, \qquad x \in \bar{C} \cap X.$$

Due to the independence of preferences (section 2.6), $\cap\, \hat{P}_i(x) = \Pi P_i(x_i)$. So a Pareto optimum is an x such that:

$$\text{(ii)} \quad \Pi P_i(x) \cap \bar{C} = \emptyset, \qquad x \in \bar{C} \cap X.$$

It is shown that (ii) is equivalent to:

(iii) $\Sigma P_i(x_i) \cap Z = \emptyset$

$\Sigma x_i \in Z.$

For suppose first that (ii) holds and $a \in \Sigma P_i(x_i) \cap Z$ for some $a \in R^n$. Then there exists $v = (v_1, v_2, \dots, v_n) \in R^{nh}$, such that $\Sigma v_i = a$ and $\forall_i : v_i \in P_i(x_i)$. But since $a \in Z$, $v \in \bar{C}$, which is a contradiction. Let x not be a Pareto optimum, hence, there exist $z \in \Pi P_i(x_i) \cap \bar{C}$. Then $\forall_i : z_i \in P_i(x_i)$, so $\Sigma z_i \in \Sigma P_i(x_i)$. Since $\Sigma z_i \in Z$, x does not satisfy (iii).

It was noted in 6.2, that in an equilibrium:

$$\Sigma P_i(x_i) \cap Z = \emptyset \text{ and } \Sigma x_i \in Z.$$

So an equilibrium is a Pareto optimum. Note that this conclusion does not hold if preferences are not independent but only separable, (see section 2.6).

7. Intertemporal optimality.

In this section an economy will be defined in which production processes need time. The first three subsections will deal with technological economies in which consumption is absent and preferences are expressed about the capital structure (of the last period). Both superlinear and convex technologies are considered.
In the last subsection consumption will also be introduced. Although most results of the first three sections can also be found in e.g. Makarov and Rubinov [10], the presentation is such that these models are interpretations of an abstract economy introduced in section 2, and - above all - such that it allows for explicit treatment of consumption in section 4.

7.1. A dynamic technological economy.

Consider an economy over T+1 time periods, indicated by $t \in T := \{0,1,\dots,T\}$. At each time period the set of possible actions X_t is equal to $R_+^{n_t}$, the nonnegative orthant of the n_t-dimensional commodity space. Each bundle $k_t \in X_t$ is interpreted as a bundle of goods, that is used as input in a production proces $Y_{s,t}$ to produce a set of outputs $Y_{s,t}(x_t)$ in X_s. Labor and consumption goods may occupy some dimensions in X_t, in which case the evolution of the laborforce and consumption is a part of the production process. However, labor and consumption may also be excluded from X_t, and implicitly included in $Y_{s,t}$. Then X_t contains only bundles of capital goods. Let $Y_0 := \{y \in X_0 | y \leqq y_0\}$, where y_0 is a vector of initial resources.

The motion of the economy over time is described by a trajectory or program $(k_0, k_1, \ldots, k_T) =: k$, where $k \in X := \Pi X_t$. A preference correspondence $P: X \rightrightarrows X$ has to be specified

The dynamic technological economy E thus consists of the objects:

$$E := \{T, X_t, P: X \rightrightarrows X, Y_{t,s}, Y_0\}$$

Assumption 7.1: For each $t \in T$, the commodity space X_t equals $R_+^{n_t}$. Each production process $Y_{t,s} : X_s \rightrightarrows X_t$, with $0 \leqq s < t \leqq T$, is a superlinear and monotonous correspondence (see Def. A.14) such that $Y_{t,\tau} \circ Y_{\tau,s} = Y_{t,s}$, for $s < \tau < t$, $s, \tau, t \in T$. The set Y_0 is compact, convex and contains zero as well as an interior point.

A program $k \in X$ is said to be feasible, if:
(i) $k_t \in Y_{t,s}(k_s)$, for $0 \leqq s < t \leqq T$;
(ii) $k_0 \in Y_0$.

Since $Y_{t,s}(k,s) = \bigcup_{k_\tau \in Y_{\tau,s}(k_s)} Y_{t,\tau}(k_\tau)$, for $s < \tau < t$,

by assumption 7.1, a program k is feasible if all states between k_0 and k_T can be produced and can produce the succeeding state (see fig. 7.a).

This is expressed by a correspondence $F : X \rightrightarrows X$, defined by:

$$F(k) := Y_0 \times Y_{1,0}(k_0) \times \ldots \times Y_{T,T-1}(k_{T-1}).$$

Since each projection of F into X_t for $t \geqq 1$, gives the set of outputs resulting from a given input in the preceding period, $F_t(k) = Y_{t,t-1}(k_{t-1})$, F is called the output correspondence in E.

A program k is feasible if and only if $k \in F(k)$. The set of feasible programs in E is defined by $B := \{k \in X | k \in F(k)\}$.

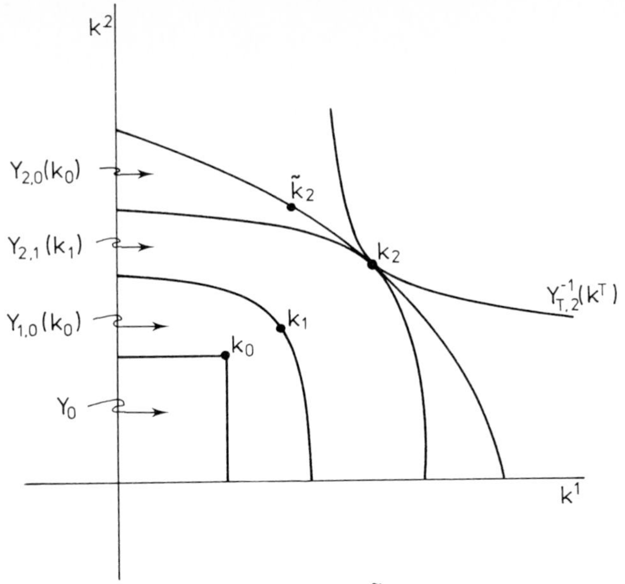

Fig. 7.a $\tilde{k}_2 \in Y_{2,0}(k_0)$, but $(k_0, k_1, \tilde{k}_2)$ is not feasible.

Property 7.2.

The set B of feasible programs in E is compact, convex and contains $k = 0$.

Proof:

Since $Y_{t,s}$ is a monotonous Gale map, it is compact-valued and starred; it follows that $k = 0 \in X$ is feasible.
Take any sequence $\{k^i\}_{i=1,2,\ldots}$ such that $k^i \in F(k^i)$ and $k^i \to k$. Then for each i and t, $k^i_t \in Y_{t,t-1}(k^i_{t-1})$. Since the graph of $Y_{t,t-1}$ is closed, $k_t \in Y_{t,t-1}$, for $t \in T$, and $k \in F(k)$.
Finally, choose $k^1, k^2 \in B$ and consider $k := \lambda k^1 + (1-\lambda)k^2$, for $0 \leqq \lambda \leqq 1$. Since each $Y_{t,s}$ has a convex graph $G(Y_{t,s})$, and Y_0 is convex, it follows that: $k^1_0, k^2_0 \in Y_0$ and $(k^1_t, k^1_{t+1}), (k^2_t, k^2_{t+1}) \in G(Y_{t+1,t})$ imply that $k_0 \in Y$ and $(k_t, k_{t+1}) \in G(Y_{t+1,t})$. Thus B is convex. □

Next, we consider the optimality criterion $P: X \rightrightarrows X$. Since no consumption is possible in this economy, the investment decisions are determined by technological requirements, for all t, except for the last or terminal period T. For this period, preferences about the capital structure k_T can be expressed.

Assumption 7.3: $P_T : X_T \rightrightarrows X_T$ is such that:

(i) it has an open and convex graph, $x_T \notin P(x_T), x_T \in \mathrm{Cl}\, P(x_T)$, and $P(x_T) + X_T = P(x_T)$, for all $x_T \in X_T$;

(ii) it is irreflexive, transitive and complete;

(iii) $X_t = Y_t$.

Although preferences are expressed only for the last or terminal period, they determine implicitly an ordering on inputs in the preceding period. For, let some output $k_T \in X_T$ be given; then the set of inputs required at (T-1) to produce k_T at T is determined by $Y^{-1}_{T,T-1}(k_T) \subset X_{T-1}$. For every k_t, such a set $Y^{-1}_{t,t-1}(k_t)$ of input-requirements in the preceding period can be determined. This procedure defines a correspondence K: $X \rightrightarrows X$, called the input-correspondence:

$$K(k) := Y^{-1}_{1,0}(k_1) \times \ldots \times Y^{-1}_{T,T-1}(k_T) \times X_T.$$

The input-correspondence of some program $k \in X$ owns all programs which, if invested in the production process, can produce at least sufficient outputs to guarantee the desired output in the succeeding period, and notably the output of the terminal period T. It consists of a cartesian product of aureoled, convex and closed sets, which are all but one inverses of components of the output correspondence F.

The input correspondence K is constructed recursively from the terminal period T to the initial period 0. In this simple technological economy E, feasibility of a program $k \in K(k)$ is implied by the condition $k_0 \in Y_0$.

The output correspondence F is constructed forwards from t = 0 to t = T, determining feasible sets in the succeeding period. Although it is not the inverse of K, it is very close to the inverse, as is metioned above.

The interpemporal preference correspondence P: $X \rightrightarrows X$ is defined by:

$$P(k) := K(k) + [\,\mathrm{Int}\, X_0 \times \ldots \times \mathrm{Int}\, X_{T-1} \times P_T(k_T)]$$

$$= \mathrm{Int}\, [Y^{-1}_{1,0}(k_1) \times \ldots \times Y^{-1}_{T,T-1}(k_T)] \times P_T(k_T).$$

A special preference correspondence is the <u>efficiency criterion</u> P^E: $X \rightrightarrows X$, in which the terminal preferences are defined by: $P^E_T(k_T) :=$ $\{\hat{k}_T \in X_T | \hat{k}_T > k_T\} = \{k_T\} + \text{Int } X_T$.
It may be noticed that this criterion is weak in the sense that it permits an efficient point interior relative to a facet of the feasible set $Y_{T,0}(k_0)$, which means that the characteristic price has at least one zero component. A slightly stronger criterion is given by $\{\hat{k}_T \in X_t | \hat{k}_T \geqq k_T \text{ and } \hat{k}_T \neq k_T\}$, just like the definition of a weak Pareto optimum. However, this set (or correspondence) is not open, as required above. Therefore, we will restrict ourselves to the criterion firstly mentioned.

In order to show the existence of an optimum program in E, an abstract economy $\mathcal{E}_0 := (X, P: X \rightrightarrows X, F)$ is defined using the definitions above. It is easily checked that the conditions of theorem 2.2 are met, if assumptions 7.1 and 7.3 (i) hold. From $[k \in F(k)] \Leftrightarrow [k_T \in Y_{T,0}(k_0)]$, and $[P(k) \cap F(k) = \emptyset] \Leftrightarrow [P_T(k_T) \cap Y_{T,0}(k_0) = \emptyset]$, it follows that an optimal program in E is equivalently characterized by an optimal terminal bundle in the economy $\{X_T, P_T, Y_{T,0}(k_0)\}$. Finally, if $Y_{t,s}$ or F are monotonous, i.e. $(F(k)-X) \cap X = F(k)$, then P may be replaced by $\tilde{P}(k) := \text{Mon } P(k)$, without loss of generality. Since $P^E(k) \subset \tilde{P}(k)$ for all k such that $P(k) \neq \emptyset$, it follows that an optimal program is always efficient. Therefore, the following proposition holds:

<u>Proposition 7.4.</u>

1. A program k is optimal in E, if and only if it is optimal in the economy $E_T := \{X_T, P_T, Y_{T,0}(k_0)\}$, i.e. $k_T \in Y_{T,0}(k_0)$ and $P_T(k_T) \cap Y_{T,0}(k_0) = \emptyset$.
2. An optimal program in E is efficient, if assumption 7.1 is satisfied and P(k) is not empty for any feasible k.
3. Given assumptions 7.1 and 7.3, there exists an optimal program k in E.

An efficient program k in E (i.e. optimal for P^E), can equivalently be characterized by the following condition:
there exists a nonzero price $p_T \in X^*_T$ such that

$$\max\{p_T \cdot k_T | k_T \in Y_{T,0}(k_0)\} \text{ is positive.}$$

A program meeting this condition is elsewhere called "optimal" (see Makarov and Rubinov, [10] p. 101).

This corresponds with the so called first principle of optimality, which says that if k is efficient in E, then for any $\tilde{T} < T$, $\tilde{k} := (k_0,\dots,k_{\tilde{T}})$ is efficient in $\tilde{E} := \{\tilde{T},\tilde{X},\tilde{P},\tilde{F}\}$, with $\tilde{X} := (X_0 \times \dots \times X_{\tilde{T}})$, and $\tilde{P}$ and $\tilde{F}$ defined on $\tilde{X}$.

If an optimal program $\hat{k}$ in E exists, then there also exists a characteristic price $\hat{p}$ corresponding to $\hat{k}$. This price is a trajectory $(\hat{p}_0,\dots,\hat{p}_T)$, which sustains in every period the optimal bundle $(\hat{x}_0,\dots,\hat{x}_T)$; see fig. 7.a. If these prices were known or given, separation of consumption and production decisions is possible.
However, this characteristic price $\hat{p}$ can also be considered as a (special) program in the dual representation of the technological economy E.

7.2. The dual economy of E.

A dynamic technological economy $E := \{T,X_t,P,Y_{t,s},Y_0\}$ satisfying assumptions 7.1 and 7.3, permits a dual representation E^* that has the assumptions as properties. Since X_t is the nonnegative orthant, the price space for production is equal to the upper dual cone X_t^0, for each t.
As assumption 7.3 implies that assumption 3.9 is satisfied, a dual preference relation can be defined on X_t^0 (see 3.10). The graph-dual correspondence of a production process $Y_{t,s} : X_s \rightrightarrows X_t$ is called a <u>price development process</u> (given the unit amount of profits), $Y^*_{t,s} : X_s^0 \rightrightarrows X_t^0$.
Since $Y_{t,s}$ is a superlinear correspondence (and its graph a convex cone), the production technology has constant returns of scale and profits are equal to zero at each t. Therefore:

$$Y^*_{t,s}(p_s) = \{p_t \in X_t^0 \mid \forall k_s, \forall k_t \in Y_{t,s}(k_s) : p_t \cdot k_t \leqq p_s \cdot k_s\}.$$

The set of initial prices $Y_0^* := (Y_0)^*_- \cap X_0^0$.

The dual of the output-correspondence $F : X \rightrightarrows X$ is called the <u>output-price correspondence</u> and defined by $F^* : X^0 \rightrightarrows X^0$, with:

$$F^*(p) := Y_0^* \times Y^*_{1,0}(p_0) \times \dots \times Y^*_{T,T-1}(p_{T-1}).$$

Similary, the <u>input-price correspondence</u> $K : X \rightrightarrows X$ is defined by $K^* : X^0 \rightrightarrows X^0$ such that:

$$K^*(p) := Y^{*-1}_{1,0}(p_1) \times \dots \times Y^{*-1}_{T,T-1}(p_T) \times X_T^0.$$

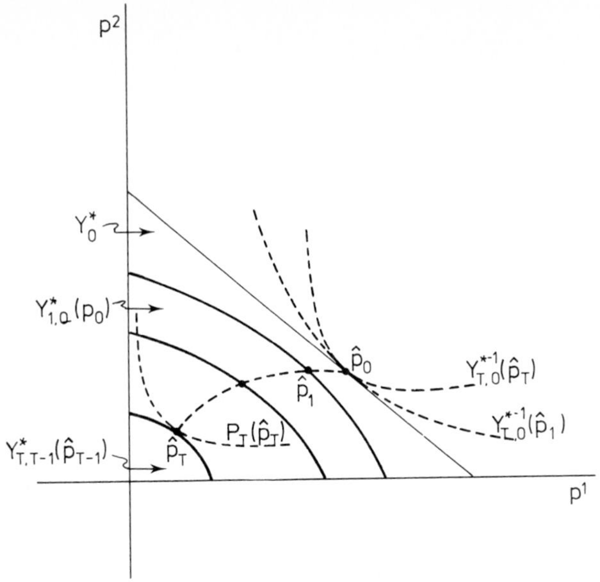

Fig. 7.b A trajectory $\hat{p}$ in E^*, with X_t constant over t.

The output-price correspondence F^* assigns to any $p \in X^0$ a set of prices in each period t that cannot give a value to any feasible output at t higher than a value given to any feasible output in the preceding period. For this concept of feasibility, the set of feasible trajectories B^* is defined by:

$$B^* := \{p \in X^0 \mid p \in F^*(p)\}.$$

The input-price correspondence K^* assigns to any $p \in X^0$ a set of prices in each period t that cannot give a lower value to any input at t (sufficient to produce any output at the following period) than a value given to the output in the succeeding period.

Just as in the previous section, the intertemporal preference correspondence $P^* : X^0 \rightrightarrows X^0$ is constructed from the input-price correspondence K^* and the dual preference correspondence $P_T^* : X_T^0 \rightrightarrows X_T^0$, defined in (3.6) or (3.7):

$$P^*(p) := \text{Int}\, K^*(p) + [X_0^0 \times \ldots \times X_{T-1}^0 \times P_T^*(p_T)] .$$

Thus the <u>dual economy</u> E^* of the technological economy E is defined by:

$$E^* := \{T, X^0_T, P^*: X^0 \rightrightarrows X^0, Y^*_{t,s}: X^0_s \rightrightarrows X^0_t, Y^*_0\}.$$

The following proposition follows from the properties 3.8, 3.11, A.5, A.15, and theorem A.18.

<u>Proposition 7.5:</u>
For the dual economy E^* of the technological economy E meeting assumptions 7.1 and 7.3, identical conditions hold as properties, after substituting the dual concepts from E^* for the primal concepts from E.

The motion of the dual "economy" E^* over time is represented by a trajectory $p := (p_0, p_1, \ldots, p_T) \in X^0$, as in fig. 7.b. In order to apply optimality criteria on these trajectories, the abstract economy $\mathcal{E}^*$ is derived:

$$\mathcal{E}^* := (X^0, P^*: X^0 \rightrightarrows X^0, B^*)$$

A trajectory p is feasible in E^*, as remarked above, if $p \in F^*(p)$, on $p \in B^*$. From the definition of F^* it follows that a trajectory p is <u>feasible in E^*</u>, if and only if for any program k feasible in E the following condition holds:

$$(7.6) \qquad 1 \geqq p_0 \cdot k_0 \geqq p_1 \cdot k_1 \geqq \cdots \geqq p_T \cdot k_T .$$

A trajectory $\hat{p}$ is <u>optimal in E^*</u> if it is both feasible and maximal in $\mathcal{E}^*$, i.e. $\hat{p} \in B^*$ and $B^* \cap P^*(\hat{p}) = \emptyset$. From the definitions of P^* and K^* it can be deduced that $\hat{p}_0 \cdot k_0 \geqq \cdots \geqq \hat{p}_T \cdot k_T \geqq 1$, for any feasible k, is necessary for optimality of $\hat{k}$. Thus a trajectory $\hat{p}$ is optimal, only if for some $\bar{k}$ feasible in E, the condition holds:

$$(7.7) \qquad \hat{p}_0 \cdot \bar{k}_0 = \ldots = \hat{p}_T \cdot \bar{k}_T = 1.$$

If P^* is the <u>efficiency criterion</u> constructed from $P^*_T(p_T) := \mathrm{Int}[p_T + X^0_T]$, then the above condition is also sufficient. An efficient trajectory in E^* for some $\bar{k}$ feasible in E, is thus characterized by (7.7).

The interesting point is that such a program $\bar{k}$ in E is not only feasible, but also itself efficient in E in order to admit an efficient trajectory p in E^*. This efficient program $\bar{k}$ plays the same role as the characteristic price of an optimum in E, and generates a hyperplane separating B^* and $P^*(\hat{p})$ in $\mathcal{E}^*$. It also follows that efficient trajectories $\bar{k}$ in E can be characterized by means of the existence of efficient trajectories $\bar{p}$ in E^*:

Property 7.8: (second principle of optimality).
A necessary and sufficient condition for a feasible program $\bar{k}$ to be
(1) efficient in E, is that there exists an efficient trajectory $\bar{p}$ in E^* for $\bar{k}$;
(2) optimal in E, is that there exists an optimal trajectory $\hat{p}$ in E^* for $\bar{k}$ such that

$$p_T \in [P_T(\bar{k}_T)]^*_+.$$

It is evident that the optimal trajectory $\hat{p}$ corresponding to $\hat{k}$ is equal to the characteristic price $\hat{p}$, mentioned at the end of the previous section.

7.3. Von Neumann growth.

The notion of a technological economy was introduced by von Neumann [23] in order to proof the existence of a particular efficient program, viz. one that has proportional growth, and is called stationary. His idea was to look only after stationary programs in an economy, each having a specific rate of growth. He showed that there was one stationary program that has a maximum rate of growth, called the von Neumann rate of growth, using Brouwer's fixed point theorem. A stationary program which has a Neumann rate of growth is called a Neumann ray or a turnpike.

Consider the dynamic technological economy:

$$E := (T, X_t, P: X \rightrightarrows X,\ Y_{t,s}: X_s \rightrightarrows X_t,\ Y_0)$$

which satisfies assumptions 7.1. Define the preference correspondence P by:

$$P(k) := \left\{ \tilde{k} \in X \;\middle|\; \begin{array}{l} k < \tilde{k}, \text{ and } \exists\alpha : \forall t, \alpha k_t \leqq k_{t+1}, \ \alpha k_t \not< k_{t+1} \\ \\ \text{and } \alpha k_t < \tilde{k}_{t+1}. \end{array} \right\}$$

This definition implies that also assumption 7.3 holds.

By proposition 7.4, there exists an optimal program $\hat{k}$ such that for each t, $k_{t+1} = \alpha k_t \in Y_{t+1,t}(k_t)$.

Since $\hat{k}$ is optimal, there exists a characteristic trajectory $\hat{p}$, which is an optimal trajectory in E^*, and so: $\hat{p} \in B^*$ and $B^* \cap P^*(p) = \emptyset$, or: $p_{t+1} \in Y^*_{t+1,t}(p_t)$, and $p_0 . k_0 = \dots = p_T . k_T = 1$.
This implies that: $\alpha p_{t+1} = p_t$, $\forall_t$.

The conditions: $k_{t+1} = \alpha k_t$, and $\alpha p_{t+1} . k_t = p_{t+1} . k_{t+1} = 1$, $\forall (k_t, k_{t+1})$: $k_{t+1} \in Y_{t+1,t}(k_t)$ are used by von Neumann to construct an equilibrium notion in an economy with a constant technology, called <u>a Neumann-Gale</u>

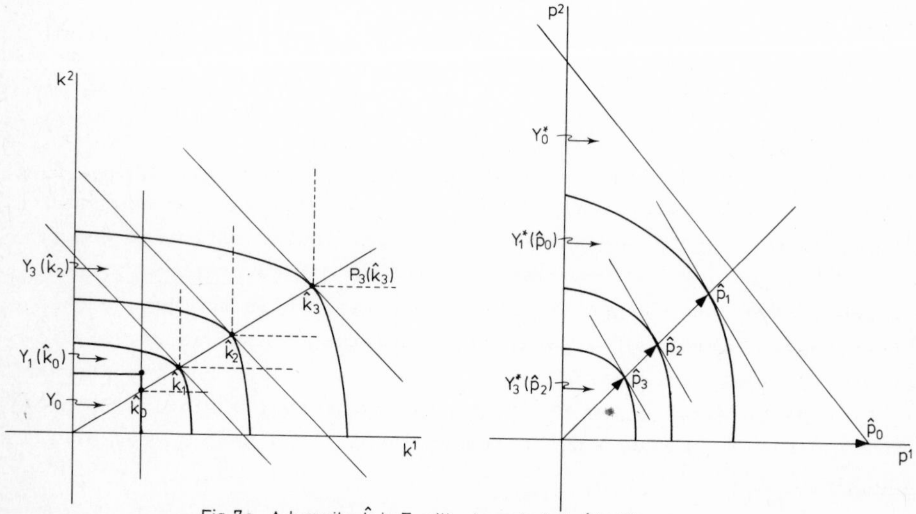

Fig. 7.c A turnpike $\hat{k}$ in E, with characteristic $\hat{p}$ in E*.

<u>economy</u>. Let $X_t = X_0 = R^n_+$, for all $t \in T$, and let $Y_{t+1,t} : X_0 \rightrightarrows X_0$ be constant for $t \geqq 1$, denoted by Y. If only the rate of growth is analyzed, this can be done irrespective of the initial bundle k_0, or the terminal bundle k_T. In fact, the economy can be reduced to two successive period without loss of generality. Thus consider the economy:

$$E^N := \{X_0 \times X_0,\ P: X \rightrightarrows X,\ B^N\},$$

with P as defined above:

$$P(k_1,k_2) := \left\{ (\tilde{k}_1,\tilde{k}_2) \in X \;\middle|\; \begin{array}{l} \exists\alpha: [\alpha k_1 \leqq k_2 \text{ and } \alpha k_1 \not< k_2], \\ \text{and } k_1 < \tilde{k}_1,\ \alpha k_1 < \tilde{k}_2 \end{array} \right\}$$

and B^N is constrained (arbitrarily) to the unit circle:

$$B^N := \{k \in X | k_2 \in Y(k_1) \text{ and } \|k\| \leqq 1\}.$$

An equilibrium in E^N consists of a feasible program $(\hat{k}_1,\hat{k}_2)$, a positive number α, and a price $\hat{p} \in X_0^0$, such that:

(i) $\alpha\hat{k}_1 \leqq \hat{k}_2$;

(ii) $\alpha\hat{p}.k_1 \geqq \hat{p}.k_2$, for all k_1 and $k_2 \in Y(k_1)$;

(iii) $\hat{p}.\hat{k}_2 > 0$.

The scalar α is the rate of growth in E^N, and is not necessarily the maximum or Neumann rate of growth $\hat{\alpha}$. The Neumann rate of growth is defined by:

$$\hat{\alpha}(Y) := \max \{\alpha | \exists k \in \text{Graph } Y : \|k\| \leqq 1 \text{ and } \alpha k_1 \leqq k_2\}.$$

It is easy to see that an optimal program in E^N (which exists under above mentioned conditions), has a Neumann rate of growth, and is part of an equilibrium state. Notice that condition (ii) is equivalent to saying that $p \in \alpha Y^*(p)$.

An example of a von Neumann model is a correspondence $Y : R_+^n \rightrightarrows R_+^n$, defined by use of two given $(n\times m)$ matrices A and B;

$$Y(k_1) := \{k_2 | \exists x \in R_+^m : k_2 = Bx \text{ and } k_1 = Ax\}$$

Its dual model is $Y^* : R_+^{n*} \rightrightarrows R_+^{n*}$, with

$$Y^*(p_1) := \{p_2 | p_1 A \geqq p_2 B\}.$$

7.3. A convex technological economy.

This economy $E := \{T, X_t, P: X \rightrightarrows X, Y_{t,s}: X_s \rightrightarrows X_t, Y_0\}$, satisfying assumptions 7.1 and 7.3 has a production technology characterized by constant returns to scale, represented by superlinear correspondences $Y_{t,s}$. In this section a more general production technology will be considered, allowing also for decreasing returns to scale. This mainly causes complications in the dual economy.

Assume that each production process $Y_{t,s} : X_s \rightrightarrows X_t$ is represented by a convex-star correspondence instead of a superlinear correspondence, and let further assumptions 7.1 and 7.3 hold for E. A convex-star correspondence has a closed and convex graph, and is a starred Gale map; both its cone-closure and its cone-interior are superlinear correspondences (see def. A.12).

Since in the proof of compactness and convexity of the set B of feasible programs in E (property 7.2), no use is made of positive homogeneity ($Y_{t,s}$ was assumed superlinear), it is also valid in this case where $Y_{t,s}$ is assumed to be a convex-star correspondence. Therefore, the necessary conditions for the existence of an optimal program are satisfied (proposition 7.4).

The dual economy E^* can be defined by using the same operations as in section 7.1, but the consistency condition in assumption 7.1 will be violated. This condition requires that: $Y^*_{t,\tau} \circ Y^*_{\tau,s} = Y^*_{t,s}$ for $t > \tau > s$, which means that price information between s and t must correspond with intermediate price formation. This is precluded, of course, if profits between consecutive periods (equal to unity) are equal to unit profits between any two periods, say t and s.

In order to solve this problem, a (nonnegative) distribution of profits over time $\pi := (\pi_0, \pi_1, \ldots, \pi_T)$ is introduced, which replaces the unit profits in the duality operations and allows the price development to be consistent over time.

Define the graph-duality operation with respect to π_t by:

$$Y^{\otimes}_{t+1,t}(p_t,\pi_t) := \left\{ p_{t+1} \,\middle|\, \begin{array}{l} \forall k_t, \forall k_{t+1} \in Y_{t+1,t}(k_t); \\ p_{t+1}\cdot k_{t+1} \leqq p_t \cdot k_t + \pi_t \end{array} \right\}$$

$$= \pi_t Y^{\otimes}_{t+1,t}(p_t/\pi_t).$$

The consistency condition then implies that for all $k \in F(k)$:

$$\begin{array}{lcl} p_0 \cdot k_0 + \pi_0 & \geqq & p_1 \cdot k_1 \\ \cdots\cdots\cdots & & \\ p_{T-1}\cdot k_{T-1} + \pi_{T-1} & \geqq & p_T \cdot k_T \\ \hline p_0 \cdot k_0 + \Sigma \pi_t & \geqq & p_T \cdot k_T \end{array}$$

with: $Y^*_{t,\tau}(.,\pi_{\tau,t}) \circ Y^*_{\tau,s}(.,\pi_{s,\tau}) = Y^*_{t,s}(.,\pi_{s,t})$,

where: $\pi_{s,t} := \sum_{\tau=s}^{t} \pi_\tau$ and $\pi_{0,T} = \Sigma\pi_t$.

Thus: $p_0.k_0 + \pi_{0,T} \geqq p_1.k_1 + \pi_{1,T} \geqq \dots \geqq p_{T-1}.k_{T-1} + \pi_{T-1,T} \geqq p_T.k_T$, for all $k \in F(k)$.

It follows that $(\pi_{0,T}, \pi_{1,T}, \dots, \pi_{T-1,T}, \pi_{T,T})$ is a decreasing sequence with $\pi_{0,T} = \Sigma\pi_t$ and $\pi_{T,T} = \pi_T = 0$.

Since each efficient path $\hat{k}$ is sustained by a characteristic price $\hat{p}$, it is also implicitly sustained by a profit distribution $\hat{\pi}$, and a turn-over value $\hat{\beta}$, satisfying:

$$\hat{p}_0.\hat{k}_0 + \hat{\pi}_{0,T} = \dots = \hat{p}_{T-1}.\hat{k}_{T-1} + \hat{\pi}_{T-1,T} = \hat{p}_T.\hat{k}_T =: \hat{\beta}.$$

The value $\hat{\beta}$ represents turn-over at each period, which is equal in case of efficient programs. The turn-over value β can also be given a priori to determine the initial price level; it has to be used in the point-duality operations:

$$p_0 \in Y^*_0 := \{p_0 \mid \forall k_0 \in Y_0 : p_0.k_0 \leqq \beta\},$$

and in $P^*(p_T) \subset X^*_T$.

Let the dual economy E^* be defined by:

$$\{T, X^0_t, P^*: X^0 \rightrightarrows X^0,\ Y^*_{t,s} : X^0_s \times R_+ \rightrightarrows X^0_t,\ Y^*_0\}.$$

The turn-over value β is implicitly given through P^* and Y^*_0. A <u>program</u> in E^* consists now of a price path p and a profit or income distribution π. This is feasible if: $p_t \in Y^*_{t,s}(p_s, \pi_{s,T})$, $t \geqq 1$, and $p_0 \in Y^*_0$. Let $F^* : X^0 \times R^T_+ \rightrightarrows X^0 \times R^T_+$ be defined by:

$$F^*(p,\pi) := Y^*_0 \times Y^*_{1,0}(p_0, \pi_{0,T}) \times \dots \times Y^*_{T,T-1}(p_{T-1}, \pi_{T-1}) \times [0,\pi].$$

The set of <u>feasible programs in E^*</u> is defined by:

$$B^* := \{(p,\pi) \in X^0 \times R^T_+ \mid (p,\pi) \in F^*(p,\pi)\}.$$

It can be shown that this set is nonempty, compact, convex. Analogously to the reasoning in section 7.1, an input-price correspondence $K^* : X^0 \times R_+^T \rightrightarrows X^0 \times R_+^T$ can be constructed and an intertemporal preference correspondence P^* on $X^0 \times R_+^T$. Again, the necessary conditions for the existence of an optimal program $(\hat{p},\hat{\pi})$ in E^* can be shown to exist, if assumption 7.1 and 7.3 hold in E.

Another approach to handle convex technological systems has been proposed by Makarov and Rubinov [10]. They define a superlinear extension of a convex production correspondence $Y : X_1 \rightrightarrows X_2$ by $\hat{Y}:(X_1 \times R_+) \rightrightarrows (X_2 \times R_+)$ with:

$$\hat{Y}(k_1,\mu) := \mu Y(k_1/\mu) \times [0,\mu], \text{ for all } (k_1,\mu) \in (X_1 \times R_+) \text{ and } \mu > 0$$

Since every convex technology admits a unique superlinear extension which meets the consistency requirement, a superlinear technological economy $\hat{E}$ is derived. A trajectory in $\hat{E}$ is (k,e), where $e := (1,\ldots,1)$. An efficient trajectory is sustained by a dual trajectory (p,ν) in $\hat{E}^*$, which itself is also efficient, and corresponds with $(p_t,\pi_{t,T})$ above.

The interesting feature of a convex technological economy is that the correspondences $Y_{1,0},Y_{2,0},\ldots,Y_{T,0}$ converge to a process that is bounded for every input (also infinite), if the largest eigenvalue of the cone-interior correspondence is smaller than one. Further, the prices may also rise during the process, contrary to prices in a superlinear economy. Finally, there may be more profit distributions that sustain an optimal or efficient program.

7.4. A dynamic economy with consumption.

The intertemporal model developed above can easily been extended to an economy E with consumption. Consider a dynamic economy (either superlinear, or convex):

$$E := \{T, X_t, P: X \rightrightarrows X,\ Y_{t,s}: X_s \rightrightarrows X_t,\ Y_0\}.$$

In this economy a program consists of a consumption bundle c_t and an investment bundle k_t at each period $t \in T$. A program (c,k) is said to be feasible if $(c,k) \in X \times X$, and $\forall_t,\ y_t := c_t + k_t \in Y_{t,t-1}(k_{t-1})$, with $Y_0 := Y_{0,-1}(k_{-1})$.

Consider the correspondence F from X×X into itself:

$$F(c,k) := \left\{ (x,k) \in X{\times}X \;\middle|\; \begin{array}{l} \forall_t : c_t \in Y_{t,t-1}(k_{t-1})-k_t, \text{ and} \\ k_t \in Y_{t,t-1}(k_{t-1})-c_t. \end{array} \right\}$$

The set of feasible programs is defined by:

$$B := \{(c,k) \mid (c,k) \in F(c,k)\}.$$

It can be shown that the set B is nonempty, compact and convex. Next, consider the <u>input-correspondence</u> K from X×X into X, determining the set of inputs that are sufficient to produce a consumption program c, and which is defined by:

$$K(c,k) := Y^{-1}_{1,0}(c_1+k_1) \times \ldots \times Y^{-1}_{T,T-1}(c_T+0) \times X_T.$$

Given an intertemporal preference correspondence $P:X \rightrightarrows X$, a <u>gross-preference correspondence</u> $\tilde{P}$ from X×X into itself is defined by

$$\tilde{P}(c,k) := P(c) \times [\,\text{Int } K(c,k)\,].$$

A program (c,k) in E is optimal, if it is feasible, $(c,k) \in B$, and if it is maximal, $\tilde{P}(c,k) \cap B = \emptyset$. It is evident that an optimal program exists, if E meets assumptions 7.1 and 7.3.

Under certain conditions it is possible to reduce intertemporal choice to the current period. This is the case if the preference structure is defined according to Rawls' Maximin criterion, see [13], which can be simplified as:

$$P(c) := \{\tilde{c} \in X \mid \forall_t,\ \tilde{c}_t \in \bigcup_{s \in T} P_0(c_s)\},$$

where P_0 is a given one period preference correspondence. An intertemporal program is thus judged by the worst period in that program. The set of programs which are better than today's consumption continued over time is given by a correspondence $P:X_0 \rightrightarrows X$, defined by:

$$P(c_0) := \{\tilde{c} \in X \mid \forall_t : \tilde{c}_t \in P_0(c_0)\}.$$

If today's consumption $\bar{c}_0$ is too high, it is possible that the future consumption aspirations $P(\bar{c}_0)$ and the necessary investments given by K are not feasible any more, i.e. there exists no $(\bar{c},\bar{k})$ in:

$$B \cap [\mathrm{Cl}\ P(\bar{c}_0) \times K(\bar{c},\bar{k})].$$

On the other hand, if today's consumption $\bar{c}_0$ is too low, it is possible to improve on the projected program. The constraint set of feasible programs is thus dependent on current consumption, i.e.:

$$B_0(c_0) := \{\tilde{c}_0 \in X_0 \mid \exists(\tilde{c},\tilde{k}) : (\tilde{c},\tilde{k}) \in B \times [\mathrm{Cl}\ P(c_0) \times K(\tilde{c},\tilde{k})]\}.$$

The model $(X_0, P_0 \rightrightarrows X_0, B_0 : X_0 \rightrightarrows X_0)$ results in a <u>relative optimum</u> $\hat{c}_0$, which is today's optimal consumption bundle if a consumption program which is at every period not worse than current consumption must also be feasible. It is evident that there exists an optimal program $(\hat{c},\hat{k})$ in E associated with each relative optimal current consumption bundle $\hat{c}_0$.

Appendix.

A.1. Duality operations on sets and correspondences.

The duality concepts which are used here, are based on the notion of separation of sets in R^n. A typical separation theorem gives necessary and sufficient conditions for the existence of a hyperplane separating two sets. Such a hyperplane divides R^n into two halfspaces, each of which contains one set mentioned above.

Let X be a set in R^n and let a hyperplane be called a bounding hyperplane of X, if one halfspace associated with that hyperplane contains X. The set X can be characterized (and perfectly if X is convex) by the set of all bounding hyperplanes of X, not just ∩ of -(ie, not conv. hull). Since each hyperplane in R^n can be represented by a vector $p \in R^{n*}$ and a scalar $\alpha \in R$:

$$H(p;\alpha) := \{x \in R^n | p.x = \alpha\},$$

it is fruitful to consider the set of all linear functions als having their domain in R^n and values in R. This set is again a real euclidean n-space denoted by R^{n*} and called the dual space of R^n. The spaces R^n and R^{n*} are isomorphic and do not need to be distinguished, but a distinction has sense if this theory is applied to economics. The primal space R^n will be identified with the quantity (or action) space, the dual space R^{n*} with the price or valuation space.

Let

$$H_-(p;\alpha) := \{x \in R^n | p.x \leq \alpha\}$$

$$H_+(p;\alpha) := \{x \in R^n | p.x \geq \alpha\},$$

and $H(p) := H(p;1)$, $H_-(p) := H_-(p;1)$, $H_+(p) := H_+(p;1)$.
The idea expressed above that a set $X \subset R^n$ can be characterized by the set of all bounding hyperplanes of X, is made precise by means of the dual relation between hyperplanes in R^n and prices (covectors) in R^{n*}.[1]

---

[1] Since this distiction is mathematically not necessary in case of a finite euclidean space, all properties derived here can be applied both in R^n and R^{n*}. Also $(R^{n*})^* = R^n$.

A.1.1. Dual cones, sets, and correspondences.

Definition A.1: Let X be a set in R^n. The dual sets of X are defined by:

$$X_-^* := \{p \in R^{n*} | X \subset H_-(p)\} = \{p \in R^{n*} | \forall x \in X: p.x \leqq 1\}$$

$$X_+^* := \{p \in R^{n*} | X \subset H_+(p)\} = \{p \in R^{n*} | \forall x \in X: p.x \geqq 1\}$$

and are called the lower dual set, resp. upper dual set.
The dual cones of X are defined by:

$$X_-^0 := \{p \in R^{n*} | X \subset H_-(p;0)\} = \{p \in R^{n*} | \forall x \in X: p.x \leqq 0\}$$

$$X_+^0 := \{p \in R^{n*} | X \subset H_+(p;0)\} = \{p \in R^{n*} | \forall x \in X: p.x \geqq 0\}$$

and are called the lower, resp. upper dual cone of X.

The upper dual set X_+^* contains all $p \in R^{n*}$ such that the hyperplanes H(p) separate X and {0}, see fig. A.1a.
The lower dual set X_-^* contains all $p \in R^{n*}$ such that X and {0} are on one side of H(p). The dual cones contain all p such that the hyperplanes H(p;0) have X on the negative, resp. positive side.

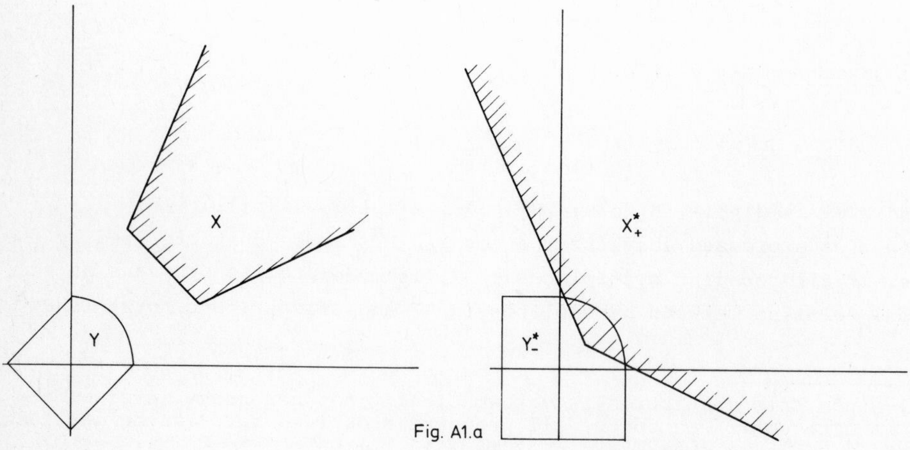

Fig. A1.a

The following hull (or closure) operations are defined:

Definition A.2: Let $X \subset R^n$.

The affine hull of X:

$$\text{Aff } X := \{x \in R^n | x = \sum_{i=1}^{n+1} \lambda_i x_i, \text{ for } x_i \in X \text{ and } \Sigma\lambda_i = 1\};$$

The convex hull of X:

$$\text{Conv } X := \{x \in R^n | x = \sum_{i=1}^{n+1} \lambda_i x_i, \text{ for } x_i \in X \text{ and } \Sigma\lambda_i = 1,\ \lambda_i \geqq 0\};$$

The aureole hull of X:

$$\text{Aur } X := \{x \in R^n | x = \lambda y, \text{ for } y \in X \text{ and } \lambda \geqq 1\};$$

The star hull of X:

$$\text{Star } X := \{x \in R^n | x = \lambda y, \text{ for } y \in X \text{ and } 0 \leqq \lambda \leqq 1\};$$

The cone closure of X:

$$\text{Cone } X := \{x \in R^n | x = \lambda y, \text{ for } y \in X \text{ and } \lambda \geqq 0\};$$

The normal hull with respect to the cone K [1]:

$$\text{Norm}_K X := (X-K) \cap K;$$

The monotone hull with respect to the cone K [1]:

$$\text{Mon}_K X := (X+K) \cap K.$$

Sets which are equal to their hull are called accordingly affine, convex, etc.

The following "opening" operation is used:

---

1) If $K = R^n_+$, no mention is made of K in the notation.

Definition A.3: Let $X \subset R^n$;

The interior cone of X is:

$$\text{Conint } X := \{x \in R^n \mid \forall \lambda \geqq 0: \lambda x \in X\}.$$

Definition A.4:
Apart from the usual operations on sets (λX, $X+Y$, $X \cap Y$, $X \cup Y$), we shall use an operation called dual addition [25], convex intersection [18], or inverse addition (Rockafellar [15]):

$$\bigcup_{\lambda \in [0,1]} [\lambda X \cap (1-\lambda) Y].$$

In general, if $X_i \subset R^n$ are sets, $i \in I := \{1,2,\ldots,n\}$ and $L := \{\lambda \in R^n \mid \Sigma \lambda_i = 1 \text{ and } \lambda_i \geqq 0\}$, then the expression becomes:

$$\bigcup_L \bigcap_I \lambda_i X_i.$$

Sometimes we use the notation:[1)]

$$X \mathring{\cap} Y := \bigcup_{\lambda \in [0,1]} [\lambda X \cap (1-\lambda) Y].$$

The following properties of polar sets are given without proof; their proofs, or references to their proofs, can be found in [16], [18], [24], [25], [26].

Property A.5 (valid for both positive and negative dual operations; the suffix is therefore omitted):

1. $X^* = (\text{Rint } X)^* = (\text{Cl } X)^* = (\text{Conv } X)^*$;
2. X^* is closed and convex;
3. $p \in \text{Bnd } X^* \Leftrightarrow H(p;1)$ supports X;
4. $X \subset Y \Leftrightarrow X^* \supset Y^*$;

---

1) Analogously, one may define an operation convex addition:

$$X \mathring{+} Y := \bigcup_{\lambda \in [0,1]} [\lambda X + (1-\lambda) Y] = \text{Conv } [X \cup Y].$$

5. $(\lambda X)^{*} = \lambda^{-1}X^{*}$, for $\lambda > 0$;

6. $(X \cup Y)^{*} = X^{*} \cap Y^{*}$;

7. $(X \cap Y)^{*} = \mathrm{Conv}(X^{*} \cup Y^{*})$;

8. $(X + Y)^{*} = \mathrm{Cl}\,[\bigcup_{\lambda \in [0,1]} (\lambda X^{*} \cap (1-\lambda)Y^{*})]$.

Property A.6 (on negative dual sets):

1. $0 \in \mathrm{Int\,Conv}\,X \Leftrightarrow X^{*}_{-}$ is bounded;

2. $X^{*}_{-} = (\mathrm{Star}\ X)^{*}_{-}$;

3. $X^{*}_{-} = \mathrm{Star}\ (X^{*}_{-})$, and thus contains 0;

4. $X^{*}_{-} \supset X^{0}_{-} = \mathrm{Conint}(X^{*}_{-}) = (\mathrm{Cone}\ X)^{*}_{-} = (\mathrm{Cone}\ X)^{0}_{-}$;

5. $X \subset K \Rightarrow [X^{*}_{-} \cap K^{0}_{+}]$ is K^{0}_{+}-normal, for some K; $(X^{*}_{-} - K^{0}_{+}) \cap K^{0}_{+} = X^{*}_{-}$.

Property A.7 (on positive dual sets):

1. $0 \in \mathrm{Cl\,Conv}\,X \Leftrightarrow X^{*}_{+} = \emptyset$;

2. $X^{*}_{+} = (\mathrm{Aur}\ X)^{*}_{+}$;

3. $X^{*}_{+} = \mathrm{Aur}(X^{*}_{+})$, and does not contain 0;

4. $X^{*}_{+} \subset X^{0}_{+} = \mathrm{Cl\ Cone}(X^{*}_{+}) = (\mathrm{Cone}\ X)^{*}_{+} = (\mathrm{Cone}\ X)^{0}_{+}$;

5. $X \subset K \Rightarrow X^{*}_{+} + K^{0}_{+} = X^{*}_{+}$, i.e. K^{0}_{+}-monotone.

Property A.8 (reflexivity conditions):

Let X be a closed and convex set. Then:

1. $[(X^{*}_{+})^{*}_{+} = X] \Leftrightarrow$ X is aureoled and $0 \notin X$;

2. $[(X^{*}_{-})^{*}_{-} = X] \Leftrightarrow$ X is starred (so $0 \in X$);

3. $[(X^{0}_{+})^{0}_{+} = X] \Leftrightarrow$ X is a cone;

4. $[(X^{0}_{-})^{0}_{-} = X] \Leftrightarrow$ X is a cone.

Property A.9 (dual separation theorem):

Let X be closed, convex, aureoled and not containing 0 (i.e. aureole-reflexive), and Y be closed, convex and containing 0 (i.e. star-reflexive), then:

1. $[X \cap Y = \emptyset] \Rightarrow [X^{*}_{+} \cap Y^{*}_{-} \neq \emptyset]$;

2. If $[\text{Cl Cone } X \cap \text{Conint } Y] \subset \{0\}$, then:

$[(X \cap Y) \neq \emptyset \text{ and } (\text{Rint } X \cap \text{Rint } Y) = \emptyset] \Leftrightarrow$

$[(X_+^* \cap Y_-^*) \neq \emptyset \text{ and } (\text{Rint } X_+^* \cap \text{Rint } Y_-^*) = \emptyset]$.

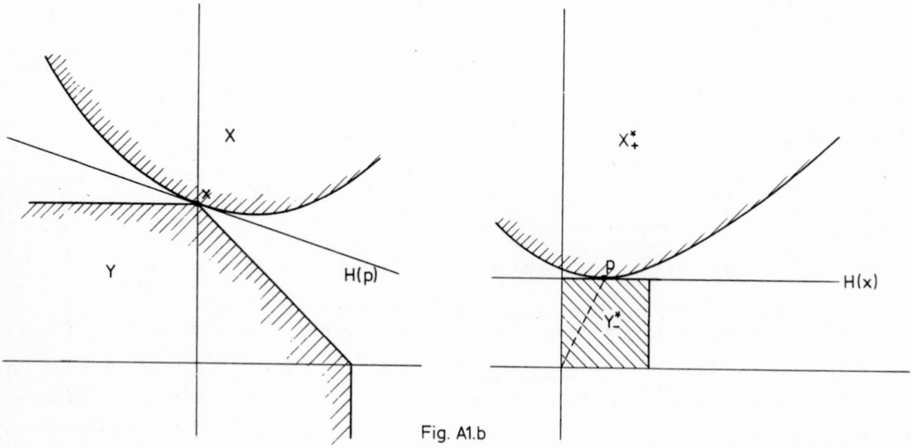

Fig. A1.b

A.1.2. Dual correspondences.

We distinguish two types of dual correspondences, the point-dual correspondence and the graph-dual correspondence. The point-dual of a correspondence F is obtained by taking the dual set (upper or lower) of each image F(x):

Definition A.10: Given a correspondence $F: X \rightrightarrows Y$, for $X \subset R^m$ and $Y \subset R^n$, we call point-dual correspondences the correspondences $F_+^* : X \rightrightarrows R^{n*}$ and $F_-^* : X \rightrightarrows R^{n*}$ defined by:

$$F_+^*(x) := [F(x)]_+^* \text{ and } F_-^*(x) := [F(x)]_-^*, \text{ for all } x \in X.$$

Property A.11 (on point-dual correspondences; see [26]):
Let $F : X \rightrightarrows Y$ be a correspondence. If F is point-closed, point-convex, point-aureoled and $0 \notin F(x)$, $\forall x$, then:

1. F is lhc $\Rightarrow F_+^*$ is closed.

2. [F is closed and for all $x \in X$ and for some neighborhood N of 0, $F_+^*(x) \cap N = \emptyset$] $\Rightarrow F_+^*$ is lhc.

If F is point-closed, point-convex and point-starred, then

1. F is lhc $\Rightarrow F^{*}_{-}$ is closed.

2. F is closed $\Rightarrow F^{*}_{-}$ is uhc.

The graph-dual correspondence is obtained by taking the dual (upper or lower) of the graph of a correspondence.

Definition A.12. Let $X \subset R^m$ and $Y \subset R^n$ be closed, convex and solid cones, and $F : X \rightrightarrows Y$ a correspondence. The upper and lower graph-dual correspondences $F^{\otimes}_{+} : X^0_{+} \rightrightarrows Y^0_{+}$ and $F^{\otimes}_{-} : X^0_{+} \rightrightarrows Y^0_{+}$ are defined by:

$$F^{\otimes}_{+}(p) := \{q \in Y^0_{+} | (p,-q) \in [Gr(F)]^{*}_{-}\}, \text{ and}$$

$$F^{\otimes}_{-}(p) := \{q \in Y^0_{+} | (-p,q) \in [Gr(F)]^{*}_{-}\}.$$

The inverse of this correspondence has been introduced by Ruys [18, p. 191], and is called the adjoint of F. If the graph of F is a convex cone, it corresponds with the (sup-, or inf-oriented) adjoint defined by Rockafellar [14, p. 4]. If F is a linear function, both adjoints coincide and correspond with the usual definition.

The graph-dual correspondences are equivalently described by:

$$F^{\otimes}_{+}(p) := \{q | \forall x, \forall y \in F(x) : p.x \leqq q.y + 1\};$$

$$F^{\otimes}_{-}(p) := \{q | \forall x, \forall y \in F(x) : p.x + 1 \geqq q.y\}.$$

Property A.13 (on graph-dual correspondences; see [18, p. 199]): Let $X \subset R^m$ and $Y \subset R^n$ be closed convex and solid cones, and $F : X \rightrightarrows Y$ be a correspondence with a closed and convex graph. Then

1. F and $F^{\otimes}$ are closed and lhc.
2. $(F^{\otimes})^{\otimes} = F$.

It may be noticed that for each $\pi > 0$:

$$\pi F^{\otimes}_{+}(p/\pi) = \{q | \forall x, \forall y \in F(x) : p.x \leqq q.y + \pi\};$$

$$\pi F^{\otimes}_{-}(p/\pi) = \{q | \forall x, \forall y \in F(x) : p.x + \pi \geqq q.y\}.$$

This formulation comes close to the conjugate operation, in which one component of the vector is fixed (on +1) instead of the scalar. Compare e.g. Makarov and Rubinov [10, p. 145]:

$$p.x + \pi \geqq q.y + \rho \quad , \qquad \text{for all } x,y \in F(x).$$

Definition A.14: Let X and Y be closed, convex cones in R^n, resp. R^m, and F be a correspondence from X into Y.
F is said to be superlinear if it is:

1) superadditive: $F(x+y) \supset F(x) + F(y)$;
2) positive homogeneous: $F(\lambda x) = \lambda F(x)$, $\forall \lambda > 0$;
3) closed: Gr(F) is closed in $X \times Y$;
4) a Gale map: $F(0) = \{0\}$;
5) nondegenerate: $F(X) \cap [\text{Int } Y] \neq \emptyset$.

F is said to be a convex-star map, if its graph is a closed and convex set, if the cone closure and the cone interior of graph F meet the conditions on the graph of a superlinear correspondence, and if $0 \in F(x)$ for all $x \in X$.

F is said to be a convex-aureole map, if its inverse is a convex-star correspondence.
The correspondence $F_c : X \rightrightarrows Y$ defined by:

$$F_c(x) := \{y \mid (x,y) \in \text{Cone Gr}(F)\}$$

is called the cone-closure of F, and analogously the cone-opening of F, F_0 is defined. Then it is clear that F_c and $F_0^{\otimes}$ describe the behavior of F, resp. $F^{\otimes}$ near the origin, and F_0, resp. $F_c^{\otimes}$, the behavior of F, resp. $F^{\otimes}$ in the infinite. If F is a superlinear map, then evidently F, F_0 and F_c coincide.

The following properties of convex-star and convex-aureole correspondences can be derived, see [18].

Property A.15: Let $F : X \rightrightarrows Y$ be a convex-star correspondence.
Then:

1. F is point-compact, point-starred, and increasing: i.e.:

$$[x,y, \text{ and } (y-x) \in X] \Rightarrow [F(x) \subset F(y)].$$

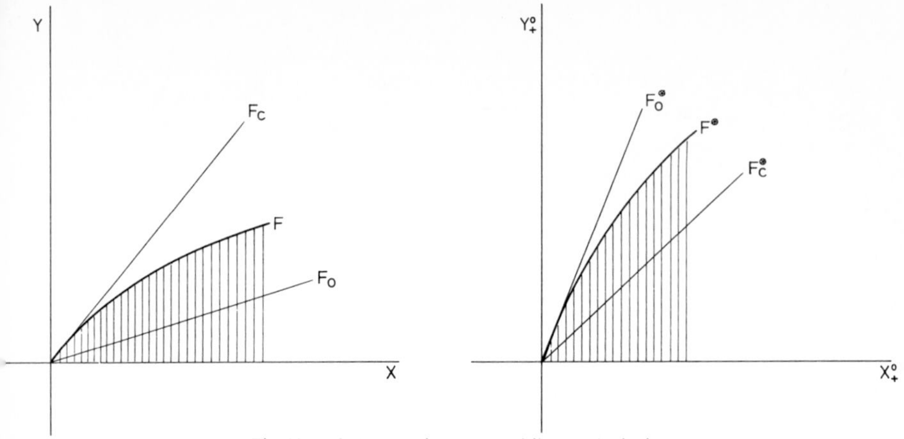

Fig. A1.c A convex-star map and its graph-dual

2. $F^{\otimes}$ is a convex-star map, and also Y-<u>normal</u>, i.e.:

$$\text{for all } p \in X^0 : F^{\otimes}(p) = [F^{\otimes}(p) - Y^0] \cap Y^0 .$$

3. (reflexivity) $[F^{\otimes\otimes} = F] \Leftrightarrow [F \text{ is } Y\text{-normal}]$.

4. (composition) GoF is a convex-star map; $(G : Y \rightrightarrows Z)$

$$(GoF)^{\otimes} = G^{\otimes} o F^{\otimes} .$$

5. F is uhc and lhc.

6. If Gr(F) is a cone, then F is superlinear.

<u>Property A.16:</u> Let $F : X \rightrightarrows Y$ be a convex-aureole correspondence. Then:

1. F is point-aureoled and <u>decreasing</u>, i.e.:

$$[x,y \text{ and } (y-x) \in X] \Rightarrow [F(x) \supset F(y)] .$$

2. $F^{\otimes}$ is a <u>convex-aureole</u> map, and also Y^0-<u>monotone</u>, i.e.:

$$\text{for all } p \in X^0 : F^{\otimes}(p) = [F^{\otimes}(p) + Y^0] \cap Y^0 .$$

3. (reflexivity) $[F^{\otimes\otimes} = F] \Leftrightarrow$ [F is Y-supernormal] .

4. (composition) GoF a convex-aureole correspondence, if both F and $G : Y \rightrightarrows Z$ are so; and $(G \circ F)^{\otimes} = G^{\otimes} \circ F^{\otimes}$;

5. F is lhc.

<u>Property A.17</u> (duality):

1. If F is a convex-star map, then:

$$\max_{y \in F(x)} q.y = \inf_{p \in (F^{\otimes})^{-1}(q)} p.x + 1.$$

2. If F is a convex-aureole map. then:

$$\inf_{y \in F(x)} q.y = \max_{p \in (F^{\otimes})^{-1}(q)} p.x - 1.$$

If X is a convex cone, then we have

$$X_-^0 = X_-^*$$

i.e. the lower dual cone and the lower dual set coincide, because: $\forall x \in X : p.x \leqq 1$ is in this case equivalent to: $\forall x \in X : p.x \leqq 0$.

Now let $F : X \rightrightarrows Y$ be <u>superlinear.</u> Then the graph of F is a cone. Consequently

$$F_+^{\otimes}(p) = \{q \in Y_+^0 \mid (p,-q) \in [\,Gr(F)]_-^0\}$$

$$= \{q \in Y_+^0 \mid \forall x, \forall y \in F(x) : p.x \geqq q.y\}$$

The relation between the graph-dual correspondence and dual sets can be indicated as follows, for $A \subset X$, $B \subset Y$; $A_-^* \subset X_+^0$ and $B_-^* \subset Y_+^0$:

$$\begin{array}{ccc} A & \xrightarrow{F} & B \\ {\scriptstyle *}\downarrow & & \downarrow{\scriptstyle *} \\ A_-^* & \xrightarrow{F^{\otimes}} & B_-^* \end{array}$$

and we get the following theorem:

Theorem A.18: Let F be a superlinear correspondence of the cone $X \subset R^m$ into the cone $Y \subset R^n$. Then

$$F_-^{\otimes}(A_-^*) = [F(A)]_-^*$$

for all closed subsets $A \subset X$.

Proof:

(1) Let $q \in F^{\otimes}(A^*)$, hence

$$y \in F(x) \text{ and } p \in A^* \Rightarrow p.x \geqq q.y,$$

so a fortiori:

$$y \in F(x),\ p \in A^* \text{ and } x \in A \Rightarrow p.x \geqq q.y;$$

but since

$$x \in A \text{ and } p \in A^* \Rightarrow p.x \leqq 1,$$

it follows:

$$\forall y \in F(A) : q.y \leqq 1,$$

hence $q \in [F(A)]^*$.

(2) Let $q \in [F(A)]^*$

Since by definition: $\forall y \in F(A) : q.y \leqq 1$, for $M := \{y \in Y | q.y > 1\}$,

$$M \cap F(A) = \emptyset,$$

so also

$$F^{-1}(M) \cap A = \emptyset.$$

Since $H_+(q)$ is convex, and aureoled, M also convex and aureoled, so there exists a hyperplane H(p) separating $F^{-1}(M)$ and A, and $p \in A^*$, hence

$$F^{-1}(M) \cap H_-(p) = \emptyset,$$

for $H_-(p) = \{x \in X | p.x \leqq 1\}$.
Let $x \in X$ and $y \in F(x)$, so also $\lambda y \in F(\lambda x)$ for $\lambda > 0$;

(a) if $p.x > 1$, choose λ such that $p.\lambda x = 1$. Then $\lambda y \in F(\lambda x)$, $\lambda y \notin F^{-1}(M)$, hence $\lambda y \in M$. Therefore $q.\lambda y \leqq 1 = p.\lambda x$.
(b) if $p.x = 0$, find $\bar{x}$ such that $p.\bar{x} > 0$. Then by (a) and superlinearity: for all $\mu > 0$:

$$p.(\mu\bar{x}+x) \geqq \sup q.F(\mu\bar{x}+x)$$

and therefore by the closedness of F : $p.x = 0 = q.y$.
So $q \in F^{\otimes}(p) \subset F^{\otimes}(A^{*})$ □

For a correspondence $F : X \rightrightarrows X$, defined by $F(x) := \{y \in X | Ay \leqq x\}$, and A regular, this theorem has been formulated in [17] and proven in [18] as

$$F_-^{\otimes}(p) = \bigcap_{x \in H(p)} F_-^{*}(x).$$

In [18], finally, this has been generalized for a convex-star correspondence $F: X \rightrightarrows Y$:

$$F_-^{\otimes}(p) = \bigcap_{x \in H_-(-p)} (p.x+1)\, F_-^{*}(x).$$

A.2. Dual programs.

A.2.1. Linear optimization and duality.

The purpose of this subsection is twofold: (a) it serves as an illustration of the theory of the preceding sections; (b) it shows the relation that exists between the concept of duality of this paper and the duality concept that occurs in optimization theory (dual linear program etc.).

In linear optimization models, preferences are given by a linear utility function $u(x) := a.x$. The preference correspondence that follows from this function is $P(x) = \{\tilde{x} \in R^n | a.\tilde{x} > a.x\}$. Clearly this correspondence satisfies the Assumption 3.2.(B) that we need to ensure that it also has a dual preference correspondence in terms of prices, as defined in 3.6. Two models are considered:
(1) linear constraints, but no sign constraint;

(2) linear constraints and the requirement that the solution should be non-negative (linear programming).

(1) Consider the following problem:
max $a.x$ with constraints[1] $Ax \leqq \ell$ for $x \in R^n$, $a \in R^{n*}$, $\ell = \{1,1,\ldots,1\} \in R^m$ and A an $n \times m$-matrix

$$A = \begin{bmatrix} a_1 \\ a_2 \\ \vdots \\ a_m \end{bmatrix}, \text{ with } a_k \in R^{n*}.$$

The abstract economy $\mathcal{E}_0 = \{X,P,\bar{C}\}$ is now defined by[2]:

$$X := \{x \in R^n | a.x \geqq 0\}$$

$$P(x) := \{\tilde{x} \in X | a.\tilde{x} > a.x\}$$

$$\bar{C} := \{y \in R^n | Ay \leqq 1\}$$

P is a preference correspondence satisfying Assumptions 3.2.(B) and we have, applying (3.3):

$$R(x) = X \setminus P^{-1}(x) = \{\tilde{x} \in X | a.x \geqq a.x\}.$$

In an optimum we have

$$P(x) \cap \bar{C} = \emptyset \text{ and } x \in \bar{C}.$$

We define the dual economy (see section 2.3) $\mathcal{E}_0^* = \{V^*,P^*,Y^*\}$ by

$$V^* := \{p \in R^{n*} | p = \lambda a,\ \lambda \geqq 0\}$$

---

1) Clearly any set of constraints $a_k.x \leqq b$, for which an $\bar{x}$ exists such that $a_k.\bar{x} \leqq b$ for all k, can be put in the required form by writing

$$a_k' = \frac{a_k}{b-a_k.\bar{x}} \text{ and } x' = x-\bar{x}, \text{ hence } a_k'.x' = \frac{a_k}{b-a_k.\bar{x}} \leqq \frac{b-a_k.\bar{x}}{b-a_k.\bar{x}} = 1.$$

2) X and V^* contain 0 in their boundary contrary to assumptions made in preceding sections. In this case this can do no harm.

$$P^*(p) := \{p \in V^* | \tilde{p} > p\}$$

$$\bar{C}^* := \mathrm{Conv}\,\{a_1, a_2, \ldots, a_m, 0\} = \bar{C}^*_-$$

For an optimum price in $\mathcal{E}^*_0$, we have

$$P^*(p) \cap \bar{C}^* = \emptyset \text{ and } p \in \bar{C}^*$$

Clearly p is colinear with a.

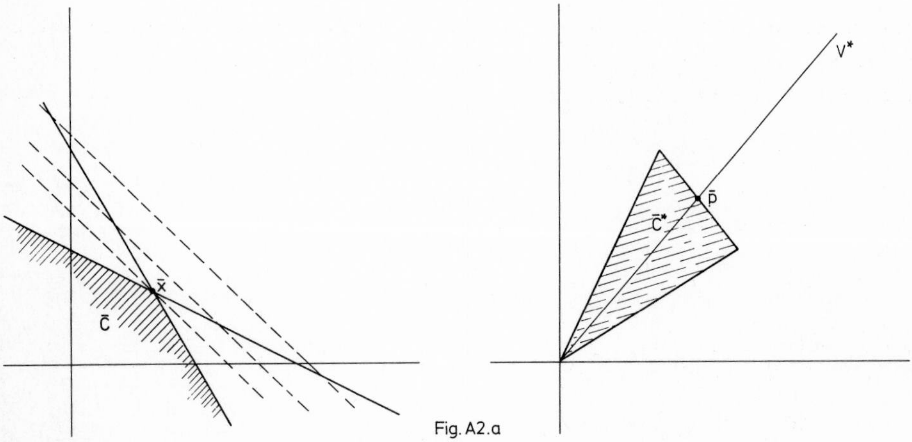

Fig. A2.a

This is equivalent to finding $p = \lambda a$, such that:

$$\lambda a \in \bar{C}^* \text{ and } \lambda' > \lambda \Rightarrow \lambda' a \notin \bar{C}^*.$$

Since we may write:

$$\bar{C}^* = \{p \in R^{n*} | \exists r \in R^{m*} : p = rA,\ r \geqq 0 \text{ and } r.\ell \leqq 1\}.$$

we have that p is optimal if $p = \lambda a$, such that:

$$\lambda = \max\{\lambda' \in R_+ | \lambda a = rA,\ r \geqq 0,\ r.\ell \leqq 1\}.$$

or equivalently: $p = \lambda a$ and

$$\frac{1}{\lambda} = \min \{\mu \in R_+ | a = qA,\ q \geqq 0 \text{ and } q.\ell \leqq \mu\}.$$

This precisely corresponds to the dual program of the original problem.

$$\min q\ell, \text{ with constraints } qA = a \text{ and } q \geqq 0.$$

(2) The following problem is a <u>true linear programming problem:</u>

$$\max ax, \text{ with constraint } Ax \leqq \ell$$
$$x \geqq 0.$$

From this, an abstract economy $\&_0$ can be derived in two ways: by introducing the sign constraint in either X or in $\bar{C}$ (or in both).
First define $\&_0 := \{X,R,\bar{C}\}$ by:

$$X := \{x \in R^n | a.x \geqq 0\}$$

$$P(x) := \{\tilde{x} \in X | a.\tilde{x} > a.x\}$$

$$\bar{C} := \{x \in R^n | Ax \leqq \ell \text{ and } x \geqq 0\}.$$

Then as before $\&_0^* = \{V^*, P^*, \bar{C}^*\}$, where

$$V^* := \{p \in R^{n*} | p = \lambda a,\ \lambda \geqq 0\},$$

$$P^*(p) := \{\tilde{p} \in V^* | \tilde{p} > p\}.$$

But now (see fig. A2.b):

$$\bar{C}^* := \text{Conv}\ \{a_1, a_2, \ldots, a_m\} + R^n_-$$

$$= \text{Norm Conv}\ \{a_1, a_2, \ldots, a_m\}$$

For an optimum price in $\&_0^*$ we have again: $p = \lambda a$ such that:

$$\lambda a \in \bar{C}^* \text{ and } \lambda' > \lambda \Rightarrow \lambda' a \notin \bar{C}^*$$

We now have:

$$\bar{C}^* := \{p \in R^{n*} \mid \exists r \in R^{m*} : p \leqq rA,\ r \geqq 0,\ r.\ell \leqq 1\}$$

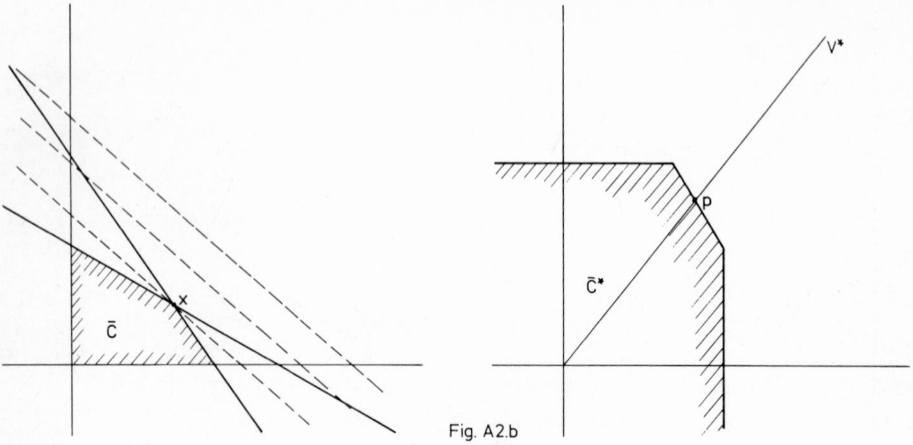

Fig. A2.b

(so $p = rA$ has been replaced by $p \leqq rA$).
So $p = \lambda a$ is optimal if:

$$\lambda = \max \{\lambda' \in R_+ \mid \lambda a \leqq rA).$$

or equivalently:

$$\frac{1}{\lambda} = \min \{\mu \in R_+ \mid a \leqq qA,\ q \geqq 0,\ q.\ell \leqq \mu\}.$$

This corresponds to the dual l.p. problem:

$$\max\ q.\ell$$

$$\text{s.t. } qA \geqq a$$
$$q \geqq 0.$$

Provided that $a > 0$, we could also define $\tilde{\mathcal{E}}_0^* := (\tilde{V}^*, P^*, \tilde{\bar{C}})$:

$$V^* = \{p \in R^n \mid p \geqq \lambda a \text{ and } p \geqq 0\}$$

$$P^*(p) := \{\tilde{p} \in V^* \mid \tilde{p} > p\}$$

$$\tilde{\bar{C}}^* := \mathrm{Conv}\ \{a_1, a_2, \ldots, a_m, 0\}.$$

Now an optimum price is $p \geqq \lambda a$, $p \in X^*$ and

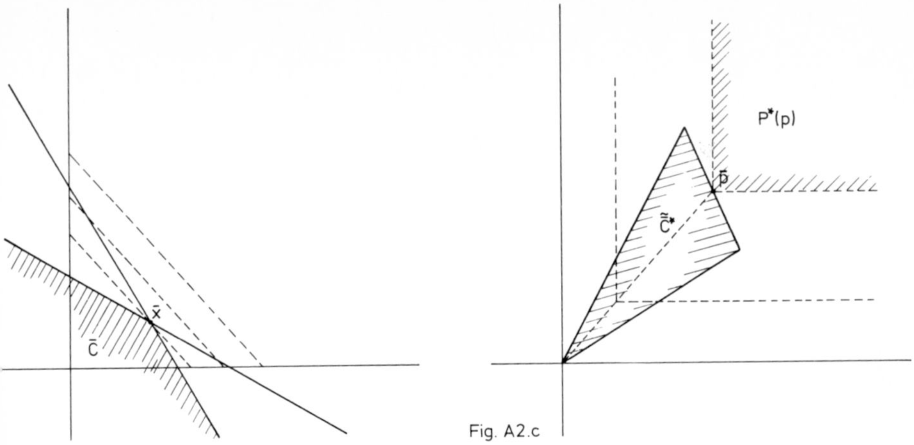

Fig. A2.c

$$\lambda = \max \{\lambda \in R_+ | \lambda a \leqq rA,\ r \geqq 0,\ r.\ell \leqq 1\},$$

$$\frac{1}{\lambda} = \min \{\mu \in R_+ | a \leqq qA,\ r \geqq 0,\ r.\ell \leqq \mu\},$$

which is identical to the corresponding formula above.
In $\mathcal{E}_0^*$ only prices colinear with a can be optimum; in $\tilde{\mathcal{E}}_0^*$ all prices such that $p \geqq \lambda a$ may be optimum (but clearly not $p > \lambda a$).
The dual variable p in the model is the optimum price, whereas the prices q (or r) are the shadow prices of the restrictions.
Above we considered a maximum L.P. problem. A minimum L.P.-problem also has a dual, but then the preference correspondence in star shaped and the set of restrictions aureoled (min $a.x$, given $Ax \geqq b$, $b > 0$). Particularly the dual program of the L.P. problem above (min $q.\ell$, given $qA \geqq a$, or $q'A \geqq \ell$, for $a > 0$) is a minimum problem: clearly this problem has a dual optimum problem, that corresponds to the original L.P.-program.

A.2.2. The general structure of Convex Programming.

The dual correspondences defined above make it possible to describe the general structure of convex programming as follows.

Consider the economy:

$$E := \{X \times Y,\ P:X \rightrightarrows X,\ C:Y \rightrightarrows X\},$$

where X and Y are closed convex cones in R^n, resp. R^m; P is a complete and transitive preference correspondence which has an open and convex graph; C is a superlinear correspondence (Def. A.14). Consider the graph-dual operation on C (Def. A.12).

Define $\tilde{P} : Y \rightrightarrows Y$ by:

$$\tilde{P}(y) := \left\{ \tilde{y} \in Y \;\middle|\; \begin{array}{l} \forall x \in X: \quad P(x) \cap C(y) = \emptyset \\ \text{implies } P(x) \cap C(\tilde{y}) = \emptyset \end{array} \right\}$$

Since $P^{*} : X^0 \rightrightarrows X^0$ has been defined by (see 3.11):

$$P^{*}(p) := \left\{ \tilde{p} \in X^0 \;\middle|\; \begin{array}{l} \forall x \in X: \quad P(x) \cap H(p) = \emptyset \\ \text{implies } P(x) \cap H(\tilde{p}) = \emptyset \end{array} \right\}$$

we can define $\tilde{P}^{*} : Y^0 \rightrightarrows Y^0$ by:

$$\tilde{P}^{*}(q) := \left\{ \tilde{q} \in Y^0 \;\middle|\; \begin{array}{l} \forall p \in X_0 : P^{*}(p) \cap C^{\otimes}(q) = \emptyset \\ \text{implies } P^{*}(p) \cap C^{*}(\tilde{q}) = \emptyset \end{array} \right\}$$

$$= \left\{ \tilde{q} \in Y^0 \;\middle|\; \begin{array}{l} \forall y \in Y : \tilde{P}(y) \cap H(q) = \emptyset \\ \text{implies } \tilde{P}(y) \cap H(\tilde{q}) = \emptyset \end{array} \right\}$$

And the dual economy:

$$E^{*} := \{X^0 \times Y^0, P^{*} : X^0 \rightrightarrows X^0, C^{\otimes} : Y^0 \rightrightarrows X^0\}.$$

The optimum (or programming) problem in E is defined by:

(i) given $y \in Y$, find $x \in X$ such that:

$x \in C(y)$ and $P(x) \cap C(y) = \emptyset$.

Three other problems in E or in the dual economy E^{*} can be formulated which have the same structure as (i) and are also in other ways closely related to (i). These are:

(ii) given $q \in Y^0$, find $p \in X^0$ such that:

$p \in C^{\otimes}(q)$ and $P^{*}(p) \cap C^{\otimes}(q) = \emptyset$;

(iii) given $x \in X$, find $y \in Y$ such that

$$y \in C^{-1}(x) \text{ and } \tilde{P}(y) \cap C^{-1}(x) = \emptyset;$$

(iv) given $p \in X^0$, find $q \in Y^0$ such that

$$q \in C^{-1\otimes}(p) \text{ and } \tilde{P}^*(q) \cap C^{-1\otimes}(p) = \emptyset.$$

The constraint correspondences are represented by the following diagram on the next page.

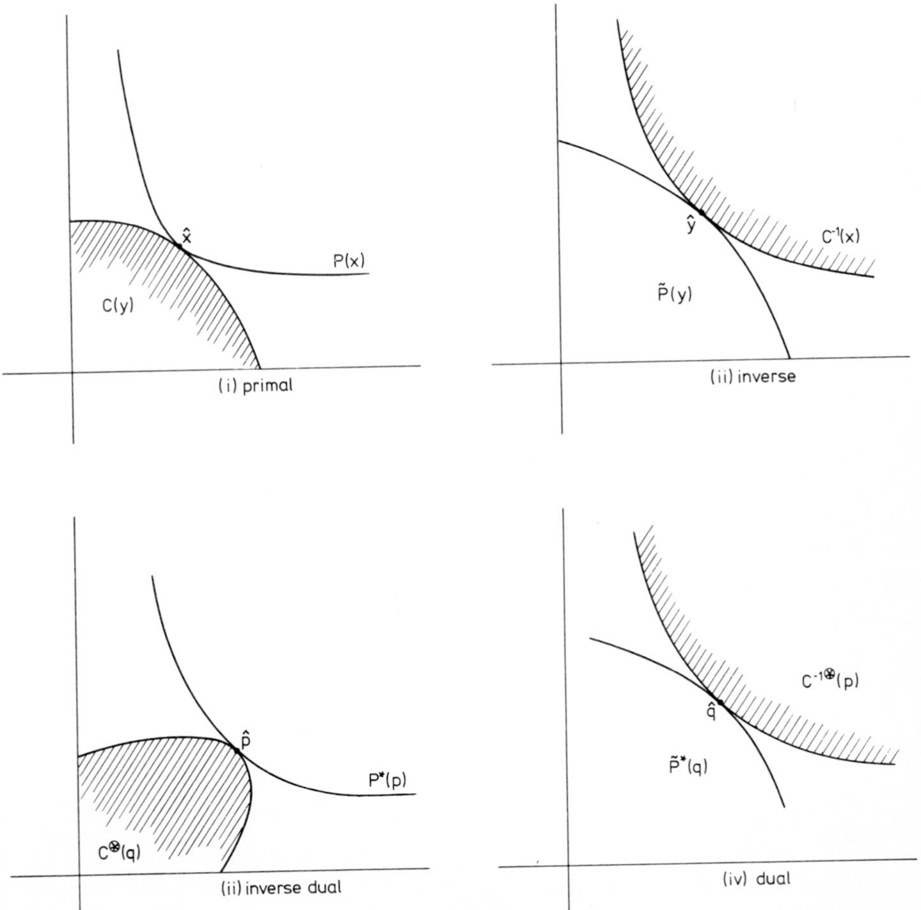

Fig. A2.d

The four problems (see also fig.A2.d) are called (i) primal, (ii) inverse, (iii) inverse dual, and (iv) dual. The fact that the inverse of the graph-dual correspondence is used to define the dual problem is caused by the fact that this correspondence is the adjoint of the constraint correspondence (see definition A.12).

From the inverse-dual problem (iii), the dual formulation of the previous section can be derived, using theorem A.18:

$$[C(y)]^*_- = C^{\otimes}(\{y\}^*_-) = \bigcup_{q \in \{y\}^*} C^{\otimes}(q),$$

$$[P(x)]^*_+ = \bigcup_{p \in \{x\}^*} P^*(p).$$

The dual problem (iv) is the usual dual programming problem.

This structure has been introduced by Ruys [17] for a simple linear programming problem, which can now serve as an example given a linear and regular constraint matrix A, and the vectors p and y for (i) and (iv), resp. q and x for (ii) and (iii):

(i) $P(x) := \{\tilde{x} \in X \mid p.\tilde{x} > p.x\}$
$C(y) := \{x \in X \mid Ax \leqq y,\ x \geqq 0\}$

(ii) $\tilde{P}(y) := \{\tilde{y} \in Y \mid q.\tilde{y} < q.y\}$
$C^{-1}(x) := \{y \in Y \mid A^{-1}y \geqq x,\ y \geqq 0\}$

(iii) $P^*(p) := \{\tilde{p} \in X^0 \mid \tilde{p}.x > p.x\}$
$C^{\otimes}(q) := \{p \in X^0 \mid p\,A^{-1} \leqq q,\ p \geqq 0\}$

(iv) $\tilde{P}^*(q) := \{\tilde{q} \in Y^0 \mid \tilde{q}.y < q.y\}$
$C^{-1\otimes}(p) := \{q \in Y^0 \mid Aq \geqq p,\ q \geqq 0\}$

The constraint correspondences are represented in the following diagram:

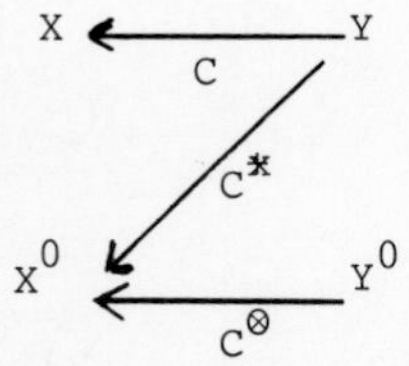

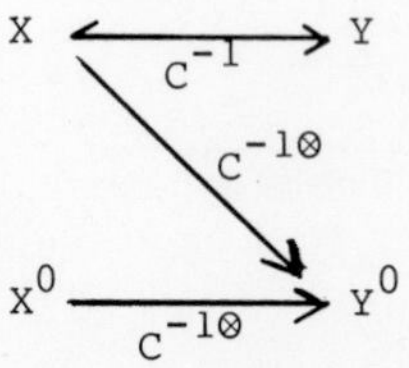

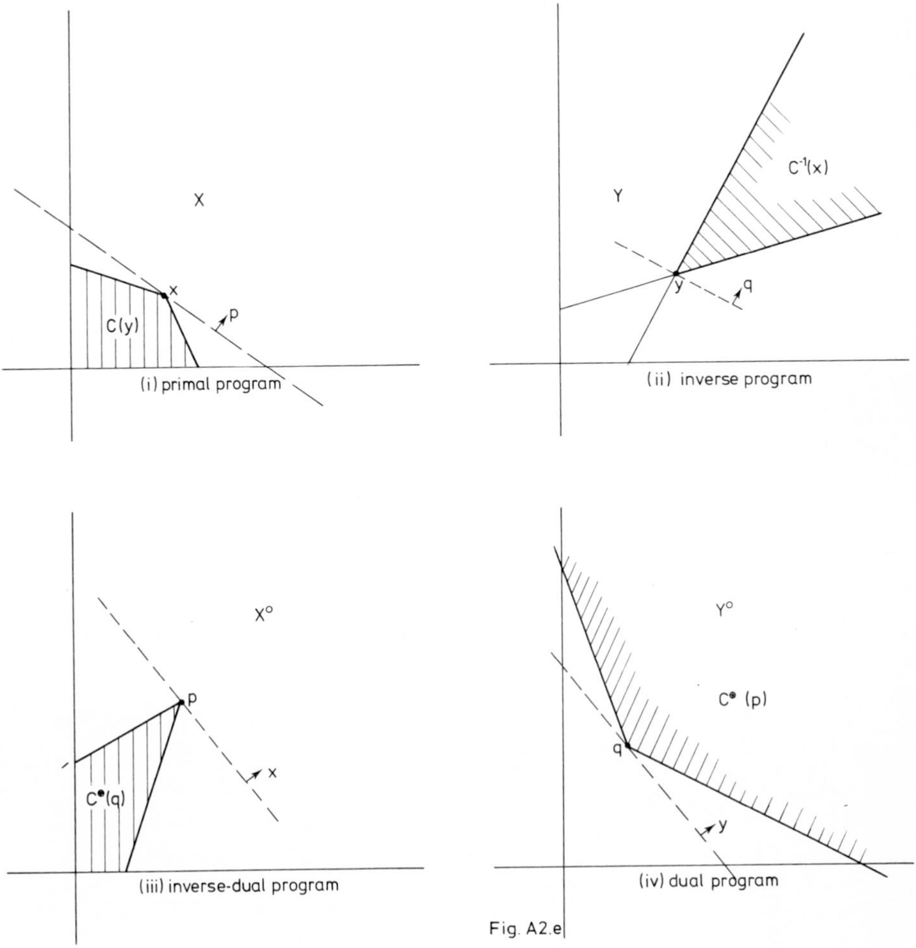
X
x
p
C(y)
(i) primal program
Y
C⁻¹(x)
y
q
(ii) inverse program
X°
p
x
C•(q)
(iii) inverse-dual program
Y°
C• (p)
q
y
(iv) dual program

Fig. A2.e

References.

[1] Arrow, K.J. and F.H. Hahn, General competitive analysis, Holden Day/Oliver and Boyd, San Francisco, Edinburgh, 1971.

[2] Borglin, A. and H. Keiding, "Existence of equilibrium actions and of equilibrium, a note on the 'new' existence theorems", Journal of Mathematical Economics, 3, (1976), 313-316.

[3] Debreu, G., "A social equilibrium existence theorem", Proceedings of the National Academy of Sciences, 38, no. 10, (1952), 886-893.

[4] Debreu, G., Theory of Value, Wiley, New York 1959.

[5] Diewert, W.E., "Applications of duality theory", in: Intrilligator, M.D. and D.A. Kendrick (ed.), Frontiers in Quantitative Economics, Vol. II, North Holland Publishing Company, Amsterdam, 1974.

[6] Fan, K., "A generalization of Tychynoff's fixed point theorem", Math. Annals, 142, (1961), 305-310.

[7] Foley, D.K., "Lindahl's solution and the core of an economy with public goods", Econometrica, 38, (1970), 66-72.

[8] Gale, D. and A. Mas-Collel, "An equilibrium existence theorem for a general model without ordered preferences", Journal of Mathematical Economics, 1, (1975), 277-294.

[9] Greenberg, J., "Quasi-equilibrium in abstract economics without ordered preferences", Journal of Mathematical Economics, 4, (1977), 163-166.

[10] Makarov, V.L. and A.M. Rubinov, Mathematical Theory of Economic Dynamics and Equilibria, Springer Verlag, Berlin (1977).

[11] Michael, E., "Continuous selections I", Annals of Mathematics, 63, (1956), 361-382.

[12] Milleron, J.C., "Theory of value with public goods, a survey article", Journal of Economic Theory, 5 (1972), 419-477.

[13] Rawls, J. A Theory of Justice, Harvard UP, Cambridge, (1971).

[14] Rockafellar, R.T., Monotone Processes of Convex and Concave Type, Memoirs A.M.S. No 77, (1967).

[15] ---------------- , Convex Analysis, Princeton University Press, (1970).

[16] Ruys, P.H.M., "On the existence of an equilibrium for an economy with public goods only", Zeitschrift für Nationalökonomie, 32, (1972), 189-202.

[17] ------------, "The relation between dual linear programs and their programs in the dual spaces", KHT, mimeographed, (1972).

[18] ------------, Public goods and Decentralization, Tilburg University Press, (1974).

[19] ------------, "Production correspondences and convex algebra" in: Production Theory (eds. W. Eichhorn, R. Henn, O. Opitz and R.W. Shephard), Lecture Notes in Economics and Mathematical Systems, 99, Springer, Berlin, 1974.

[20] ------------, "Reduction of intertemporal optimal choice", KHT, (july 1978).

[21] Shafer, W. and H. Sonnenschein, "Equilibrium in abstract economies", Journal of Mathematical Economics, 2, (1975), 345-348.

[22] Shephard, R., Theory of cost and production functions, Princeton University Press, (1970).

[23] Von Neumann, J. "Über ein Ökonomisches Gleichungssystem und eine Veralgemeinerung des Brouwerschen Fixpunktsatzes" Ergebnisse eines Math. Kolloquiums, No. 8, Wien, (1937).

[24] Weddepohl, H.N., Axiomatic choice models and duality, Rotterdam University Press, (1970).

[25] ------------, (1972), "Duality and equilibrium", Zeitschrift für Nationalökonomie, 32, (1972), 163-187.

[26] ------------, "Dual sets and dual correspondences and their application to equilibrium theory", E.I.T. Research Memorandum 38, (1973).

[27] ------------, "Equilibrium in a market with incomplete preferences, where the number of consumers may be finite", in: G. Schwödiauer (ed.), Equilibrium and Disequilibrium in Economic Theory, Reidel Publishing Company, Dordrecht-Boston (1978), 13-26.

Department of Econometrics,
Tilburg University,
Box 90153 - 5000 LE Tilburg,
The Netherlands.

II. THE DYNAMICS OF CONCAVE INPUT/OUTPUT PROCESSES

Joseph J.M. Evers

TWENTE UNIVERSITY OF TECHNOLOGY, NETHERLANDS.

1. Input/output processes; logic and economic relevance.

In economic theory, production is considered as a process - or as a complex of processes - transforming bundles of commodities - called inputs - into other bundles of commodities - called outputs.
With commodity spaces of inputs and outputs, R^m and R^n respectively, the production process is specified by its set of feasible input/output combinations $S \subset R^m \times R^n$; i.e. concerning a pair $(x,y) \in S$, vector $x \in R^m$ is taken as the input vector and $y \in R^n$ represents the output vector. Concerning such a set S - in this context called <u>production set</u> - we shall impose some conditions, emphasizing the nature of production: (i) non-negativity of the inputs: $S \subset R^m_+ \times R^n$, (ii) free disposal of inputs: $\forall (x,y) \in S : \forall \bar{x} \geqq x : (\bar{x},y) \in S$, (iii) convexity of S, (iv) closedness of S.

In a similar manner, consumption is considered as the process of transforming inputs, like food, housing etc., into a bundle of output, for instance containing labor. The set of feasible input/output combinations $C \subset R^m \times R^n$ is called the <u>consumption set</u>. Further we assume that there is a preference ordering on C, being expressed by a utility function $\mu : C \to R^1$; i.e. a pair $(\bar{x},\bar{y}) \in C$ is preferred over $(\tilde{x},\tilde{y}) \in C$, if and only if $\mu(\bar{x},\bar{y}) > \mu(\tilde{x};\tilde{y})$. Thus a consumer is represented simply by a function $\mu : C \subset R^m \times R^n \to R^1$ satisfying the hypotheses: (i) non-negativity of inputs: $C \subset R^m_+ \times R^n$, (ii) free disposal of inputs: $\forall (x,y) \in C$: $\forall\, \bar{x} \geqq x$: $(\bar{x},y) \in C$, $\mu(\bar{x};y) \geqq \mu(x;y)$, (iii) concavity of $\mu : C \to R^1$ (implying convexity of C), (iv) closedness of the hypograph of $\mu : C \to R^1$.

Obviously, any production process can be represented by such a function $\mu : S \subset R^m_+ \times R^n \to R^1$ as well; simply by defining the function identical to zero. For that reason we shall introduce the general concept of I/O-process, which covers both production and consumptive aspects in economic models.

1.1. The concept of Input/Output process.

Formally an I/O-process is defined as a function $\mu: S \subset R^m \times R^n \to R^1$ satisfying the hypotheses:

(1) $S \subset R_+^m \times R^n$,

(2) $\forall (x,y) \in S,\ x \in R^m,\ y \in R^n: \forall\ \bar{x} \in R^m | \bar{x} \geqq x: (\bar{x},y) \in S,\ \mu(\bar{x};y) \geqq \mu(x;y)$,

(3) $\mu: S \to R^1$ is concave (implying convexity of S),

(4) the hypograph, $\text{hypo}(S;\mu) := \{(x,y,\nu) \in S \times R^1 | \nu \leqq \mu(x;y)\}$ is closed.

We conceive $\mu: S \subset R^m \times R^n \to R^1$ as a bi-function. The domain with respect to the first argument - denoted $D_1(S)$ - is the set $\{x \in R^m | \exists y \in R^n: (x,y) \in S\}$; in the symmetric manner, we have the domain of argument 2, denoted $D_2(S)$. For any fixed $x \in D_1(S)$, we have a partial function $\mu(x;.)$ on the set $\{y \in R^n | (x,y) \in S\}$; notation $\mu(x;.): S \to R^1$. Changing the arguments, we have the partial function $\mu(.;y): S \to R^1$, y being fixed in $D_2(S)$. We shall denote such a bi-function with the short notation $(\mu: S \to R^1,\ m \times n)$; in the case that the bi-function is improper by $(\mu: S \to]-\infty, +\infty],\ m \times n)$ etc. We shall call a (bi-) function closed-concave if its hypograph is closed and convex; a (bi-) function $\mu: S \to R^1$ (or $\mu: S \to [-\infty, +\infty[$) is called closed-convex if its epigraph $\text{epi}(S;\mu) := \{(z,\alpha) \in S \times R^1 | \alpha \geqq \mu(z)\}$ is closed and convex.

1.2. I/O-processes and production functions.

In the classic theory, production is specified by a production function $F: R_+^m \to R_+^n$, where the outputs are given as a non-decreasing function of the inputs; i.e. for every $\bar{x}, \tilde{x} \in R_+^m$, $\bar{x} \geqq \tilde{x}$, it holds: $F(\bar{x}) \geqq F(\tilde{x})$. Evidently, defining $(\mu: S \to R^1,\ m \times n)$:

$$(1) \quad \begin{cases} S := \{(x,y) \in R_+^m \times R_+^n | y \leqq F(x)\}, \\ \mu(x;y) := 0, \end{cases}$$

we arrive at an I/O-process, provided $F: R_+^m \to R_+^n$ is closed-concave.

The other way round, we may specify inputs as a non-decreasing function $G: R_+^n \to R_+^m$ of the outputs. Now defining $(\mu: S \to R^1,\ m \times n)$:

$$(2) \quad \begin{cases} S := \{(x,y) \in R_+^m \times R_+^n | G(y) \leqq x\}, \\ \mu(x;y) := 0, \end{cases}$$

it turns out that $(\mu:S\to R^1,\ m\times n)$ is an I/O-process, indeed, provided $G:R^n_+\to R^m_+$ is closed-convex.

Further we have the standard representation of linear activity analysis. Here the production process is supposed to be composed of a finite number - k - subprocesses. The operation intensities can be chosen at any (non-negative) level; the quantities of commodities involved as inputs and outputs of each subprocess are proportional with respect to its intensity level of operation. Thus, representing the set of intensity levels by R^k_+ - the j-th component of an $r \in R^k_+$ being the operation level of the subprocess numbered j -, representing the input rates by a non-negative $m\times k$-matrix A of "input coefficients", and finally, representing the output rates by a non-negative $n\times k$-matrix B of "output coefficients", the inputs and the outputs associated with any intensity vector $r \in R^k_+$ are specified as Ar and Br respectively. Then, defining $(\mu:S\to R^1,\ m\times n)$:

$$(3)\quad \begin{cases} S := \{(x,y) \in R^m_+\times R^n_+ \mid \exists r \in R^k_+ : x \geqq Ar,\ y = Br\}, \\ \mu(x;y) := 0, \end{cases}$$

we have an I/O-process, again.

1.3. Composed I/O-processes.

In order to illustrate that the concept of I/O-process is extremely flexible, we consider a system where the consumptive activities are specified by an I/O-process $(\mu:S\to R^1,\ n\times m)$, and where production is given as a closed convex set $P \subset R^m_+\times R^n_+$ with free disposal of inputs. Let us compose these processes as suggested in the scheme:

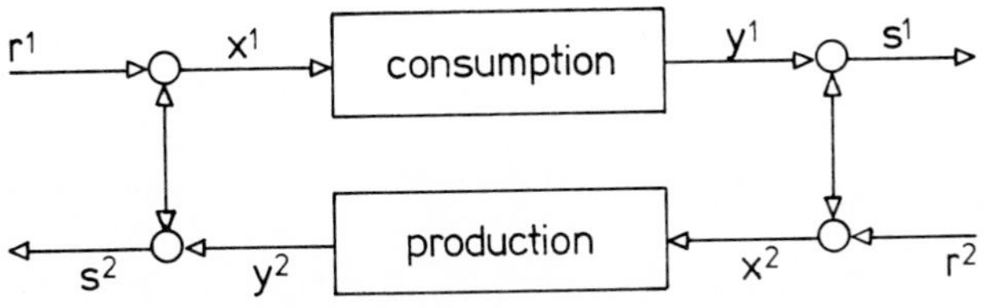

where (r^1,r^2) plays the role of an inputvector and (s^1,s^2) represents external outputs. Formally, the total process is characterized as $(\varphi:C\to]-\infty,+\infty],(n+m)\times(m+n))$:

(1)
$$\begin{cases} C := \{(r^1,r^2,s^1,s^2) \in R^n_+\times R^m_+\times R^m\times R^n \mid \\ \qquad \exists (x^1,y^1) \in S,\ (x^2,y^2) \in P:\ x^2-y^1 = r^2-s^1,\ y^2-x^1 = s^2-r^1\}, \\ \varphi((r^1,r^2);(s^1,s^2)) := \sup \mu(x^1;y^1), \text{ over } (x^1,y^1) \in S,\ (x^2,y^2) \in P, \\ \qquad \text{s.t. } x^2-y^1 = r^2-s^1,\ y^2-x^1 = s^2-r^1. \end{cases}$$

It is elementary to verify that the conditions 1.1-(1) to -(3) concerning I/O-processes are satisfied. Generally, relevant conditions can be imposed implying $\varphi(C) \subset R^1$ and closedness of hypo$(C;\varphi)$.

As a matter of fact, one may combine any finite number of I/O-processes in any manner, provided the signs of inputs and outputs are placed in the physical correct manner and provided reasonable conditions concerning boundedness are satisfied, the result will be an I/O-process. For that reason the I/O-process might be considered as a strongly unifying concept in micro-economic modelling under free disposal and convexity assumptions. As an example of such a general approach, we consider a finite number of I/O-processes $(\mu^i:S^i\to R^1,m^i\times n^i)$, $i=1,\ldots,k$, with the help of a closed convex cone $K \subset R^m\times R^n$, $m := \Sigma_{i=1}^k m^i$, $n := \Sigma_{i=1}^k n^i$, being composed into $(\varphi:C\to]-\infty,+\infty],m\times n)$:

(2)
$$\begin{cases} \varphi((r^i)_1^k;(s^i)_1^k) := \sup \Sigma_{i=1}^k \mu^i(x^i;y^i), \text{ over } (x^i,y^i)_1^k \in (S^i)_1^k \cap (K+(r^i,s^i)_1^k), \\ C := \{((r^i)_1^k,(s^i)_1^k) \mid r^i \in R^{m^i}_+,\ s^i \in R^{n^i},\ i=1,\ldots,k,\ (S^i)_1^k \cap (K+(r^i,s^i)_1^k) \neq \emptyset\}. \end{cases}$$

Concerning the notations: $(x^i,y^i)_1^k$ stands for the composed vector $(x^1, y^1,x^2,y^2,\ldots,x^k,y^k)$. The cartesian product set $S^1\times S^2\times\ldots\times S^k$ is denoted $(S^i)_1^k$. In the context of a sequence of bi-functions $(\mu^t:S^t\to R^1,m^t\times n^t)$, $t=1,\ldots,k$, the expression $(x^t,y^t)_1^k \in (S^t)_1^k$ stands for the composed vector $(x^1,y^1,x^2,y^2,\ldots,x^k,y^k)$ with $(x^t,y^t) \in S^t$, $x^t \in R^{m^t}$, $y^t \in R^{n^t}$, $t = 1,\ldots,k$. If there is no danger of confusion, these notations will be used in a flexible way; for instance $(x^t,y^{t-1})_1^\infty := (x^1,y^0,x^2,y^1,\ldots)$. The expression $K+(r^i,s^i)_1^k$ is the translation of K with $(r^1,s^1,r^2,s^2, \ldots,r^k,s^k)$.

Putting $K := \{(x^1,y^1,x^2,y^2) \mid x^2-y^1 = 0,\ y^2-x^1 = 0\}$, it should be clear that I/O-system (1) can be written in the scheme of (2). However, instead of studying the specific form (2), we shall consider an abstract formulation $(\varphi : C \to]-\infty,+\infty], m\times n)$:

$$(3) \qquad \begin{cases} \varphi(r;s) := \sup \mu(x;y), \text{ over } (x,y) \in S \cap (K+(r,s)), \\ C := \{(r,s) \in R^m \times R^n \mid S \cap (K+(r,s)) \neq \emptyset\}, \end{cases}$$

where $(\mu : S \to R^1, m\times n)$ is any bi-function and where K is a closed-convex cone in $R^m\times R^n$. If we are interested in specific I/O-properties, we assume that $(\mu : S \to R^1, m\times n)$ is an I/O-process and we restrict the domain of φ to $C \cap (R^m_+ \times R^n)$. In that context it is natural to impose some conditions on K; to be specific $K \subset R^m\times R^n$ is called a <u>composition cone</u> if:

(4) K is a closed-convex cone,
(5) $\forall (x,0) \in K$: $x \not\geq 0$ (or equivalently $\forall (x,y) \in K \mid x \geq 0$: $y \neq 0$),
(6) $\exists (p,q) \in -K$: $p > 0$.

Note that $x \geq 0$ means $x \geqq 0$, $x \neq 0$.

Clearly, if $(\mu : S \to R^1, m\times n)$ is an I/O-process, then, as a consequence of the free disposal assumption, (5) is a necessary condition for the sets $S \cap (K+(r,s))$, given $(r,s) \in R^m\times R^n$, to be bounded. Condition (6) might be taken as the facility of supplying a positive amount of inputs to the complex without changing the internal activities. The question whether or not $(\varphi : C \cap (R^m_+\times R^n) \to]-\infty,+\infty])$ is an I/O-process is answered in 1.5.

A second operation on an I/O-process $(\mu : S \to R^1, m\times n)$, which can be used in reducing the dimensions, is defined with the help of two non-negative matrices $A(m\times p)$ and $B(n\times q)$, resulting into $(\nu : W \to R^1, p\times q)$:

$$(7) \qquad \begin{cases} \nu(u;v) := \mu(Au;Bv), \\ W := \{(u,v) \in R^p_+ \times R^q \mid (Au,Bv) \in S\}. \end{cases}$$

Evidently, the above is an I/O-process, provided $W \neq \emptyset$. Of course, it is very well possible to combine the operations (3) and (7). Returning to (3), with the help of standard methods from convex analysis one may verify:

1.4. Proposition.

Suppose concerning $(\varphi:C\to]-\infty,+\infty],m\times n)$ defined by 1.3-(3), that hypo$(S;\mu)$ and K are both closed, and suppose that all level sets of the form $\{(x,y) \in S \cap (K+(p,q))\,|\,\mu(x;y) \geqq \alpha\}$, with $(r,s) \in R^m\times R^n$, $\alpha \in R^1$ are bounded. Then: (i) $\varphi(C) \subset R^1$, (ii) hypo$(C;\varphi)$ is closed, (iii) for every $(r,s) \in C$, there exist an $(\hat{x},\hat{y}) \in S \cap (K+(r,s))$ so that $\mu(\hat{x};\hat{y}) = \varphi(r;s)$.

In the case that $(\mu:S\to R^1,m\times n)$ is an I/O-process and K is a closed-convex cone, it is easy to verify that $(\varphi:C\to R^1,m\times n)$ is concave and satisfies the free disposal condition. Thus, as a consequence of 1.4, we have:

1.5. Theorem.

Suppose concerning $(\varphi:C\to]-\infty,+\infty],m\times n)$ defined by 1.3-(3), that $(\mu:S\to R^1,m\times n)$ is an I/O-process, that K is a closed-convex cone, and that all level sets of the form $\{(x,y) \in S \cap (K+(r,s))\,|\,\mu(x;y) \geqq \alpha\}$ are bounded. Then (i) $\varphi(C) \subset R^1$, (ii) $\varphi(C \cap (R^m_+\times R^n)\to R^1,\ m\times n)$ is an I/O-process.

We observe that the provisio "the signs of inputs and outputs are placed in the physical correct manner", mentioned before, is hidden in the boundedness condition. For instance, composing $(\mu^1:S^1\to R^1,m\times n)$, $(\mu^2:S^2\to R^1,m\times n)$ by $K:=\{(x^1,x^2,y^1,y^2) \in R^m_+\times R^m_+\times R^n\times R^n\,|\,x^1-x^2 = 0,\ y^1+y^2=0\}$, it should be clear that, under free disposal, the boundedness condition is violated.

1.6. The hypographic recession function of an I/O-process.

In order to study boundedness, we introduce the concept recession cone of a set $S \cap R^n$ - notation: rec(S) -, defined as the set $\{y \in R^n\,|\ \forall\ x \in S:\ \forall\ \lambda \in R^1_+:x+\lambda y \in S\}$ (cf. [12]). The concept is justified by its property that a closed convex set $C \subset R^n$ is bounded, if and only if rec(C) = {0}. Further it is known that rec(C) is a closed convex cone. Now let us consider the recession cone of the hypograph of a closed-concave function $\rho:U \subset R^n\to R^1$: rec(hypo$(U;\rho)$). Evidently, this recession cone satisfies the specific hypographic property:

$\forall\ x \in R^n|(\{x\}\times R^1) \cap \text{rec(hypo}(U;\rho)) \neq \emptyset:\ \exists\ \alpha \in R^1:(\{x\}\times R^1) \cap$ rec(hypo$(U;\rho)$) $= \{x\}\times]-\infty,\alpha]$. Obviously, one may take rec(hypo$(U;\rho)$) as the hypograph of a function; we shall call this function the hypographic recession function of $\rho:U\to R^1$, to be denoted $\mathring{\rho}:\mathring{U}\to R^1$. Provided $\rho:U\to R^1$ is closed-concave the theory concerning the recession cone (cf. [12])

implies: (i) $\text{hypo}(\mathring{U};\mathring{\rho})$ is a closed-convex cone, thus $\mathring{\rho}:\mathring{U}\to R^1$ is positive homogeneous of degree one, (ii) a level set $\{x \in U|\rho(x) \geqq \alpha\} \neq \emptyset$ is bounded if and only if $\{y \in \mathring{U}|\mathring{\rho}(y) \geqq 0\} = \{0\}$, (iii) if $\sup_{x\in U} \rho(x) < +\infty$, then for every $y \in \mathring{U}$ it holds $\mathring{\rho}(y) \leqq 0$. Of course, in the opposite orientation the same can be said from the epigraph of a closed-convex function. In that context, the function generated by the recession cone of the epigraph will be called the <u>epigraphic recession function.</u>

Now let us consider the hypographic recession function $(\mathring{\mu}:\mathring{S}\to R^1,m\times n)$ of an I/O-process $(\mu:S\to R^1,m\times n)$, generated by $\text{hypo}(S;\mu)$. Then, as an immediate consequence of the free disposal axiom and of $S \subset R^m_+\times R^n$, we have: (i) $\mathring{S} \subset R^m_+\times R^n$, (ii) $\forall\ (x,y) \in \mathring{S}$: $\forall\ \bar{x} \geqq x$: $(\bar{x},y) \in \mathring{S}$, $\mathring{\mu}(\bar{x};y) \geqq \mathring{\mu}(x;y)$. Obviously, since $(\mathring{\mu}:\mathring{S}\to R^1,m\times n)$ is closed-concave we have:

1.7. <u>Theorem.</u>
The hypographic recession function of an I/O-process, is an I/O-process, positive homogeneous of degree one.

The following applications are based on the well-known property: $\text{rec}(A \cap B) = \text{rec}(A) \cap \text{rec}(B)$, with A,B closed convex and $A \cap B \neq \emptyset$:

1.8. <u>Proposition.</u>
Given $(\mu:S\to R^1,m\times n)$ closed-concave, given a closed convex cone $K \subset R^m\times R^n$ and vectors $p \in R^m$, $q \in R^n$ so that $S \cap (K+(p,q)) \neq \emptyset$. Let $(\mathring{\mu}:\mathring{S}\to R^1,m\times n)$ be the hypographic recession function of $(\mu:S\to R^1,m\times n)$:

1) The hypographic recession function of $(\mu:S \cap (K+(p,q))\to R^1,m\times n)$ is the function $(\mathring{\mu}:\mathring{S} \cap K\to R^1,m\times n)$.
2) The level sets $\{(x,y) \in S \cap (K+(p,q))|\mu(x;y) \geqq \alpha\}$ are all bounded, if and only if $\{(\mathring{x},\mathring{y}) \in \mathring{S} \cap K|\mathring{\mu}(\mathring{x};\mathring{y}) \geqq 0\} = \{(0,0)\}$.

1.9. <u>Theorem (Corollary of 1.8, 1.4 and 1.5).</u>
Given I/O-process $(\mu:S\to R^1,m\times n)$ and its hypographic recession function $(\mathring{\mu}:\mathring{S}\to R^1,m\times n)$. Let $K \subset R^m\times R^n$ be a closed-convex cone. Suppose $\{(\mathring{x},\mathring{y}) \in \mathring{S} \cap K|\mathring{\mu}(\mathring{x};\mathring{y}) \geqq 0\} = \{(0,0)\}$. Then, concerning $(\varphi:C^+\to R^1,m\times n)$, $C^+:=\{(r,s) \in R^m_+\times R^n|S \cap (K+(r,s)) \neq \emptyset\}$, $\varphi(r;s):= \sup \mu(x;y)$, over $(x,y) \in S \cap (K+(r,s))$:

(1) $\varphi(C^+) \subset R^1$ and $(\varphi:C^+\to R^1,m\times n)$ is an I/O-process.
(2) For every $(r,s) \in C^+$, there is an $(\hat{x},\hat{y}) \in S \cap (K+(r,s))$ so that $\mu(\hat{x};\hat{y}) = \varphi(r;s)$.

Later on we shall use the following evident property.

1.10. Proposition.

Given a closed-concave function $\rho:U \subset R^n \to R^1$ and its hypographic recession function $\mathring{\rho}:\mathring{U}\to R^1$. Let $f:R^n\to R^1$ be a linear function. Then the hypographic recession function of $\rho(.)+f(.):U\to R^1$ is the function $\mathring{\rho}(.)+f(.):\mathring{U}\to R^1$.

2. Prices and dual Input/Output processes.

Let $(\mu:S\to R^1, m\times n)$ be an I/O-process. Suppose the input and output prices are given by vectors $u \in R^m_+$ and $v \in R^n_+$ respectively. Then the net-value of an I/O-combination $(x,y) \in S$ is defined $\mu(x;y)-u.x+v.y$ (note: the inner product of vectors $a,b \in R^n$ is denoted a.b). Thus, net-value maximization leads to the following transformation.

2.1. Duality transformations.

With any bi-function $(\mu:S\to R^1, m\times n)$ we associate the (max-oriented) dual as a bi-function $(\underline{\wedge}\mu:\underline{\wedge}S\to R^1, m\times n)$:

$$(1)\qquad \begin{cases} \underline{\wedge}\mu(u;v) := \sup_{(x,y)\in S}(\mu(x;y)-u.x+v.y), \\ \underline{\wedge}S := \{(u,v) \in R^m\times R^n \mid \underline{\wedge}\mu(u;v) < +\infty\}, \end{cases}$$

provided $\underline{\wedge}S \neq \emptyset$. As a matter of fact this dual is exactly Rockafellar's (max-oriented) adjoint of a bi-function. Rockafellar's adjoint - and so our dual $\underline{\wedge}\mu:\underline{\wedge}S\to R^1$ - is a closed-convex bi-function (provided $\underline{\wedge}S \neq \emptyset$), in addition, concavity of $\mu:S\to R^1$ implies $\underline{\wedge}S \neq \emptyset$. The corresponding inverse transformation is the min-oriented dual, concerning any $(\nu:W\to R^1, m\times n)$, defined as a bi-function $(\underline{\vee}\nu:\underline{\vee}W\to R^1, m\times n)$:

$$(2)\qquad \begin{cases} \underline{\vee}\nu(x;y) := \inf_{(u,v)\in W}(\nu(u;v)+x.u-y.v), \\ \underline{\vee}W := \{(x,y) \in R^m\times R^n \mid \underline{\vee}\mu(x;y) > -\infty\}, \end{cases}$$

provided $\underline{\vee}W \neq \emptyset$). Namely, the min-oriented dual of $(\underline{\vee}\mu:\underline{\wedge}S\to R^1, m\times n)$ - notation: $(\underline{\vee\wedge}\mu:\underline{\vee\wedge}S\to R^1, m\times n)$ is equivalent to $(\mu:S\to R^1, m\times n)$, if and only if $(\mu:S\to R^1, m\times n)$ is closed-concave. In the opposite orientation the max-oriented dual is the inverse of the min-oriented dual.

A geometric interpretation of the max-oriented dual can be given in terms of supergradients; being, concerning $(\mu:S\to R^1, m\times n)$, defined as an $(\bar{u},\bar{v}) \in R^m\times R^n$ so that there is an $\alpha \in R^1$ with $\mu(x;y) \leq \alpha+\bar{u}.x+\bar{v}.y$, for all $(x,y) \in S$. More specific: $(\bar{u},\bar{v})$ is called a supergradient at a point $(\bar{x},\bar{y}) \in S$, if it is a supergradient and if, in addition, $\mu(\bar{x};\bar{y}) - \bar{u}.\bar{x} - \bar{v}.\bar{y} = \sup_{(x,y)} (\mu(x;y) - \bar{u}.x - \bar{v}.y)$. The evident relations with the dual are given below; property 2.2-(3) can be established with the help of separation arguments.

2.2. Proposition.

Let $(\underline{\wedge}\mu : \underline{\wedge}S \to R^1, m\times n)$ be the max-oriented dual of $(\mu : S \to R^1, m\times n)$. Then concerning the supergradients of $(\mu : S \to R^1, m\times n)$:

(1) $\{(\bar{u},\bar{v}) \in R^m \times R^n \mid (\bar{u},-\bar{v}) \in \underline{\wedge}S\}$ is the set of supergradients.

(2) Suppose $\mu(\bar{x};\bar{y}) = \inf_{(u,v) \in \underline{\wedge}S} (\underline{\wedge}\mu(u;v) + \bar{x}.u - \bar{y}.v)$ (with $(\bar{x},\bar{y}) \in S$). Then, $(\bar{u},\bar{v}) \in R^m \times R^n$ is a supergradient at $(\bar{x},\bar{y})$, if and only if $(u,v) := (\bar{u},-\bar{v})$ is optimal in $\inf_{(u,v) \in \underline{\wedge}S} (\underline{\wedge}\mu(u;v) + \bar{x}.u - \bar{y}.v)$.

(3) If $(\mu : S \to R^1, m\times n)$ is concave, then, for every $(\bar{x},\bar{y}) \in \mathrm{rint}(S)$, there exists a supergradient (implying the equality $\mu(\bar{x},\bar{y}) = \inf_{(u,v) \in \underline{\wedge}S} (\underline{\wedge}\mu(u;v) + \bar{x}.u - \bar{y}.v)$, for every $(\bar{x},\bar{y}) \in \mathrm{rint}(S)$).

Returning to an I/O-process $(\mu : S \to R^1, m\times n)$: concavity implies the existence of the dual $(\underline{\wedge}\mu : \underline{\wedge}S \to R^1, m\times n)$. As an immediate consequence of the free disposal hypothesis we have: (i) $\underline{\wedge}S \subset R^m_+ \times R^n$, and (ii) $\forall\ (u,v) \in \underline{\wedge}S$: $\forall\ \bar{u} \in R^m \mid \bar{u} \geqq u$: $(\bar{u},v) \in \underline{\wedge}S$, $\underline{\wedge}\mu(\bar{u};v) \leqq \underline{\wedge}\mu(u;v)$. Moreover, we know that the dual is closed-convex. Thus it appears that $(-\underline{\wedge}\mu : \underline{\wedge}S \to R^1, m\times n)$ is an I/O-process. This justifies the introduction of the following concept.

2.3. Dual I/O-processes.

We define the dual I/O-process as $(\nu : W \to R^1, m\times n)$ satisfying:

(1) $W \subset R^m_+ \times R^n$,

(2) $\forall (u,v) \in W : \forall \bar{u} \in R^m \mid \bar{u} \geqq u$: $(\bar{u},v) \in W$, $\nu(\bar{u};v) \leqq \nu(u;v)$,

(3) $\nu : W \to R^1$ is convex,

(4) $\mathrm{epi}(W;\nu)$ is closed.

2.4. Theorem.

The max-oriented dual of an I/O-process is a dual I/O-process.

2.5. Partial duals.

With respect to any bi-function $(\mu : S \to R^1, m\times n)$ we associate:

(1) The partial max-oriented dual in argument 1: $(\wedge_1\mu : \wedge_1 S \to R^1, m\times n)$,

$\wedge_1\mu(u;y) := \sup\ \mu(x;y) - u.x$, over $x \in R^m$, subject to (abbreviated s.t.) $(x,y) \in S$, $\wedge_1 S := \{(u,y) \in R^m \times D_2(S) \mid \wedge_1\mu(u;y) < +\infty\}$, provided $\wedge_1 S \neq \emptyset$.

(2) The <u>partial max-oriented dual in argument 2:</u> $(\wedge_2\mu : \wedge_2 S \to R^1, m\times n)$,

$\wedge_2\mu(x;v) := \sup \mu(x;y) + v.y$, over $y \in R^n$, s.t. $(x,y) \in S$,

$\wedge_2 S := \{(u,v) \in D_1(S)\times R^n \mid \wedge_2\mu(x;v) < +\infty\}$, provided $\wedge_2 S \neq \emptyset$.

In the case that the partial functions $\mu(.;y):S\to R^1$ are closed-concave, the inverse transformation of (1) is the partial min-oriented dual in argument 1, being defined in the symmetric manner. The same can be said concerning the partial dual in the second argument. The economic interpretation should be clear: partial dual (2) can be taken as value maximization, given the inputs; partial dual (1) might be taken as net cost minimization under fixed outputs. The dual, simultaneously over both arguments, and the partial duals are closely related (cf. [12]):

2.6. <u>Proposition.</u>
Let $(\mu:S\to R^1, m\times n)$ be closed-concave. Then; concerning the duals $(\underline{\wedge}\mu:\underline{\wedge}S\to R^1, m\times n)$, $(\wedge_1\mu:\wedge_1 S\to R^1, m\times n)$, it holds:

(1) $D_1(\underline{\wedge}S)\times D_2(S) \subset \wedge_1 S \subset cl(D_1(\underline{\wedge}S))\times D_2(S)$.

(2) The partial min-oriented dual in argument 1 of the bi-function $(\wedge_1\mu:D_1(\underline{\wedge}S)\times D_2(S)\to R^1, m\times n)$ is equivalent to $(\mu:S\to R^1, m\times n)$.

(3) The partial max-oriented dual in argument 2 of the bi-function $(\wedge_1\mu:D_1(\underline{\wedge}S)\times D_2(S)\to R^1, m\times n)$ is equivalent to $(\underline{\wedge}\mu:\underline{\wedge}S\to R^1, m\times n)$.

(4) $(\wedge_1\mu:D_1(\underline{\wedge}S)\times D_2(S)\to R^1, m\times n)$ is concave-convex.

In the symmetric matter the same is true for the partial duals in the second argument. Duality also can be related to the boundedness of level sets. For instance, exploring the closedness of a hypographic recession function, it is not hard to prove that, concerning a concave bi-function $(\nu:U\to R^1, m\times n)$, the level sets $\{(u,v) \in U \mid \nu(u;v) \geqq \alpha\}$ are all bounded, if and only if there is an $\varepsilon > 0$ so that, for every $({}^\circ u, {}^\circ v) \in R^m\times R^n$, $\|({}^\circ u, {}^\circ v)\| \leqq \varepsilon$: $\sup_{(u,v)\in U}(\nu(u;v) - {}^\circ u.u + {}^\circ v.v) < +\infty$. The latter is equivalent to the condition that $0 \in int(\underline{\wedge}U)$. Combining these relations with 1.8 and 1.10 we arrive at the equivalent characterizations:

2.7. <u>Proposition.</u>
Let $(\nu:U\to R^1, m\times n)$ be closed-concave, and let $(\mathring{\nu}:\mathring{U}\to R^1, m\times n)$ be its hypographic recession function. Let $(p,q) \in R^m\times R^n$. Then the following statements are equivalent:

(1) The level sets $\{(x,y) \in U \mid \nu(x;y) - p.x + q.y \geqq \alpha\}$ are compact.

(2) $\{(\mathring{x},\mathring{y}) \in \mathring{U} \mid \mathring{\nu}(\mathring{x};\mathring{y})-p.\mathring{x}+q.\mathring{y} \geqq 0\} = \{(0,0)\}$.

(3) $(p,q) \in \mathrm{int}(\underline{\wedge}U)$.

Now we shall study duality of composed systems; firstly by Lagrangian methods and next with the help of the max-oriented dual.

2.8. <u>Duality of composed systems by Lagrangian methods.</u>

A <u>Lagrangian representation</u> of a max-problem $\sup_{x\in C} f(x)$, where $f:X\to R^1, C \subset X$, is a bi-function $L:X\times W\to R^1$ satisfying the conditions: $\forall x \in C: f(x) = \inf_{w\in W} L(x;w)$, and $\forall x \in X, \notin C : \inf_{w\in W} L(x;w) = -\infty$. A vector $\hat{w} \in W$ is called a <u>Lagrange vector</u> if $\sup_{x\in C} f(x) = \sup_{x\in X} L(x;\hat{w})$. A necessary condition for the existence of a Lagrange vector is, that the representation satisfies the equality: $\sup_x \inf_w L(x;w) = \inf_w \sup_x L(x;w)$; in that case the representation is called <u>normal</u>. The so called <u>dual problem</u>, associated with the representation is defined: $\inf_{w\in W}(\sup_{x\in X} L(x;w))$. Clearly, if $L:X\times W \to R^1$ is normal, then the Lagrange vectors are the dual optimal solutions. Now let us consider the max-problem:

$$(1) \qquad \bar{\varphi} := \sup \mu(x;y) - {}^*r.x + {}^*s.y, \text{ over } (x,y) \in S \cap (K+(r,s)),$$

given the concave bi-function $(\mu:S\to R^1, m\times n)$, the closed convex cone $K \subset R^m\times R^n$, and given the vectors $r,s,{}^*r,{}^*s$ with appropriate dimensions. In order to construct a suitable Lagrangian representation, we introduce the concept <u>dual cone</u> of a set $C \subset R^m\times R^n$, denoted ${}^*C$:

$$(2) \qquad {}^*C := \{(u,v) \in R^m\times R^n \mid \forall (x,y) \in C : u.x-v.y \leqq 0\}.$$

Realizing that, as a matter of fact, the dual cone is a modification of the well-known concept polar cone, we know: (i) ${}^*C$ is a closed-convex cone, (ii) the dual cone of ${}^*C$ is equal to C, if and only if C is a closed-convex cone. Then, with the hypothesis that K is a closed-convex cone, it is easy to verify that:

$$(3) \qquad \begin{cases} L:S\times({}^*K+({}^*r,{}^*s))\to R^1. \\ L((x,y);(u,v)) := \mu(x;y)-u.(x-r)+v.(y-s)-{}^*r.r+{}^*s.s, \end{cases}$$

satisfies the Lagrangian conditions. The corresponding dual problem can be elaborated to:

(4) $\bar{\Psi} := \inf \underline{\wedge}\mu(u;v)+u.r-v.s$, over $(u,v) \in \underline{\wedge}S \cap (^{*}K+(^{*}r,^{*}s))$,

$(\underline{\wedge}\mu:\underline{\wedge}S\to R^1,m\times n)$ being the max-oriented dual of $(\mu:S\to R^1,m\times n)$; however, in such a manner that:

(5) $\bar{\Psi}-{}^{*}r.r+{}^{*}s.s = \inf_{(u,v)\in {}^{*}K+({}^{*}r,{}^{*}s)} \sup_{(x,y)\in S} L((x,y);(u,v))$.

The symmetry between the primal problem (1) and its dual counter part is remarkable. Particularly, in the case that $(\mu:S\to R^1,m\times n)$ is an I/O-process, the symmetry is complete in the sense that, changing the sign of the dual, we have a problem with the same logical structure as the primal problem. As a matter of fact, in the opposite orientation (3) might be considered as a Lagrangian representation of (4), and, consequently, (1) can be conceived as the dual of (4).

As an immediate consequence of the min-max inequality and of (5) we have the inequality:

(6) $\bar{\varphi} \leqq \bar{\Psi}-{}^{*}r.r+{}^{*}s.s$.

So the representation is <u>normal</u> if $\bar{\varphi} = \bar{\Psi}-{}^{*}r.r+{}^{*}s.s$. The so called weak duality relations can be deduced easily.

2.9. <u>Theorem (weak duality relations between 2.8-(1) and 2.8-(4)).</u>

Concerning any $(\hat{x},\hat{y}) \in S \cap (K+(r,s))$, $(\hat{u},\hat{v}) \in \underline{\wedge}S \cap (^{*}K+(^{*}r,^{*}s))$, it holds

(1) If $\hat{\mu}(\hat{x};\hat{y})+\hat{v}.\hat{y} = \underline{\wedge}\mu(\hat{u};\hat{v})+\hat{u}.\hat{x}$, $(\hat{u}-{}^{*}r).(\hat{x}-r) = (\hat{v}-{}^{*}s).(\hat{y}-s)$, then $(\hat{x},\hat{y})$ and $(\hat{u},\hat{v})$ are primal and dual optimal solutions; moreover, the existence of such an $(\hat{x},\hat{y})$, $(\hat{u},\hat{v})$ implies normality.

(2) If the representation is normal, then satisfying the equalities in (1), is a necessary condition for optimality.

(3) Corollary: suppose the representation is normal, suppose $(\hat{u},\hat{v})$ is dual optimal, and suppose $\sup_{(x,y)\in S}(\mu(x;y)-\hat{u}.x+\hat{v}.y)$ possesses at most one optimal solution. Then $(\tilde{x},\tilde{y}) \in S$ is primal optimal, if and only if $(\tilde{x},\tilde{y})$ is optimal in $\sup_{(x,y)\in S}(\mu(x;y)-\hat{u}.x+\hat{v}.y)$.

We observe that in 2.9-(3), the condition $(x,y) \in K+(r,s)$ is eliminated. For that reason this property might be used for decomposition purposes. Below, the existence of optimal solutions and Lagrangian vectors will be studied in terms of the max-oriented dual.

2.10. Duality of composed I/O-processes by duality transformations.

Now we focus our attention on the max-oriented dual of the bi-function $(\Psi:P\to]-\infty,+\infty],m\times n)$:

$$(1)\quad \begin{cases} \Psi(r;s):=\sup \mu(x;y)-{}^{*}r.x+{}^{*}s.y, \text{ over } (x,y)\in S\cap(K+(r,s)) \\ P:=\{(r,s)\in R^{m}\times R^{n}\mid S\cap(K+(r,s))\neq\emptyset\}, \end{cases}$$

where $(\mu:S\to R^{1},m\times n)$ is concave, $K\subset R^{m}\times R^{n}$ a closed-convex cone, and where ${}^{*}r\in R^{m}$, ${}^{*}s\in R^{n}$. In terms of these data, the max-oriented dual $(\underline{\wedge}\Psi:\underline{\wedge}P\to R^{1},m\times n)$ (provided $\underline{\wedge}P\neq\emptyset$) can be deduced with the help of
$\underline{\wedge}\Psi(u;v) := \sup \mu(x;y)-{}^{*}r.x+{}^{*}s.y-u.r+v.s$, over $(x,y)\in S$, $(r,s)\in R^{m}\times R^{n}$, s.t. $(x-r,y-s)\in K$, to be written:
$\underline{\wedge}\Psi(u;v) := \sup \mu(x;y)-({}^{*}r+u).x+({}^{*}s+v).y+u.(x-r)-v.(y-s)$, over $(x,y)\in S$, $(r,s)\in R^{m}\times R^{n}$, s.t. $(x-r,y-s)\in K$. The latter implies:

$$(2)\quad \begin{cases} \underline{\wedge}\Psi(\tilde{u};\tilde{v}) = \underline{\wedge}\mu({}^{*}r+\tilde{u};{}^{*}s+\tilde{v}), \\ \underline{\wedge}P = \{(\tilde{u},\tilde{v})\in R^{m}\times R^{n}\mid({}^{*}r+\tilde{u},{}^{*}s+\tilde{v})\in\underline{\wedge}S,\ (\tilde{u},\tilde{v})\in{}^{*}K\}. \end{cases}$$

Consequently, the supergradients (cf. proposition 2.2) of $\Psi:P\to R^{1}$ at a point $(r,s)\in P$ can be found as an optimal solution of:
$\inf \underline{\wedge}\Psi(\tilde{u};\tilde{v})+r.\tilde{u}-s.\tilde{v}$, over $(\tilde{u},\tilde{v})\in\underline{\wedge}P$. Thus it appears that $(\bar{u},\bar{v})$ is a supergradient of $(\Psi:P\to R^{1},m\times n)$ at $(r,s)\in P$, if and only if $(u,v) := (\bar{u}+{}^{*}r,-\bar{v}-{}^{*}s)$ is optimal with respect to:

$$(3)\qquad \tilde{\Psi} := \inf \underline{\wedge}\mu(u;v)+(u-{}^{*}r).r-(v-{}^{*}s).s,$$
$$\text{over } (u,v)\in\underline{\wedge}S\cap({}^{*}K+({}^{*}r,{}^{*}s)).$$

Apart from the constant term $-{}^{*}r.r+{}^{*}s.s$, we see that the above is equivalent to the dual problem 2.8-(4) generated by the Lagrangian representation. In fact 2.8-(5) implies $\tilde{\Psi} = \inf_{(u,v)}\sup_{(x,y)} L((x,y);(u,v))$.

In order to formulate, with the help of 2.2-(3), sufficient conditions for the existence of Lagrange vectors, we introduce the following concepts: max-problem 2.8-(1) - given $(r,s)\in R^{m}\times R^{n}$ - is called <u>primal feasible</u> if $S\cap(K+(r,s))\neq\emptyset$, and <u>strictly primal feasible</u> if $0\in\operatorname{int}((S-(r,s))\cap K)$; the problem - given $({}^{*}r,{}^{*}s)\in R^{m}\times R^{n}$ - is called <u>dual feasible</u> if $\underline{\wedge}S\cap({}^{*}K+({}^{*}r,{}^{*}s))\neq\emptyset$, and <u>strictly dual feasible</u> if $0\in\operatorname{int}((\underline{\wedge}S-({}^{*}r,{}^{*}s))\cap{}^{*}K)$.
As will be pointed out in theorem 2.14, dual strict feasibility is equi-

valent to the assumption: $\{(\mathring{x},\mathring{y}) \in \mathring{S} \cap K | \mathring{\mu}(\mathring{x};\mathring{y}) - {}^{*}r.\mathring{x} + {}^{*}s.\mathring{y} \geqq 0\} = \{(0,0)\}$, $(\mathring{\mu}:\mathring{S}\to R^1, m\times n)$ being the hypographic recession function of $(\mu:S\to R^1, m\times n)$. In the opposite orientation, the same relation holds concerning primal strict feasibility on one side and the epigraphic recession function of $(\underline{\wedge}\mu:\underline{\wedge}S\to R^1, m\times n)$ and the dual cone ${}^{*}K$ on the other. Now, as a consequence of 2.2-(3), we have:

2.11. Theorem (strong duality relations).
Concerning the primal and dual problem 2.8-(1) and 2.8-(4) respectively it holds:

(1) If the problem is dual feasible and primal strictly feasible, then $\bar{\varphi} = \bar{\Psi} - {}^{*}r.r + {}^{*}s.s$ and there exists a dual optimal solution.
(2) If the problem is primal feasible and dual strictly feasible, then $\bar{\varphi} = \bar{\Psi} - {}^{*}r.r + {}^{*}s.s$ and there exists a primal optimal solution.

Returning to the original composed system 1.3-(3), it is clear that its max-oriented dual is given by 2.10-(2) with $({}^{*}r, {}^{*}s) := (0,0)$. Thus we have:

2.12. Theorem.
Let $(\mu:S\to R^1, m\times n)$ be concave, let $K \in R^m\times R^n$ be a closed-convex cone. Let $(\varphi:C\to]-\infty,+\infty], m\times n)$ be defined $\varphi(r;s) := \sup \mu(x;y)$, over $(x,y) \in S \cap (K+(r,s))$, $C := \{(r,s) \in R^m\times R^n | S \cap (K+(r,s)) \neq \emptyset\}$. Then, if $\varphi(C) \subset R^1$, its max-oriented dual exists and is equivalent to $(\underline{\wedge}\mu:\underline{\wedge}S \cap {}^{*}K\to R^1, m\times n)$.

Earlier we observed that, in case $(\mu:S\to R^1, m\times n)$ is an I/O-process and the domain of φ is restricted to $C \cap (R^m_+\times R^n)$ we obtain a composed I/O-process, provided $\varphi(C \cap (R^m_+\times R^n)) \subset R^1$. However, since the domain is restricted, the dual of this I/O-process differs from the dual given in 2.12. Therefore we prove the following theorem:

2.13. Theorem.
Let $(\mu:S\to R^1, m\times n)$ be an I/O-process, let $K \subset R^m\times R^n$ be a closed-convex cone. Let $(\varphi:C^+\to R^1, m\times n)$ be defined $\varphi(r;s) := \sup \mu(x;y)$, over $(x,y) \in S \cap (K+(r,s))$, $C^+ := \{(r,s) \in R^m\times R^n | S \cap (K+(r,s)) \neq \emptyset\}$. Then, if $\varphi(C^+) \subset R^1$, its max-oriented dual exists and is equivalent to $(\underline{\wedge}\mu:\underline{\wedge}S \cap ({}^{*}K+(R^m_+\times\{0\}))\to R^1, m\times n)$.

Proof. Let $(\underline{\vee\wedge}\varphi:\underline{\vee\wedge}\, C\to R^1, m\times n)$ be the min-max dual of $(\varphi:C\to R^1, m\times n)$, then $(\nu:W\to R^1, m\times n)$ is the max-oriented dual of $(\varphi:C^+\to R^1, m\times n)$, if and only if

$\text{hypo}(\underline{\vee\wedge}\ C \cap (R^m_+ \times R^n);\ \underline{\vee\wedge}\varphi) = \text{hypo}(\underline{\vee}w;\underline{\vee}\nu)$. By virtue of 2.12, the latter is true if and only if, simultaneously:

(i) $\forall(r,s) \in C \cap (R^m \times R^n)$: $(\inf \underline{\wedge}\mu(u;v)+r.u-s.v,$ over $(u,v) \in \underline{\wedge}S \cap {}^*K) =$
$= (\inf \nu(u;v)+r.u-s.v,$ over $(u,v) \in W)$,

(ii) $\forall(r,s) \in R^m \times R^n,\ \notin C \cap (R^m_+ \times R^n)$:
$(\inf \nu(u;v)+r.u-s.v,$ over $(u,v) \in W) = -\infty$.

Putting $(\nu:W\to R^1, m\times n)$ equal to $(\underline{\wedge}\mu:\underline{\wedge}S \cap ({}^*K+(R^m_+ \times \{0\}))\to R^1, m\times n)$, we have:

(iii) $\forall(r,s) \in R^m \times R^n$: $(\inf \nu(u;v)+r.u-s.v,$ over $(u,v) \in W) =$
$= (\inf \nu(\bar{u}+\tilde{u};\bar{v})+r.(\bar{u}+\tilde{u})-s.\bar{v},$ over $(\bar{u},\bar{v}) \in \underline{\wedge}\ S \cap {}^*K, \tilde{u} \in R^m_+)$.

It is easy to verify that for this $(\nu:W\to R^1, m\times n)$, the conditions (i) and (ii) are satisfied. □

It is interesting to relate the strict feasibility hypothesis in theorem 2.11 to boundedness aspects. The natural starting point is presented by proposition 2.7 and theorem 2.12 where the max-oriented dual of the composed system is given. The result is the following theorem:

2.14. <u>Theorem.</u>

Let $(\mathring{\mu}:\mathring{S}\to R^1, m\times n)$ be the hypographic recession function of a closed-concave bi-function $(\mu:S\to R^1, m\times n)$ and let $K \subset R^m \times R^n$ be a closed-convex cone. Then, given $(r,s) \in R^m \times R^n$ so that $S \cap (K+(r,s)) \neq \emptyset$, and given $({}^*r,{}^*s) \in R^m \times R^n$, the following statements are equivalent:

(1) The level sets $\{(x,y) \in S \cap (K+(r,s)) \mid \mu(x;y)-{}^*r.x+{}^*s.y \geqq \alpha\}$ are compact.

(2) $\{(\mathring{x},\mathring{y}) \in \mathring{S} \cap K \mid \mathring{\mu}(\mathring{x};\mathring{y})-{}^*r.\mathring{x}+{}^*s.\mathring{y} \geqq 0\} = \{(0,0)\}$.

(3) $0 \in \text{int}((\underline{\wedge}S-({}^*r,{}^*s)) \cap {}^*K)$. (${}^*K$ being the dual cone of K).

We shall conclude this part concerning duality with a few remarks concerning the concept <u>composition cone</u>; in 1.3 being defined as a closed convex cone K satisfying (i) $\forall(x,0) \in K : x \not\geqq 0$, and (ii) $\exists(p,q) \in -K: p>0$. With the help of separation arguments it can be verified that these conditions are related to the dual cone in the following manner:

2.15. <u>Proposition.</u>

Let $K \subset R^m \times R^n$ be a closed-convex cone and let ${}^*K$ be its dual (cf. definition 2.8-(2)). Then:

(1) $K \cap (R^m_+ \times \{0\}) = \{(0,0)\}$, if and only if $-{}^*K \cap (R^m_{++} \times R^n) \neq \emptyset$.

(2) $-K \cap (R^m_{++} \times R^n) \neq \emptyset$, if and only if ${}^*K \cap (R^m_+ \times \{0\}) = \{(0,0)\}$.

(3) Corollary: K is a composition cone, if and only if ${}^*K$ is a composition cone.

3. Dynamic Input/Output processes.

Here we shall elaborate the concept composed I/O-process, in studying an economic system where the activities take place during a sequence- finite or infinite- of periods, in such a manner that inputs at the beginning of a period result into outputs which become available at the end of that period. These outputs are used as inputs for the activities during the succeeding period, and so on. The periods are numbered $t = 0,1,\dots,h$. Period $t:=0$ is considered as the last passed period. Period h is the terminal period; it is called the (time or planning) horizon. If the horizon is not specified, we shall speak of an open (or infinite) horizon process. The moments of period changing are called time-points; to be indicated as "the start of period t" or as "the end of period t". The activities and their corresponding utilities for the separate periods are specified by a sequence of I/O-processes. This leads to the following formal structure.

3.1. The formal structure of dynamic I/O-processes.

The core of a dynamic I/O-process with horizon h - finite or infinite - consists of a sequence of I/O-processes $(\mu^t:S^t\to R^1, m^t\times n^t)$, $t=1,\dots,h$, with $m^{t+1} = n^t$, $t=1,\dots,h-1$. In the open horizon case we have to assume $m^t \leqq \tilde{m}$, $t=1,\dots,$ for some $\tilde{m}$. Composed vectors $(x^t,y^t)_1^h \in (S^t)_1^h$ will be called (primal) trajectories. In order to gain some generality, the notion of feasible trajectories is based on given fixed sequence of positive "scaling factors" $\{\delta^t\}_1^h$, for instance specified by an exponential form $\delta^t:=(\rho)^t, t=1,\dots,h, \rho \in R^1_{++}$. Then, a trajectory $(x^t,y^t)_1^h$ is called (primal) feasible with respect to a given $(r^t,s^t)_1^h \in (R^{m^t}\times R^{n^t})_1^h$ if $\delta^1(x^1-r^1) = 0$, $\delta^{t+1}(x^{t+1}-r^{t+1}) = \delta^t(y^t-s^t)$, $t=1,\dots,h-1$; observe that s^h is dummy and that, for $h < +\infty$, the terminal output y^h is free. In this and in the following sections, the constituting I/O-processes and the scaling factors are supposed to be fixed given data; thus the set of trajectories $(x^t,y^t)_1^h$, being feasible with respect to an $(r^t,s^t)_1^h$ will be denoted $F^h((r^t,s^t)_1^h)$. Vector r^1 can be taken as a given initial state vector.

Generally, there is no natural principle to bundle the objective functions of the separate periods together into one single objective function (cf. [10]). Of course the concept Pareto-efficiency can serve a leading principle; i.e. given $(r^t,s^t)_1^h$, a feasible trajectory $(\hat{x}^t,\hat{y}^t)_1^h$ is called Pareto-efficient if there is no $(x^t,y^t)_1^h \in F^h((r^t,s^t)_1^h)$ so that $\mu^t(x^t;y^t) \geqq \mu^t(\hat{x}^t,\hat{y}^t)$, $t=1,\dots,h$, with at least for one period the strict inequality. In the finite horizon case, we shall restrict ourselves to an objective function of the form $\Sigma_{t=1}^{h}\gamma^t\delta^t(\mu^t(x^t;y^t)-{}^{*}r^t.x^t+{}^{*}s^t.y^t)$, given $({}^{*}r^t,{}^{*}s^t)_1^h \in (R^{m^t}\times R^{n^t})_1^h$, given the positive scalars γ^t, to be called (time) discount factors and given the scaling factors $\delta^t \in R^1_{++}$, being introduced before. The time discount factors, as the I/O-processes and the scaling factors, are supposed to be fixed data. Thus $(\hat{x}^t,\hat{y}^t)_1^h \in F^h((r^t,s^t)_1^h)$ (h being finite) will be called (primal) optimal (with respect to $({}^{*}r^t,{}^{*}s^t)_1^h$) if $\Sigma_{t=1}^{h}\gamma^t\delta^t(\mu^t(\hat{x}^t;\hat{y}^t)-{}^{*}r^t.x^t+{}^{*}s^t.y^t)=$ $= \sup \Sigma_{t=1}^{h}\gamma^t\delta^t(\mu^t(x^t;y^t)-{}^{*}r^t.x^t+{}^{*}s^t.y^t)$, over $(x^t,y^t)_1^h \in F^h((r^t,s^t)_1^h)$. In the ∞-horizon case, a trajectory $(\hat{x}^t,\hat{y}^t)_1^\infty \in F^\infty((r^t,s^t)_1^\infty)$ will be called (primal) optimal (with respect to $({}^{*}r^t,{}^{*}s^t)_1^\infty$) if there is no $(x^t,y^t)_1^\infty \in F^\infty((r^t,s^t)_1^\infty)$ such that for some period T and some $\varepsilon \in R^1_{++}$: $\Sigma_{t=1}^{h}\gamma^t\delta^t(\mu^t(x^t;y^t)-{}^{*}r^t.x^t+{}^{*}s^t.y^t) \geqq \varepsilon+\Sigma_{t=1}^{h}\gamma^t\delta^t(\mu^t(\hat{x}^t;\hat{y}^t)-{}^{*}r^t.\hat{x}^t+{}^{*}s^t.\hat{y}^t)$, $h=T,T+1,\ldots$. Observe that in this "no better on the long run" optimality principle, convergency of the sequences $\{\Sigma_{t=1}^{h}\gamma^t\delta^t(\mu^t(x^t;y^t)-{}^{*}r^t.x^t+{}^{*}s^t.y^t)\}_{h=1}^{\infty}$ is not required. One may verify that in both the finite and infinite horizon case, optimal trajectories are Pareto-efficient, as well.

3.2. The finite horizon system as a composed I/O-process.

With the conventions mentioned above we arrive, in the finite horizon case, at a bi-function $(\varphi:C\to]-\infty,+\infty],m\times n)$, with $m:=\Sigma_{i=1}^{h} m^t$, $n:=\Sigma_{i=1}^{n} n^t$;

(1)
$$\begin{cases} \varphi((r^t)_1^h;(s^t)_1^h) := \sup \Sigma_{t=1}^{h} \gamma^t\delta^t(\mu^t(x^t;y^t)-{}^{*}r^t.x^t+{}^{*}s^t.y^t) \\ \text{over } (x^t,y^t)_1^h\in (s^t)_1^h, \text{ s.t. } \delta^1(x^1-r^1)=0,\ \delta^{t+1}(x^{t+1}-r^{t+1})=\delta^t(y^t-s^t), t=1,..,h, \\ C:=\{((r^t)_1^h,(s^t)_1^h) \in ((R^{m^t})_1^h\times(R^{n^t})_1^h) \mid F^h((r^t,s^t)_1^h) \neq \emptyset\}. \end{cases}$$

In order to fit this bi-function in the abstract form 1.3-(3), we define $(\mu:S\to R^1,m\times n)$ and $\bar{K} \subset R^m\times R^n$ as follows:

(2)
$$\begin{cases} \bar{\mu}((x^t)_1^h;(y^t)_1^h) := \Sigma_{t=1}^{h} \gamma^t\delta^t\mu^t(x^t;y^t), \\ \bar{S}:= \{((x^t)_1^h,(y^t)_1^h) \in (R^{m^t})_1^h\times(R^{n^t})_1^h \mid (x^t,y^t) \in S^t,\ t=1,\ldots,h\} \\ \bar{K}:= \{((x^t)_1^h,(y^t)_1^h) \in (R^{m^t})_1^h\times(R^{n^t})_1^h \mid x^1=0,\ \delta^{t+1}x^{t+1} = \delta^t y^t,\ t=1,\ldots,h-1\}. \end{cases}$$

Putting: $r:=(r^t)_1^h$, $s:=(s^t)_1^h$, ${}^{*}r:=(\gamma^t\delta^t{}^{*}r^t)_1^h$, ${}^{*}s:=(\gamma^t\delta^t{}^{*}s^t)_1^h$, $x:=(x^t)_1^h$, $y:=(y^t)_1^h$, it should be clear that (1) can be written:
$\varphi(r;s):= \sup \bar{\mu}(x;y)$, over $(x,y) \in \bar{S} \cap (\bar{K}+(r,s))$, $C:=\{(r,s) \in R^m\times R^n|$

$\bar{S} \cap (K+(r,s)) \neq \emptyset\}$. One may verify that $\bar{K}$ is a composition cone. Thus it appears that all properties concerning composed systems fully apply to the dynamic system. For instance, concerning the dual process we have:

$$(3)\quad \begin{cases} \underline{\wedge}\bar{\mu}((u^t)_1^h;\ (v^t)_1^h) = \Sigma_{t=1}^h\ \gamma^t\delta^t\ \underline{\wedge}\mu^t((\gamma^t\delta^t)^{-1}u^t;(\gamma^t\delta^t)^{-1}v^t), \\ \underline{\wedge}\bar{S} = \{((u^t)_1^h,(v^t)_1^h) \in (R^{m^t})_1^h \times (R^{n^t})_1^h \mid (\gamma^t\delta^t)^{-1}(u^t,v^t) \in \underline{\wedge}S^t,\ t=1,\dots,h\}, \\ {}^*\bar{K} = \{((u^t)_1^h,(v^t)_1^h) \in (R^{m^t})_1^h \times (R^{n^t})_1^h \mid (1/\delta^{t+1})u^{t+1} = (1/\delta^t)\ v^t, t=1,\dots,h-1, v^h=0\} \end{cases}$$

and consequently, the dual 2.8-(4): $\bar{\Psi} := \inf \underline{\wedge}\bar{\mu}(u;v)+u.r-v.s$, over $(u,v) \in \underline{\wedge}\bar{S} \cap ({}^*\bar{K}+({}^*r,{}^*s))$ can be written:

$$(4)\quad \begin{cases} \bar{\Psi} := \inf \Sigma_{t=1}^h \gamma^t\delta^t(\underline{\wedge}\mu^t(u^t;v^t)+r^t.u^t-s^t.v^t),\ \text{over}\ (u^t,v^t)_1^h \in (\underline{\wedge}S^t)_1^h, \\ \text{s.t.}\ \gamma^{t+1}(u^{t+1}-{}^*r^{t+1}) = \gamma^t(v^t-{}^*s^t),\ t=1,\dots,h-1,\ v^h={}^*s^h; \end{cases}$$

related to the abstract formulation with $(u,v):=(\gamma^t\delta^t u^t,\gamma^t\delta^t v^t)_1^h$. Observe that, unlike the primal version (1), the initial vector u^1 is free, while ${}^*s^h$ represents a fixed terminal valuation. We shall denote the set of <u>dual feasible trajectories</u> $(u^t,v^t)_1^h$, given $({}^*r^t,{}^*s^t)_1^h$: ${}^*F^h(({}^*r^t,{}^*s^t)_1^h)$. It should be clear that, in terms of the original data, the duality inequality 2.8-(6) can be written:

$$(5)\quad \begin{cases} \Sigma_{t=1}^h\ \gamma^t\delta^t(\mu^t(x^t;y^t)-{}^*r^t.x^t + {}^*s^t.y^t) \leqq \\ \leqq \Sigma_{t=1}^h\ \gamma^t\delta^t(\underline{\wedge}\mu^t(u^t;v^t)+r^t.u^t-s^t.v^t-{}^*r^t.r^t+{}^*s^t.s^t). \end{cases}$$

Consequently, given $(r^t,s^t)_1^h,({}^*r^t,{}^*s^t)_1^h$, we call the system <u>normal</u> if the supremum of the left hand side is equal to the infimum of the right hand side. Elaborating the additive form of the objective function and equality of the feasibility conditions, the weak duality relations 2.9 can be written:

3.3. <u>Theorem (weak duality of 3.2-(1),-(2), given $(r^t,s^t)_1^h,({}^*r^t,{}^*s^t)_1^h$)</u>

Let $(\hat{x}^t,\hat{y}^t)_1^h \in F^h((r^t,s^t)_1^h)$, $(\hat{u}^t,\hat{v}^t)_1^h \in {}^*F^h(({}^*r^t,{}^*s^t)_1^h)$:

(1) If $\mu^t(\hat{x}^t;\hat{y}^t)+\hat{v}^t.\hat{y}^t = \underline{\wedge}\mu^t(\hat{u}^t;\hat{y}^t)+\hat{u}^t.\hat{x}^t$, $t=1,2,\dots,h$, then $(\hat{x}^t,\hat{y}^t)_1^h$, $(\hat{u}^t,\hat{v}^t)_1^h$ are optimal; moreover, the existence of such $(\hat{x}^t,\hat{y}^t)_1^h$, $(\hat{u}^t,\hat{v}^t)_1^h$ implies normality.

(2) If the system is normal, then satisfying the equalities in (1) is a necessary condition for optimality.

(3) Corollary: suppose the system is normal, suppose $(\hat{u}^t,\hat{v}^t)_1^h$ is dual optimal, and suppose each problem $\sup_{(x,y)\in S^t}(\mu^t(x;y)-\hat{u}^t.x+\hat{v}^t.y)$ possesses at most one optimal solution. Then $(\tilde{x}^t,\tilde{y}^t)_1^h \in (S^t)_1^h$ is primal optimal, if and only if each $(\tilde{x}^t,\tilde{y}^t)$ is optimal with respect to the corresponding problem $\sup_{(x,y)\in S^t}(\mu^t(x;y)-\hat{u}^t.x+\hat{v}^t.y)$.

Concerning strong duality theorem 2.11, the free disposal hypothesis and the particular structure of the dynamic system make it possible to give simple characterization of strict feasibility: the dynamic system, given $(r^t,s^t)_1^h$ is called primal strictly feasible if for some $\varepsilon > 0$, there exists a feasible trajectory such that $(\tilde{x}^t-\varepsilon e,\tilde{y}^t) \in S^t$, $t=1,\dots,h$, e being the vector with all components equal to one (and with appropriate dimension); the trajectory $(\tilde{x}^t,\tilde{y}^t)_1^h$ is called a primal strictly feasible trajectory. The notion of dual strict feasibility is defined in the symmetric manner: given $({}^*r^t,{}^*s^t)_1^h$, a trajectory $(\tilde{u}^t,\tilde{v}^t)_1^h$ is called dual strictly feasible if $(\tilde{u}^t,\tilde{v}^t)_1^h \in {}^*F^h(({}^*r^t,{}^*s^t)_1^h)$ and, in addition for some $\varepsilon > 0$: $(\tilde{u}^t-\varepsilon e,\tilde{v}^t) \in \underline{\wedge}S^t$, $t=1,\dots,h$. Then, as a consequence of theorem 2.11, we have:

3.4. Theorem (strong duality relations).

The strong duality relations of 3.2-(1) and -(4), given $(r^t,s^t)_1^h$ and $({}^*r^t,{}^*s^t)_1^h$ are:

(1) If the dynamic system is dual feasible and primal strictly feasible, then the system is normal and there exists a dual optimal trajectory.

(2) If the dynamic system is primal feasible and dual strictly feasible, then the system is normal and there exists a primal optimal trajectory.

3.5. Weak duality relations of open horizon dynamic systems.

Since the open horizon system consists of an infinite number of I/O-processes, there is no direct manner to establish a relation to our standard composition. Nevertheless, we shall introduce the dual of the open horizon system as a straightforward generalization of the finite horizon case. Thus a dual feasible (infinite horizon) trajectory, corresponding to $({}^*r^t,{}^*s^t)_1^\infty$ is a trajectory $(u^t,v^t)_1^\infty \in (\underline{\wedge}S^t)_1^\infty$ satisfying: $\gamma^{t+1}(u^{t+1}-{}^*r^{t+1}) = \gamma^t(v^t-{}^*s^t)$, $t=1,2,\dots$; the set of dual feasible trajectories will be denoted ${}^*F^\infty(({}^*r^t,{}^*s^t)_1^\infty)$. Given $({}^*r^t,{}^*s^t)_1^\infty$ and $(r^t,s^t)_1^\infty$, $(\hat{u}^t,\hat{v}^t)_1^\infty \in {}^*F^\infty(({}^*r^t,{}^*s^t)_1^\infty)$ is called a dual optimal trajectory, if there is no $(u^t,v^t)_1^\infty \in {}^*F^\infty({}^*r^t,{}^*s^t)_1^\infty)$ so that, for some $\varepsilon>0$ and some period T: $\Sigma_{t=1}^h \gamma^t\delta^t(\underline{\wedge}\mu^t(u^t;v^t)+r^t.u^t-s^t.v^t) \leqq -\varepsilon+\Sigma_{t=1}^h \gamma^t\delta^t(\underline{\wedge}\mu^t(\hat{u}^t;\hat{v}^t)+r^t.\hat{u}^t-s^t.\hat{v}^t)$, h=T,T+1,.... So, the dual optimality criterion is, in the opposite orientation and with a starting point valuation, the same as the primal infinite horizon optimality criterion.

Now, given any dual trajectory $(u^t,v^t)_1^\infty \in {}^*F^\infty(({}^*r^t,{}^*s^t)_1^\infty)$, let us consider a sequence of finite horizon problems 3.2-(1), with horizon h=1,2,..., where the terminal valuations are taken $v^1,v^2,\ldots$ respectively. Then the inequalities 3.2-(5) with the corresponding correction-terms of the terminal valuations $\gamma^h\delta^h(v^h-{}^*s^h)y^h$ and $\gamma^h\delta^h(v^h-{}^*s^h).s^h$, h=1,2,... apply to every primal trajectory $(x^t,y^t)_1^\infty \in F^\infty((r^t,s^t)_1^\infty)$ in the following manner:

$$(1)\quad \begin{cases} \gamma^h\delta^h(v^h-{}^*s^h).(y^h-s^h)+\Sigma_{t=1}^h\gamma^t\delta^t(\mu^t(x^t;y^t)-{}^*r^t.x^t+{}^*s^t.y^t) \leqq \\ \leqq \Sigma_{t=1}^h \gamma^t\delta^t(\underline{\wedge}\mu^t(u^t;v^t)+r^t.u^t-s^t.v^t-{}^*r^t.r^t+{}^*s^t.s^t),\ h=1,2,\ldots \end{cases}$$

Under the hypothesis that $r^{t+1}:=0$, ${}^*r^t:=0$, t=1,2,... we have $\delta^{t+1}x^{t+1}= = \delta^t(y^t-s^t)$, $\gamma^{t+1}u^{t+1} = \gamma^t(v^t-{}^*s^t)$, t=1,2,... and consequently (by $x^t,u^t \geq 0$, t=1,...) $(y^t-s^t).(v^t-{}^*s^t) \geq 0$, t=1,2,.... Then, the inequalities (1) imply the following sufficient conditions for optimality:

3.6. <u>Theorem (sufficient conditions for optimality ∞-horizon systems).</u>

Consider an open horizon system being composed of a sequence of I/O-processes, given $(r^t,s^t)_1^\infty$ with $r^{t+1}:=0$, ${}^*r^t:=0$, t=1,2,.... If a pair $(\hat{x}^t,\hat{y}^t)_1^\infty \in F^\infty((r^t,s^t)_1^h)$, $(\hat{u}^t,\hat{v}^t)_1^\infty \in {}^*F^\infty(({}^*r^t,{}^*s^t)_1^h)$ satisfies simultaneously:

(i) $\mu^t(\hat{x}^t;\hat{y}^t)+\hat{v}^t.\hat{y}^t = \underline{\wedge}\mu^t(\hat{u}^t;\hat{v}^t)+\hat{u}^t.\hat{x}^t$, t=1,2,...

(ii) $\lim_{h\to\infty}\gamma^h\delta^h(\hat{v}^h-{}^*s^h).(\hat{y}^h-s^h) = 0$,

then $(\hat{x}^t,\hat{y}^t)_1^\infty$ and $(\hat{u}^t,\hat{v}^t)_1^\infty$ are optimal trajectories.

Observe that, because of the special structure of the dynamic system, the provisio $r^{t+1}:=0$, ${}^*r^t:=0$, t=1,2,... is not restrictive at all. Namely, the vectors s^t, ${}^*s^t$ can be adapted by $\tilde{s}^t:=s^t-(\delta^{t+1}/\delta^t)r^{t+1}$ and by ${}^*\tilde{s}^t:={}^*s^t-(\gamma^{t+1}/\gamma^t){}^*r^{t+1}$.

In connection with the so-called <u>transitivity condition</u> (ii), it is natural to impose some additional restrictions on the system, like:

boundedness of $\{s^t\}_1^\infty$ and $\{{}^*s^t\}_1^\infty$ and $\lim_{t\to\infty}\gamma^t\delta^t=0$. Then possibly the transitivity condition might be satisfied in cases where $\lim_{h\to\infty}y^h.v^h\neq 0$.

4. Invariant dynamic processes and stationary optimal trajectories.

Particularly, the structure of open horizon dynamic processes can be made more explicit in studying processes, where the data for the separate periods are all the same. After introducing the formal set up, we shall discuss the existence of feasible trajectories, boundedness aspects, and finally the existence of stationary optimal trajectories.

4.1. Invariant dynamic processes.

We specify the invariant dynamic I/O-process as an open horizon dynamic process where: (i) for each period the I/O-process is $(\mu:S\to R^1, m\times m)$, (ii) with the exception of r^1, all vectors $r^t, s^t, {}^*r^t, {}^*s^t$ are equal to $r, s, {}^*r, {}^*s \in R^m$ respectively, and where (iii) the scaling factors $\{\delta^t\}_1^\infty$ and the time-discount factors $\{\gamma^t\}_1^\infty$ are exponential $\delta^t:=(\rho)^t$, $\gamma^t:=(\pi)^t$, $t=1,\dots,$ with $\rho,\pi > 0$, $(\rho\pi) < 1$. Consequently, the primal and dual optimality criteria are based on the series:

$$(1)\quad \begin{cases} \{\Sigma_{t=1}^h (\rho\pi)^t(\mu(x^t;y^t)-{}^*r.x^t+{}^*s.y^t)\}_{h=1}^\infty, \\ \{(\rho\pi)(r^1-r).u^1+\Sigma_{t=1}^h(\rho\pi)^t(\underline{\wedge}\mu(u^t;v^t)+r.u^t-s.v^t)\}_{h=1}^\infty, \end{cases}$$

respectively. Further it should be clear that the primal and dual feasibility conditions can be written:

$$(2)\quad \begin{cases} x^1 = r^1,\ \rho(x^{t+1}-r) = y^t-s,\ t = 1,2,\dots, \\ \pi(u^{t+1}-{}^*r) = v^t-{}^*s,\ t = 1,\dots \end{cases}$$

4.2. Theorem.

Let $(\mu:S\to R^1, m\times m)$ be an I/O-process, let $r,s \in R^m$, $\rho \in R^1_{++}$. Then the following statements are equivalent:

(1) There exists an $\{(x^t,y^t)\}_1^\infty \subset S$ so that $\rho(x^{t+1}-r) < (y^t-s-\varepsilon e)$ $t=1,2,\dots$ for some $\varepsilon > 0$.

(2) There exists an $(x,y) \in S$ so that $\rho(x-r) < (y-s)$.

Proof. Let $\{(x^t,y^t)\}_1^\infty \subset S$ satisfy $\rho(x^{t+1}-r) < y^t-s-\varepsilon e$, $t=1,2,\dots$. Then, non-negativity of all x^t implies: $(1/h)\rho\,\Sigma_{t=1}^h x^t < (1/h)\rho x^1+\rho r-s-\varepsilon e+$ $+(1/h)\,\Sigma_{t=1}^h y^t$, $h=1,2,\dots$. In addition, convexity of S implies:

$(1/h)\ \Sigma_{t=1}^{h}(x^t,y^t) \in S$, $h=1,2,\ldots$. Putting h large enough so that $(1/h)\rho x^1 < \varepsilon e$, it is clear that $(\tilde{x}^h,\tilde{y}^h):=(1/h)\Sigma_{t=1}^{h}(x^t,y^t)$ satisfies condition (2). The other way round, let $(x,y) \in S$, $\rho(x-r) < (y-s)$. Then, for $\{(x^t,y^t)\}_1^\infty$, $(x^t,y^t):=(x,y)$, $t=1,2,\ldots$ there is an $\varepsilon > 0$ so that the conditions of (1) are satisfied. □

Since $(\underline{\wedge}\mu:\underline{\wedge}S\to R^1,m\times m)$ is a dual I/O-process (cf. 2.3), a similar relation holds with respect to the dual system. Below boundedness will be studied in relation to the level sets of an I/O-process. It turns out that boundedness is directly related to dual feasibility.

4.3. Theorem.
Let $(\mu:S\to R^1,m\times m)$ be an I/O-process. Let $^*r, {}^*s \in R^m$ and let $\rho,\pi \in R^1_{++}$, $(\rho\pi) < 1$. Then the following statements are equivalent:

(1) Concerning every $\{(x^t,y^t)\}_1^\infty \subset S$ so that $\rho(x^{t+1}-r) \leqq y^t-s$, $t=1,2,\ldots$, $\Sigma_{t=1}^{h}(\rho\pi)^t(\mu(x^t;y^t)-{}^*r.x^t+{}^*s.y^t) \geqq \alpha$, $h=1,2,\ldots$, for some $r,s\in R^m$, $\alpha \in R^1$, the sequence $\{\Sigma_{t=1}^{h}\ (\rho\pi)^t(x^t,y^t)\}_{h=1}^\infty$ is bounded.

(2) $\{(\mathring{x},\mathring{y}) \in \mathring{S}\,|\,(1/\pi)\mathring{x}=\mathring{y},\ \mathring{\mu}(\mathring{x};\mathring{y})-{}^*r.\mathring{x}+{}^*s.\mathring{y} \geqq 0\} = \{(0,0)\}$, where $(\mathring{\mu}:\mathring{S}\to R^1,m\times m)$ is the hypographic recession function of $(\mu:S\to R^1,m\times m)$.

(3) There exists a $(u,v) \in \underline{\wedge}S$, so that: $\pi(u-{}^*r) < (v-{}^*s)$.

(4) There is a $\{(u^t,v^t)\}_1^\infty \subset \underline{\wedge}S$, so that $\pi(u^{t+1}-{}^*r) < (v^t-{}^*s-\varepsilon e)$, $t=1,2,\ldots$, for some $\varepsilon > 0$.

Proof. (1) ⇔ (2): given $r,s \in R^m$, $\alpha \in R^1$, let $\{(x^t,y^t)\}_1^\infty \subset S$ satisfy the conditions of (1). Defining $\{\beta^h\}_1^\infty$, $\beta^h:=(1-\rho\pi)/(\rho\pi-(\rho\pi)^{h+1})$, $h=1,2,\ldots$ (implying, each $\{\beta^h(\rho\pi)^t\}_{t=1}^h$ is a system of convex combination coefficients), and next defining $(\bar{x}^h,\bar{y}^h):=\beta^h\Sigma_{t=1}^{h}(\rho\pi)^t(x^t,y^t)$, $h=1,2,\ldots$ we have:

(i) $\{(\bar{x}^h,\bar{y}^h)\}_1^\infty \subset S$ (by convexity of S),

(ii) $\mu(\bar{x}^h;\bar{y}^h)-{}^*r.\bar{x}^h+{}^*s.\bar{y}^h \geqq \beta^h\alpha \geqq -|\alpha|/(\rho\pi)$, $h=1,2,\ldots$ (by concavity of μ and by the hypotheses in (1)).

(iii) $(1/\pi)\bar{x}^h \leqq \bar{y}^h+\rho x^1+\rho r+s$, $h = 1,2,\ldots$ (by non-negativity of $\{x^t\}_1^\infty$ and by $\rho x^{t+1} \leqq y^t+\rho r-s$, $t = 1,2,\ldots$).

Now suppose $\{\Sigma_{t=1}^{h}\ (\rho\pi)^t(x^t,y^t)\}_{h=1}^\infty$ is not bounded. Then, $\{(\bar{x}^h,\bar{y}^h)\}_1^\infty$ is not bounded, and thus (by (i), (ii), (iii), and the free disposal hypothesis, it appears that $Z:=\{(x,y) \in S\,|\,(1/\pi)x=y+\rho x^1+\rho r-s$, $\mu(x;y)-{}^*r.x+{}^*s.y \geqq -|\alpha|/(\rho\pi)\}$ is not bounded. By virtue of 1.8 and of 1.10, this implies that statement (2) is false.

The other way round, let $(\mathring{x},\mathring{y}) \in \mathring{S}$, $(\mathring{x},\mathring{y}) \neq (0,0)$ satisfy $(1/\pi)\mathring{x}=\mathring{y}$, $\mathring{\mu}(\mathring{x};\mathring{y})-{}^{*}r.\mathring{x}+{}^{*}s.\mathring{y} \geqq \nu$. Let $(x,y) \in S$, $s \in R^m$ be such that $\rho x \leqq y-s$. Then, defining $\{(x^t,y^t)\}_1^\infty$, $(x^t,y^t):=(x,y)+(\rho\pi)^{-t}(\mathring{x},\mathring{y})$, $t=1,2,\ldots$, the suppositions imply: (iv) $\{(x^t,y^t)\}_1^\infty \subset S$, (v) $\rho x^{t+1} \leqq y^t-s$, $t=1,2,\ldots$, (vi) $\Sigma_{t=1}^{h} (\rho\pi)^t(\mu(x^t;y^t)-{}^{*}r.x^t+{}^{*}s.y^t) \geqq -(1-\rho\pi)^{-1}|\mu(x;y)-{}^{*}r.x+{}^{*}s.y|$, $h=1,2,\ldots$ and finally (vii) $\{\Sigma_{t=1}^{h} (\rho\pi)^{t}(x^t,y^t)\}_{h=1}^\infty$ is not bounded. Clearly, statement (1) is false.

(2) ⇔ (3): under free disposal, a consequence of 2.15.

(3) ⇔ (4): consequence of the dual version of 4.2. □

Because of the symmetry between the primal and dual system, the same can be said of the boundedness of dual feasible trajectories. For the sake of completeness, we also give the dual version of 4.3:

4.4. Theorem (dual version of 4.3).

Let $(\mu:S\to R^1, m\times m)$ be an I/O-process. Let $r,s \in R^m$, and let $\rho,\pi \in R^1_{++}$, $(\rho\pi) < 1$. Then the following is equivalent:

(1) Concerning every $\{(u^t,v^t)\}_1^\infty \subset \underline{\wedge}S$ so that $\pi(u^{t+1}-{}^{*}r) \leqq v^t-{}^{*}s$, $t=1,2,\ldots$, $\Sigma_{t=1}^{h} (\rho\pi)^t(\underline{\wedge}\mu(u^t;v^t)+r.u^t-s.v^t) \leqq \alpha$, $h=1,2,\ldots$, for some ${}^{*}r,{}^{*}s \in R^m$, $\alpha \in R^1$, the sequence $\{\Sigma_{t=1}^{h} (\rho\pi)^t(u^t,v^t)\}_{h=1}^\infty$ is bounded.

(2) $\{(\mathring{u},\mathring{v}) \in {}^{*}S \mid (1/\rho)\ \mathring{u}=\mathring{v},\ {}^{*}\mu(\mathring{u};\mathring{v})+r.\mathring{u}-s.\mathring{v} \leqq 0\} = \{(0,0)\}$, where $({}^{*}\mu:{}^{*}S\to R^1, m\times m)$ is the epigraphic recession function of $(\underline{\wedge}\mu:\underline{\wedge}S\to R^1, m\times m)$.

(3) There exists an $(x,y) \in S$ so that $\rho(x-r) < (y-s)$.

(4) There is an $\{(x^t,y^t)\}_1^\infty \subset S$, so that $\rho(x^{t+1}-r) < (y^t-s-\varepsilon e)$, $t=1,2,\ldots$, for some $\varepsilon > 0$.

Below a stronger boundedness property is deduced under a stronger dual condition.

4.5. Theorem.

Let $(\mu:S\to R^1, m\times m)$ be an I/O-process. Let ${}^{*}r,{}^{*}s \in R^m$, $\rho \in R^1_{++}$. Then the following is equivalent:

(1) Every sequence $\{(x^t,y^t)\}_1^\infty \subset S$ so that $\rho(x^{t+1}-r) \leqq (y^t-s)$, $t=1,2,\ldots$, $\mu(x^t;y^t)-{}^{*}r.x^t+{}^{*}s.y^t \geqq \nu$, $t=1,2,\ldots$, for some $r,s \in R^m$, $\nu \in R^1$, is bounded.

(2) $\{(\mathring{x},\mathring{y}) \in \mathring{S} \mid \rho\mathring{x}=\mathring{y},\ \mu(\mathring{x};\mathring{y})-{}^{*}r.\mathring{x}+{}^{*}s.\mathring{y} \geqq 0\} = \{(0,0)\}$, where $(\mathring{\mu}:\mathring{S}\to R^1, m\times m)$ is the hypographic recession function of $(\mu:S\to R^1, m\times m)$.

(3) There exists a $(u,v) \in \underline{\wedge}S$, so that $(1/\rho)(u-{}^{*}r) < (v-{}^{*}s)$.

(4) There is a $\{(u^t,v^t)\}_1^\infty \subset \underline{\wedge}S$, so that $(1/\rho)(u^{t+1}-{}^{*}r) < (v^t-{}^{*}s-\varepsilon e)$, $t = 1,2,\ldots$, for some $\varepsilon > 0$.

<u>Proof.</u> (1) ⇔ (2). Let $\alpha \in]0,1[$ and define $\{\beta^h\}_1^\infty$: $\beta^h := (1-\alpha)/(1-(\alpha)^h)$, $h = 1,2,\ldots$, implying that each $\{\beta^h(\alpha)^{h-t}\}_{t=1}^h$ is a sequence of convex combination coefficients. Given $r,s \in R^m$, $\nu \in R^1$, let $\{(x^t,y^t)\}_1^\infty \subset S$ satisfy the conditions of (1). Defining $(\bar{x}^h,\bar{y}^h) := \beta^h \Sigma_{t=1}^h (\alpha)^{h-t}(x^t;y^t)$, it follows:

(i) $\{(\bar{x}^h,\bar{y}^h)\}_1^\infty \subset S$ (by convexity of S),

(ii) $\mu(\bar{x}^h;\bar{y}^h) - {}^*r.\bar{x}^h + {}^*s.\bar{y}^h \geqq \nu$ (by concavity of μ),

(iii) $\rho\alpha\ \bar{x}^h \leqq \bar{y}^h + \rho x^1 + \rho r - s$, $h = 1,2,\ldots$ (by non-negativity of $\{x^t\}_1^\infty$ and by $\rho x^{t+1} \leqq y^t + \rho r - s$, $t = 1,2,\ldots$).

Now, suppose $\{(x^t,y^t)\}_1^\infty$ is not bounded. Then $\{(\bar{x}^h,\bar{y}^h)\}_1^\infty$ is not bounded. In a similar manner as in the proof of 4.3, the latter implies (by virtue of (i), (ii), (iii), and the free disposal hypothesis) the existence of an $(\mathring{x},\mathring{y}) \in \mathring{S}$, $(\mathring{x},\mathring{y}) \neq (0,0)$, so that $\rho\alpha\ \mathring{x} = \mathring{y}$, $\mathring{\mu}(\mathring{x};\mathring{y}) - {}^*r.\mathring{x} + {}^*s.\mathring{y} \geqq 0$. Thus, we may conclude: the negation of statement (1) implies:

(iv) $\forall\alpha \in]0,1[: \{(\mathring{x},\mathring{y}) \in \mathring{S} \mid \mathring{\mu}(\mathring{x};\mathring{y}) - {}^*r.x + {}^*s.y \geqq 0\} \cap \{(\mathring{x},\mathring{y}) \in R^m \times R^m \mid \rho\alpha\ \mathring{x} = \mathring{y}\} \neq \{(0,0)\}$.

Using the property that the hypo $(\mathring{S};\mathring{\mu})$ is a closed-convex cone, one may verify: (iv) implies statement (2) is false.

The other way round, let $(\mathring{x},\mathring{y}) \in \mathring{S}$, $(\mathring{x},\mathring{y}) \neq (0,0)$ satisfy $\rho\mathring{x} = \mathring{y}$, $\mathring{\mu}(\mathring{x};\mathring{y}) - {}^*r.\mathring{x} + {}^*s.\mathring{y} \geqq 0$. Let $(x,y) \in S$ and $s \in R^m$ be such that $\rho(x+\mathring{x}) \leqq y-s$. Then, defining $(x^t,y^t) := (x,y) + t(\mathring{x},\mathring{y})$, $t=1,2,\ldots$, the suppositions imply that the conditions of statement (1) are satisfied; however, evidently this sequence is not bounded.

Summarizing: (1) and (2) are equivalent.

(2) ⇔ (3): under free disposal, a consequence of 2.15.

(3) ⇔ (4): consequence of the dual version of 4.2. □

Comparing 4.3 and 4.5: since by hypothesis $(\rho\pi) \in]0,1[$, it should be clear that the boundedness in 4.5-(1) is more stringent than those of 4.3-(1). Concerning the dual counterparts 4.3-(3) and 4.5-(3), the "free disposal" property of $\underline{\wedge}S$ implies that, consequently, 4.5-(3) is more stringent than 4.3-(3). Of course, like 4.3, theorem 4.5 can be formulated in a dual version. An interesting point of 4.5 is, that 4.5-(3) and its dual version appears to be directly connected with the existence of stationary optimal trajectories.

4.6. <u>Stationary optimal trajectories.</u>

Given I/O-process $(\mu:S\to R^1, m\times m)$, vectors $s, {}^*s \in R^m$ and numbers $\rho,\pi > 0$, $\rho\pi < 1$, let us consider a combination $(\hat{x},\hat{y}),(\hat{u},\hat{v}) \in R^m \times R^m$, so that

$$(1)\quad \begin{cases} (\hat{x},\hat{y}) \in S,\ (\hat{u},\hat{v}) \in \underline{\wedge}S, \\ \rho\hat{x} = \hat{y}-s,\ \pi\hat{u} = \hat{v}-{}^{*}s, \\ \mu(\hat{x};\hat{y})+\hat{v}.\hat{y} = \underline{\wedge}\mu(\hat{u};\hat{v})+\hat{u}.\hat{x}. \end{cases}$$

Defining $r^1:=\hat{x}$, $r:=0$, ${}^{*}r:=0$, it appears that $(x^t,y^t)_1^\infty$, $(u^t,v^t)_1^\infty$, $(x^t,y^t):=(\hat{x},\hat{y})$, $(u^t,v^t):=(\hat{u},\hat{v})$, $t=1,2,\ldots$ satisfy the primal and dual feasibility conditions 4.1-(2). Moreover, one may verify that $(x^t,y^t)_1^\infty$, $(u^t,v^t)_1^\infty$ fits the sufficient condition for optimality 3.6, with $\delta^t:=(\rho)^t$, $\gamma^t:=(\pi)^t$, $r^{t+1}:=0$, ${}^{*}r^t:=0$, $t=1,2,\ldots$. Thus it appears that $(x^t,y^t)_1^\infty$, $(u^t,y^t)_1^\infty$ are optimal trajectories with respect to the invariant open horizon system. We will call $(\hat{x},\hat{y})$, $(\hat{u},\hat{v})$ a <u>stationary optimal solution</u>; the corresponding trajectories will be called <u>stationary optimal trajectories.</u>

In the case that ${}^{*}s:=0$, the concept stationary optimal solution corresponds with an interesting economic interpretation. Namely, taking the dual part $(\hat{u},\hat{v})$ as input/output prices, we have the net value maximization problem:

$$(2)\qquad \sup\ \mu(x;y)-\hat{u}.x+(\pi\hat{u}).y,$$

which delivers the primal part $(\hat{x},\hat{y})$ as an optimal solution. Apart from the time discount factor, the input and output prices are the same. This looks very reasonable, for the value of the outputs is realized one period later than the input costs are made.

The existence proof consists of two steps: firstly we reduce the problem to a max-problem of type 2.8-(1) with $K:=\{(x,y) \in R^m\times R^m \mid (1/\pi)x=y\}$, ${}^{*}r:=0$, $r:=p$, and secondly, the set of optimal solutions, taken as a multi-valued function of p, will be fitted in the structure of Kakutani's fixed point theorem. Concerning the first step, we have ${}^{*}K:=\{(u,v) \in R^m\times R^m \mid \pi u=v\}$; thus we consider the following specification of 2.8-(1) and its dual 2.8-(4):

$$(3)\quad \begin{cases} \varphi(p):= \sup\ \mu(x;y)+{}^{*}s.y,\ \text{over } (x,y) \in S,\ \text{s.t. } (1/\pi)(x-p)=y-s, \\ \psi(p):= \inf\ \underline{\wedge}\mu(u;v)+p.u-s.v,\ \text{over } (u,v) \in \underline{\wedge}S,\ \text{s.t. } \pi u=v-{}^{*}s. \end{cases}$$

If (3) is normal, then by virtue of 2.9-(1), a feasible pair $(\hat{x},\hat{y})$, $(\hat{u},\hat{v})$ is primal and dual optimal respectively if and only if $\mu(\hat{x};\hat{y})+{}^{*}s.\hat{y} = \underline{\wedge}\mu(\hat{u},\hat{v})+p.\hat{u}-s.\hat{v}+{}^{*}s.s$. Now suppose that the primal part

$(\hat{x},\hat{y})$ satisfies $(1-\rho\pi)\hat{x}=p$. Then we have $\rho\hat{x}=\hat{y}-s$, and the optimality condition can be reduced to: $\mu(\hat{x};\hat{y}) = \underline{\wedge}\mu(\hat{u};\hat{v})+\hat{u}.\hat{x}-\hat{v}.\hat{y}$. Consequently, concerning optimal pairs $(\hat{x},\hat{y}),(\hat{u},\hat{v})$, the equality $(1-\rho\pi)\hat{x}=p$ implies $(\hat{x},\hat{y})$, $(\hat{u},\hat{v})$ is a stationary optimal solution (provided (3) is normal). The other way round any stationary optimal solution $(\hat{x},\hat{y}),(\hat{u},\hat{v})$ is optimal in (3) with $p:=(1-\rho\pi)\hat{x}$. In order to fit this approach in the structure of a fixed point problem that satisfies the conditions given by Kakutani we start from the hypotheses: (i) $\exists(\tilde{x},\tilde{y}) \in S:(1/\pi)\tilde{x} < \tilde{y}-s$, and (ii) $\exists(\tilde{u},\tilde{v}) \in \underline{\wedge}S:(1/\rho)\tilde{u} < \tilde{y}-{}^{*}s$. The first hypothesis implies that the primal problem is strictly feasible for every $p \in R^m_+$; the second, on account of "dual free disposal" and $\rho\pi \in]0,1[$, implies dual strict feasibility. Thus, by virtue of 2.11, we find that for every $p \in R^m_+$ the problem is normal and that primal and dual optimal solutions exist. Let $\tilde{F}:R^m_+\to R^m$ be a set-valued function:

$$\tilde{F}(p):=(1-\rho\pi)\{\hat{x}|\exists\hat{y}:(\hat{x},\hat{y}) \in S,\ (\hat{x}-p)=\pi(\hat{y}-s),\mu(\hat{x};\hat{y})+{}^{*}s.\hat{y} =\varphi(p)\}, \tag{4}$$

then, obviously we have:

4.7. <u>Proposition.</u>

If the systems $(1/\pi)x < y-s$, $(x,y) \in S$ and $(1/\rho)u < v-{}^{*}s$, $(u,v) \in \underline{\wedge}S$ are solvable, then:

(1) For every $p \in R^m_+$, the set $\tilde{F}(p)$ is non-empty and bounded,

(2) $(\hat{x},\hat{y}) \in S$, $(\hat{u},\hat{v}) \in \underline{\wedge}S$ is a stationary solution, if and only if simultaneously: $(1-\rho\pi)\hat{x} \in \tilde{F}((1-\rho\pi)\hat{x})$, $\rho\hat{x}=\hat{y}-s$, and $(\hat{u},\hat{v})$ is dual optimal in 4.6-(3) with $p=(1-\rho\pi)\hat{x}$.

4.8. <u>Stationary optimal solutions as Kakutani fixed-points.</u>

From 4.7 it appears that stationary optimal trajectories are reduced to solutions of the fixed-point problem $p \in \tilde{F}(p)$. Next we shall construct a set $P:=\{p \in R^m_+|c.p \leqq \alpha\}$, $c \in R^m_{++}$, $\alpha \in R^1$ with the particular property $\tilde{F}(P) \subset P$, being one of the Kakutani's conditions. We start from a $\xi \in]0,\rho[$ (close enough to ρ) and a $(\bar{u},\bar{v}) \in \underline{\wedge}S$ so that $\bar{u} < \xi(\bar{v}-{}^{*}s)$; the existence is a consequence of the hypothesis that $(1/\rho)u < v-{}^{*}s$, $(u,v) \in \underline{\wedge}S$ is solvable. The definition of the max-oriented dual implies: $\mu(x;y)+{}^{*}s.y \leqq \underline{\wedge}\mu(\bar{u};\bar{v})+\bar{u}.x-(\bar{v}-{}^{*}s)y$, for every $(x,y) \in S$. If $(x,y) \in S$ satisfies $(1/\pi)(x-p) = y-s$, the inequality can be elaborated to:

$$\mu(x;y)+{}^{*}s.y \leqq \underline{\wedge}\mu(\bar{u},\bar{v})-(\bar{v}-{}^{*}s).s-((1/\pi)-\xi)(\bar{v}-{}^{*}s).x+(1/\pi)(\bar{v}-{}^{*}s).p\ . \tag{1}$$

Now, let $(\bar{x},\bar{y}) \in S$ satisfy $(1/\pi)\bar{x} \leqq \bar{y}-s$. Then, by the free disposal hypothesis, it follows that, for every $p \in R^m_+$, an $(x,y) \in S$ exists so that $(1/\pi)(x-p) = y-s$, $\mu(\bar{x};\bar{y})+{}^*s.\bar{y} \leqq \mu(x;y)+{}^*s.y$. With (1), the latter implies that for every $p \in R^m$, the inequality:
$((1/\pi)-\xi)(\bar{v}-{}^*s).x \leqq -\mu(\bar{x};\bar{y})-{}^*s.\bar{y}+\underline{\wedge}\mu(\bar{u};\bar{v})-(\bar{v}-{}^*s).s+(1/\pi)(\bar{v}-{}^*s).p,$
is a necessary condition for any $(x,y) \in S$, $(1/\pi)(x-p) = y-s$, to be primal optimal with respect to 4.6-(3). Consequently, with $\beta:=|\pi(-\mu(\bar{x};\bar{y})-{}^*s.\bar{y}+\underline{\wedge}\mu(\bar{u};\bar{v})-(\bar{v}-{}^*s).s)|$, the definition of $\tilde{F}:R^m_+\to R^m$ (cf. 4.6-(4)) implies:

$$\text{(2)} \qquad \forall p \in R^m_+ : \forall x \in \tilde{F}(p) \;:\; (1-\pi\xi)(\bar{v}-{}^*s).x \leqq \beta + (\bar{v}-{}^*s).p.$$

Using the fact that $0 < \xi\pi < \rho\pi < 1$, $(\bar{v}-{}^*s) \geqq 0$, one may verify that, as a consequence of (2), we have:

$$\text{(3)} \quad \begin{cases} \forall p \in R^m_+ \,|\, (\bar{v}-{}^*s).p \leqq \beta(1-\rho\pi)/(\rho\pi-\xi\pi): \\ \forall x \in \tilde{F}(p):\; (1-\rho\pi)(\bar{v}-{}^*s).x \leqq \beta(1-\rho\pi)/(\rho\pi-\xi\pi). \end{cases}$$

Thus, defining $P:=\{p \in R^m_+ \,|\, (\bar{v}-{}^*s).p \leqq \beta(1-\rho\pi)/(\rho\pi-\xi\pi)\}$, it holds

(i) $\tilde{F}(P) \subset P$ (by (3) and by 4.7-(1)),

(ii) P is bounded (by $\underline{\wedge}S \subset R^m_+$, $\xi > 0$ and by $\bar{u} < \xi(\bar{v}-{}^*s)$),

(iii) P is convex and closed,

(iv) $\forall p \in P:\tilde{F}(p)$ is convex, not empty (by concavity of $\mu:S\to R^1$ and by 4.7-(1)),

(v) $\{(p,x) \in P\times R^m \,|\, x \in \tilde{F}(p)\}$ is compact (cf. Berge's maximum theorem); this follows from compactness of P and closedness of hypo$(S;\mu)$).

By virtue of Kakutani's fixed-point theorem, (i) to (v) imply the existence of a $\hat{p} \in P$ so that $\hat{p} \in \tilde{F}(\hat{p})$. Then, as a consequence of 4.7-(2), it follows:

4.9. <u>Theorem (existence of stationary optimal solution).</u>

If, concerning the invariant open horizon system, where $(\mu:S\to R^1, m\times m)$ is an I/O-process, where $r:=0$, and where $\rho,\pi > 0$, $(\rho\pi) < 1$, an $(x,y) \in S$, $(u,v) \in \underline{\wedge}S$ exist, with $(1/\pi)x < y-s$, $(1/\rho)u < v-{}^*s$, then there exists a stationary optimal solution.

Observe that, by virtue of 4.5, the existence of a $(u,v) \in \underline{\wedge}S$, $(1/\rho)u < r-{}^*s$ is directly related to the boundedness of primal feasible trajectories in the sense of 4.5-(1). Applying 4.5 in the dual orientation, it appears that solvability of $(1/\pi)x < y-s$, $(x,y) \in S$ is related to the boundedness of dual feasible trajectories. As a matter of fact the basic ideas of this paragraph are deduced earlier with respect to polyhedral I/O-processes (cf. [2]). The existence of stationary optimal solutions is a generalisation of earlier results by Hansen and Koopmans [9] and independently by Evers [2].

5. Existence of optimal trajectories in dynamic open horizon Input/Output-systems and approximation by finite horizon systems.

With the open horizon system, we get involved in a maximization problem in an infinite dimensional vector space. Therefore we are forced to use some notions from functional analysis. Concerning a vector $(\xi^i)_1^\infty$, $\{\xi^i\}_1^\infty \subset R^l$ we frequently will use the L_1-norm $\|(\xi^i)_1^\infty\|_1 :=$ $\sup\{\Sigma_{i=1}^h |\xi^i|\}_{h=1}^\infty$ (possibly $+\infty$) and the L_∞-norm $\|(\xi^i)_1^\infty\|_\infty :=$ $\sup\{|\xi^i|\}_{i=1}^\infty$ (possibly $+\infty$); the L_1- and L_∞-space are the set of vectors $(\xi^i)_1^\infty$ with $\|(\xi^i)_1^\infty\|_1 < +\infty$ and $\|(\xi^i)_1^\infty\|_\infty < +\infty$ respectively. Accordingly, concerning a finite dimensional vector $x \in R^k$ the L_1- and L_∞-norm are defined $\|x\|_1 := \Sigma_{i=1}^k |x_i|$, $\|x\|_\infty := \max\{x_i\}_1^k$. Concerning composed vectors - for instance of the form - $(x^t,y^t)_1^\infty \in (R^{m^t} \times R^{n^t})_1^\infty$ we define $\|(x^t,y^t)_1^\infty\|_1 := \sup\{\Sigma_{t=1}^h \|(x^t,y^t)\|_1\}_{h=1}^\infty$, $\|(x^t,y^t)_1^\infty\|_\infty :=$ $:= \sup\{\|(x^t,y^t)\|_\infty\}_{t=1}^\infty$; $(x^t,y^t)_1^\infty$ will be called L_1-bounded (respectively L_∞-bounded) if $\|(x^t,y^t)_1^\infty\|_1 < +\infty$ ($\|(x^t,y^t)_1^\infty\|_\infty < +\infty$ resp.); the set of L_1-bounded (resp. L_∞-bounded) vectors $(x^t,y^t)_1^\infty \in (R^{m^t} \times R^{n^t})$ is denoted $(R^{m^t} \times R^{n^t})_1^\infty \cap L_1$ (resp. $(R^{m^t} \times R^{n^t})_1^\infty \cap L_\infty$). We shall use this notions in a flexible way; for instance $(S^t)_1^\infty \cap L_\infty$, of course, stands for the set of L_∞-bounded $(x^t,y^t)_1^\infty \subset (S^t)_1^\infty$.

In contrast to the complexity of the proofs, the main results of this section are quite simple: under an appropriate strict primal and dual feasibility condition, theorem 5.6 affirms the existence of primal and dual optimal trajectories, theorem 5.8 gives a convergence rate of a finite horizon approximation procedure, and theorem 5.9 states that the open horizon problem is normal, implying a generalisation of the strong duality relations of the finite horizon dynamic system. Further, under a more restrictive strict feasibility condition, theorem 5.5 states that L_∞-boundedness is a necessary condition for feasible trajectories to be optimal.

5.1. Basic hypotheses and conventions.

The duality theory which will be the central theme of this section concerns the open horizon dynamic I/O-system being introduced in section 3. Throughout this section we restrict ourselves to systems, composed of a sequence of I/O-processes and in which a few extra conditions are satisfied. Firstly, we restrict ourselves to the case where $\lim_{t\to\infty} \gamma^t\delta^t = 0$, implying that the transitivity condition in 3.6 might be satisfied by trajectories where $\lim_{t\to\infty} (y^t-s^t).(v^t-{}^*s^t) \neq 0$. To be exact, concerning $\{\gamma^t\}_1^\infty$, $\{\delta^t\}_1^\infty \subset R^1_{++}$ we suppose:

$$(1) \qquad \exists \rho,\pi \in R^1_{++}, \rho\pi < 1: \delta^t \leqq (\rho)^t, \gamma^t \leqq (\pi)^t, \; t = 1,2,\ldots$$

For the sake of simplicity (cf. the observation in 3.6), we assume ${}^*r^t:=0$, $t=1,2,\ldots$, $r^t:=0$, $t=2,3,\ldots$; the vector $r^1 \in R^{m^1}$ might be considered as a given initial state. Instead of defining feasible trajectories by systems of equalities, we shall consider primal and dual systems of inequalities:

$$(2) \quad \begin{cases} x^1 \leqq r^1, \; \delta^{t+1}x^{t+1} \leqq \delta^t(y^t-s^t), \; t=1,2,\ldots \\ \gamma^{t+1}u^{t+1} \leqq \gamma^t(v^t-{}^*s^t), \; t=1,2,\ldots \end{cases}$$

Because of the free disposal hypothesis, this does not affect the nature of the dynamic system. Namely, if $(x^t,y^t)_1^\infty \in (S^t)_1^\infty$ satisfies the primal inequalities, then concerning $(\tilde{x}^t,\tilde{y}^t)_1^\infty$, $(\tilde{x}^1,\tilde{y}^1):=(r^1,y^1)$, $(\tilde{x}^t,\tilde{y}^t):= ((\delta^{t-1}/\delta^t)(y^{t-1}-s^{t-1}),y^t)$, $t=2,3,\ldots$, it holds: $\delta^1\tilde{x}^1=r^1$, $\delta^{t+1}\tilde{x}^{t+1} = \delta^t(\tilde{y}^t-s^t)$, $t=1,2,\ldots$, $(\tilde{x}^t,\tilde{y}^t)_1^\infty \in (S^t)_1^\infty$, $\mu^t(\tilde{x}^t;\tilde{y}^t) \geqq \mu(x^t;y^t)$, $t=1,2,\ldots$; the latter on account of free disposal. The similar can be said of the dual system.

Given r^1 and an $(S^t)_1^\infty$, a trajectory $(x^t,y^t)_1^\infty \in (S^t)_1^\infty$ is called primal strictly feasible if, for some $\varepsilon > 0$, $\delta^1(x^1-r^1) \leqq -\varepsilon e$, $\delta^{t+1}x^{t+1} \leqq \delta^t(y^t-s^t- e)$, $t=1,2,\ldots$, and if in addition $(x^t,y^t)_1^\infty$, $(\mu^t(x^t;y^t))_1^\infty$ are L_∞-bounded. In the symmetric manner, $(u^t,v^t)_1^\infty \in (\underline{\wedge}S^t)_1^\infty$ is called a dual strictly feasible trajectory, given $({}^*s^t)_1^\infty$, if, for some $\varepsilon > 0$, $\gamma^{t+1}u^{t+1} \leqq \gamma^t(v^t-{}^*s^t-\varepsilon e)$, $t=1,2,\ldots$ and if in addition $(u^t,v^t)_1^\infty$, $(\underline{\wedge}\mu^t(u^t;v^t))_1^\infty$ are L_∞-bounded. Comparing strict feasibility of finite and infinite horizon systems, (cf. indroduction to 3.4), it is clear that only the boundedness conditions are added. However, concerning invariant dynamic I/O-systems, theorem 4.2 and its dual version tell us that these boundedness conditions are not restrictive at all.

We shall study a special variant of the strict feasibility concept: give $(s^t)_1^\infty, ({}^*s^t)_1^\infty$ we call the system strictly feasible at a radius α - where $\alpha \geqq 1$ -, if there is an L_∞-bounded $(\underline{x}^t,\underline{y}^t)_1^\infty \in (S^t)_1^\infty$, $(\underline{u}^t,\underline{v}^t)_1^\infty \in (\underline{\wedge}\, S^t)_1^\infty$ such that for some $\varepsilon > 0$, $\theta \in N_{++}$:

$$(3)\quad \begin{cases} \alpha\delta^{t+1}\underline{x}^{t+1} \leqq \delta^t(\underline{y}^t - s^t - \varepsilon e), \ t=\theta,\theta+1,\ldots, \\ \alpha\gamma^{t+1}\underline{u}^{t+1} \leqq \gamma^t(\underline{v}^t - {}^*s^t - \varepsilon e), \ t=\theta,\theta+1,\ldots, \end{cases}$$

and if in addition $(\mu^t(\underline{x}^t;\underline{y}^t))_1^\infty$, $(\underline{\wedge}\mu^t(\underline{u}^t,\underline{v}^t))_1^\infty$ are L_∞-bounded.

Clearly, putting the feasibility radius $\alpha > 1$, close enough to 1, primal and dual strict feasibility implies strict feasibility at that radius. Because of non-negativity of all vectors $\underline{x}^t,\underline{u}^t$, this feasibility hypothesis becomes more restrictive, if the radius is taken larger. Special results will be deduced for a radius $\alpha := (\rho\pi)^{-1}$. Then, concerning an invariant dynamic system, the inequalities (3) reduce to $(1/\pi)\underline{x}^{t+1} \leqq \underline{y}^t - \underline{s} - \varepsilon e$, and $(1/\rho)\underline{u}^{t+1} \leqq \underline{v}^t - {}^*\underline{s} - \varepsilon e$, $t=1,2,\ldots$; the meaning of such an assumption is illuminated by theorem 4.5 and its dual version.

5.2. Proposition.

Given $(\underline{s}^t)_1^\infty \in (R^{n^t})_1^\infty$, $({}^*\underline{s}^t)_1^\infty \in (R^{n^t})_1^\infty$, let for $(s^t)_1^\infty := (\underline{s}^t)_1^\infty$ and $({}^*s^t)_1^\infty := ({}^*\underline{s}^t)_1^\infty$, the system be strictly feasible at a radius $\underline{\alpha} \geqq 1$.

(1) The system is strictly feasible at any radius $\alpha \in [1,\underline{\alpha}]$.

(2) There exists an $\bar{\alpha} > \underline{\alpha}$ such that the system is strictly feasible at any radius $\alpha \in [\underline{\alpha},\bar{\alpha}]$.

(3) There exist L_∞-bounded $(\tilde{s}^t)_1^\infty, ({}^*\tilde{s}^t)_1^\infty \in (R^{n^t})_{t=1}^\infty$ such that for some $\varepsilon_1 > 0$: $\tilde{s}^t \geqq \underline{s}^t - \varepsilon_1 e$, ${}^*\tilde{s}^t \geqq {}^*\underline{s}^t - \varepsilon_1 e$, $t=1,2,\ldots$, and such that for $(s^t)_1^\infty := (\tilde{s}^t)_1^\infty$, $({}^*s^t)_1^\infty := ({}^*\tilde{s}^t)_1^\infty$, the system remains strictly feasible at radius $\underline{\alpha}$.

(4) If, in addition, for $r^1 := \underline{r}^1$ the system is primal and dual strictly feasible, then there is an L_∞-bounded $(x^t,y^t)_1^\infty \in (S^t)_1^\infty$, $(u^t,v^t)_1^\infty \in (\underline{\wedge} S^t)_1^\infty$ such that for some $\varepsilon > 0$, $\theta \in N_{++}$: $\delta^1(x^1 - r^1) \leqq -\varepsilon e$, $\delta^{t+1}x^{t+1} \leqq \delta^t(y^t - s^t - \varepsilon e)$, $\gamma^{t+1}u^{t+1} \leqq \gamma^t(v^t - {}^*s^t - \varepsilon e)$, $t=1,2,\ldots,\theta-1$, $\underline{\alpha}\delta^{t+1}x^{t+1} \leqq \delta^t(y^t - s^t - \varepsilon e)$, $\underline{\alpha}\gamma^{t+1}u^{t+1} \leqq \gamma^t(v^t - {}^*s^t - \varepsilon e)$, $t=\theta,\theta+1,\ldots,$

and such that $(\mu^t(x^t;y^t))_1^\infty$, $(\underline{\wedge}\mu^t(u^t;v^t))_1^\infty$ are L_∞-bounded.

Proof. (1), (2) and (3) are straightforward consequences of the definition. Let, concerning (4), $(\bar{x}^t,\bar{y}^t)_1^\infty \in (S^t)_1^\infty$, $\varepsilon_1 > 0$ be such that $\delta^1(x^1-r^1) \leqq -\varepsilon_1 e$, $\delta^{t+1}\bar{x}^{t+1} \leqq \delta^t(\bar{y}^t-s^t-\varepsilon_1 e)$, $t=1,2,\ldots$. Let $(\underline{x}^t,\underline{y}^t)_1^\infty \in (S^t)_1^\infty \cap L_\infty$ be such that for $\varepsilon_2 > 0$, $\bar{\alpha} > \underline{\alpha}$, $k \in N_{++}$: $\bar{\alpha}\gamma^{t+1}\underline{x}^{t+1} \leqq \gamma^t(\underline{y}^t-s^t-\varepsilon_2 e)$, $t=k,k+1,\ldots$. Let $\theta \in N$, $\theta > k$ be sufficient large so that $(\bar{\alpha})^{k+1-\theta}\delta^{k+1}x^{k+1} \leqq (1/2)\delta^k\varepsilon_1 e$. Then, defining $(x^t,y^t)_1^\infty$, $(x^t,y^t) := (\bar{x}^t,\bar{y}^t)$, $t=1,\ldots,k$, $(x^t,y^t) := (1-(\bar{\alpha})^{t-\theta})(\bar{x}^t,\bar{y}^t)+(\bar{\alpha})^{t-\theta}(\underline{x}^t,\underline{y}^t)$, $t=k+1,k+2,\ldots,\theta$, $(x^t,y^t) := (\underline{x}^t,\underline{y}^t)$, $t=\theta+1,\theta+2,\ldots$, by concavity of the I/O-processes, $(x^t,y^t)_1^\infty$ satisfies the conditions. The dual part of (4) can be verified in a similar manner. □

The meaning of the first statement in the following proposition is, that piecewise at a radius $\alpha > 1$, any primal trajectory can be substituted by a primal "α-feasible" trajectory. The statements 5.3-(2) and -(3) will be used later, in decuding necessary conditions for optimality in terms of boundedness concerning feasible trajectories.

5.3. Proposition.

Suppose $(\underline{x}^t,\underline{y}^t)_1^\infty \in (S^t)_1^\infty$, $(\underline{u}^t,\underline{v}^t)_1^\infty \in (\wedge S^t)_1^\infty$, $(\underline{s}^t)_1^\infty \in (R^{n^t})_{t=1}^\infty$, $({}^{*}\underline{s}^t)_1^\infty \in (R^{n^t})_{t=1}^\infty$, $\underline{\alpha} \geq 1$, $\varepsilon \geq 0$, $\theta \in N$, $\theta \geq 2$ are such that:

(i) $\delta^{t+1}\underline{x}^{t+1} \leqq \delta^t(\underline{y}^t-\underline{s}^t)$, $\gamma^{t+1}\underline{u}^{t+1} \leqq \gamma^t(\underline{v}^t-{}^{*}\underline{s}^t-\varepsilon e)$, $t=1,\ldots,\theta-1$,

(ii) $\underline{\alpha}\delta^{t+1}\underline{x}^{t+1} \leqq \delta^t(\underline{y}^t-\underline{s}^t)$, $\underline{\alpha}\gamma^{t+1}\underline{u}^{t+1} \leqq \gamma^t(\underline{v}^t-{}^{*}\underline{s}^t-\varepsilon e)$ $t=\theta,\theta+1,\ldots$.

Let for every $h \in N$, $h > \theta$ a sequence $\{\lambda^{t,h}\}_{t=1}^\infty$ be defined $\lambda^{t,h} := (\underline{\alpha})^{\theta-h}$, $t=1,\ldots,\theta-1$, $\lambda^{t,h} := (\underline{\alpha})^{t-h}$, $t=\theta,\ldots,h-1$, $\lambda^{t,h} := 1$, $t=h,h+1,\ldots$. Then for every $(x^t,y^t)_1^k \in (S^t)_1^k$, $(s^t)_1^k \in (R^{n^t})_{t=1}^k$, $({}^{*}s^t)_1^k \in (R^{n^t})_{t=1}^k$, $k \in N \cup \{+\infty\}$, $k > 2$, so that $(s^t)_1^k \leqq (\underline{s}^t)_1^k$, $({}^{*}s^t)_1^k \leqq \cdot({}^{*}\underline{s}^t)_1^k$, $\delta^{t+1}x^{t+1} \leqq \delta^t(y^t-s^t)$, $t=1,\ldots,k$, $t < +\infty$, and for every associated $(x^{t,h},y^{t,h})_{t=1}^k$, $h \in N$, $h > \theta$ defined $(x^{t,h},y^{t,h}) := (1-\lambda^{t,h})(x^t,y^t)+\lambda^{t,h}(\underline{x}^t,\underline{y}^t)$, $t=1,\ldots,k$, $t < +\infty$, the following holds:

(1) $(x^{t,h},y^{t,h})_{t=1}^k \in (S^t)_1^k$, $\delta^{t+1}x^{t+1,h} \leqq \delta^t(y^{t,h}-s^t)$, $t=1,\ldots,k$, $t < +\infty$,
$\mu^t(x^{t,h};y^{t,h}) \geq (1-\lambda^{t,h})\mu^t(x^t;y^t)+\lambda^{t,h}\mu^t(\underline{x}^t;\underline{y}^t)$, $t=1,\ldots,k$, $t < +\infty$.

(2) If, for some $\nu \in R^1$, $T \in N_{++}$, $T < k+1$: $\Sigma_{t=1}^T\ \gamma^t\delta^t(\mu^t(x^{t,h};y^{t,h}) +$

$+ {}^{*}s^t.y^{t,h}) \leqq \nu + \Sigma_{t=1}^{T} \gamma^t \delta^t (\mu^t(x^t;y^t) + {}^{*}s^t.y^t)$, then:

$\Sigma_{t=1}^{T} \lambda^{t,h}\gamma^t\delta^t(\mu^t(\underline{x}^t;\underline{y}^t)+{}^{*}s^t.\underline{y}^t) \leqq \nu+\Sigma_{t=1}^{T} \lambda^{t,h}\gamma^t\delta^t(\mu^t(x^t;y^t)+{}^{*}s^t.y^t)$.

(3) For every $q,T,h \in N$, $1 \leqq q \leqq T < k+1$, $h > \theta$:

$$\Sigma_{t=q}^{T} \lambda^{t,h}\gamma^t\delta^t(\mu^t(x^t;y^t)+{}^{*}s^t.y^t) \leqq \lambda^{q,h}\gamma^q\delta^q\underline{u}^q.x^q-\lambda^{T,h}\gamma^T\delta^T(\underline{v}^T-{}^{*}s^T).y^T+$$
$$+\Sigma_{t=q}^{T} \lambda^{t,h}\gamma^t\delta^t\,\underline{\Lambda}\mu^t(\underline{u}^t;\underline{v}^t)-\varepsilon\Sigma_{t=q}^{T-1} \lambda^{t,h}\gamma^t\delta^t\|y^t-s^t\|_1-$$
$$-\Sigma_{t=q}^{T-1} \lambda^{t,h}\gamma^t\delta^t(\underline{v}^t-{}^{*}s^t).s^t.$$

Proof. (1): Since each $(x^{t,h},y^{t,h})$ is formed as a convex combination of (x^t,y^t) and $(\underline{x}^t,\underline{y}^t)$, concavity of the I/O-process implies $(x^{t,h},y^{t,h}) \in S^t$, $\mu^t(x^{t,h};y^{t,h}) \geqq (1-\lambda^{t,h})\mu^t(x^t;y^t)+\lambda^{t,h}\mu^t(\underline{x}^t;\underline{y}^t)$, $t=1,\ldots,k$, $t < +\infty$. The inequalities in (1) are the consequence of $x^t,\underline{x}^t \geqq 0$, and of $(s^t)_1^k \leqq (\underline{s}^t)_1^k$.

(2): Direct consequence of the inequalities $\mu^t(x^{t,h};y^{t,h}) \geqq$ $\geqq (1-\lambda^{t,h})\mu^t(x^t;y^t)+\lambda^{t,h}\mu^t(\underline{x}^t;\underline{y}^t)$.

(3): To be verified by elaborating the inequalities $\mu^t(x^t;y^t) \leqq$ $\leqq \underline{\Lambda}\mu^t(\underline{u}^t;\underline{v}^t)+\underline{u}^t.x^t-\underline{v}^t.y^t$ and $\lambda^{t,h}\gamma^t\delta^t\underline{u}^t.x^t \leqq \lambda^{t-1,h}\gamma^{t-1}\delta^{t-1}(\underline{v}^{t-1}-{}^{*}s^{t-1}-\varepsilon e).(y^{t-1}-s^{t-1})$, ${}^{*}s^t \leqq {}^{*}\underline{s}^t$, $s^t \leqq y^t$. □

Because of duality symmetry, the proposition also is valid in the dual oriented version. A first important consequence will be the following theorem, where 5.3-(2), -(3) are elaborated under the hypotheses $\delta^t \leqq (\rho)^t$, $\gamma^t \leqq (\pi)^t$, $t=1,2,\ldots$, $\rho,\pi > 0$, $(\rho\pi) < 1$, and $\alpha \in]1,(\rho\pi)^{-1}[$. Then a $\beta > 0$ exists such that for every $\{\lambda^{t,h}\}_{t=1}^{\infty}$ as defined in 5.3, $\Sigma_{t=1}^{T} \lambda^{t,h}\gamma^t\delta^t \leqq \beta(\alpha)^{-h}$, $T=1,2,\ldots$. Further, for any sequence of finite dimensional vectors $\{z^t\}_1^{\infty}$ with $((\rho\pi\alpha)^t z^t)_1^{\infty}$ L_1-bounded, these hypotheses imply $\|(\lambda^{t,h}\gamma^t\delta^t z^t)_1^{\infty}\|_1 \leqq (\alpha)^{-h}\|((\rho\pi\alpha)^t z^t)_1^{\infty}\|_1$.

5.4. Theorem (L_1-boundedness as a necessary condition for optimality).

Given $\underline{r}^1 \in R^{m^1}$, L_∞-bounded $(\underline{s}^t)_1^{\infty},({}^{*}\underline{s}^t)_1^{\infty} \in (R^{n^t})_{t=1}^{\infty}$, suppose that, for $r^1:=\underline{r}^1$, $(s^t)_1^{\infty}:=(\underline{s}^t)_1^{\infty},({}^{*}s^t)_1^{\infty}:=({}^{*}\underline{s}^t)_1^{\infty}$, the ∞-horizon system of 5.1 is primal and dual strictly feasible and strictly feasible at a radius $\alpha \in]1,(\rho\pi)^{-1}[$. Then positive numbers κ_1 to κ_4 exist, such that for every $r^1 \in R^{m^1}$, $(s^t)_1^{\infty} \in (R^{n^t})_{t=1}^{\infty},({}^{*}s^t)_1^{\infty} \in (R^{n^t})_{t=1}^{\infty}$ with $r^1 \geqq \underline{r}^1$, $(s^t)_1^{\infty} \leqq (\underline{s}^t)_1^{\infty}$, $({}^{*}s^t)_1^{\infty} \leqq ({}^{*}\underline{s}^t)_1^{\infty}$, and $\beta_1:=\|((\rho\pi\alpha)^t s^t)_1^{\infty}\|_1$, $\beta_2:=\|((\rho\pi\alpha)^t\,{}^{*}s^t)_1^{\infty}\|_1$, $\beta_3:=\|((\rho\pi\alpha)^t\|s^t\|_1\|{}^{*}s^t\|_1)_1^{\infty}\|_1$ finite, the following holds:

(1) $\|((\rho\pi\alpha)^t(x^t,y^t))_1^\infty\|_1 \leqq \kappa_1(1+\beta_1+\beta_2+\beta_3+\|r^1\|_1)$ and $\|((\alpha)^t\gamma^t\delta^t(\mu^t(x^t;y^t)+{}^{*}s^t.y^t))_1^\infty\|_\infty \leqq \kappa_2(1+\beta_1+\beta_2+\beta_3+\|r^1\|_1)$ are necessary conditions for a trajectory $(x^t,y^t)_1^\infty \in (S^t)_1^\infty$, $x^1 \leqq r^1$, $\delta^{t+1}x^{t+1} \leqq \delta^t(y^t-s^t)$, t=1,2,..., to be primal optimal.

(2) $\|((\rho\pi\alpha)^t(u^t,v^t))_1^\infty\|_1 \leqq \kappa_3(1+\beta_1+\beta_2+\beta_3+\|r^1\|_1)$ and $\|((\alpha)^t\gamma^t\delta^t(\underline{\wedge}\mu^t(u^t;v^t)-s^t.v^t))_1^\infty\|_\infty \leqq \kappa_4(1+\beta_1+\beta_2+\beta_3+\|r^1\|_1)$ are necessary conditions for a trajectory $(u^t,v^t)_1^\infty \in (\underline{\wedge}S^t)_1^\infty$, $\gamma^{t+1}u^{t+1} \leqq \gamma^t(v^t-{}^{*}s^t)$, t=1,2,..., to be dual optimal.

Proof. (1): Let $(\underline{x}^t,\underline{y}^t)_1^\infty \in (S^t)_1^\infty \cap L_\infty$, $(\underline{u}^t,\underline{v}^t)_1^\infty \in (\underline{\wedge}S^t)_1^\infty \cap L_\infty$, $\varepsilon > 0$, $\theta \in N$, $\theta > 2$, be such that $\delta^{t+1}\underline{x}^{t+1} \leqq \delta^t(\underline{y}^t-\underline{s}^t)$, $\gamma^{t+1}\underline{u}^{t+1} \leqq \gamma^t(\underline{v}^t-{}^{*}\underline{s}^t-\varepsilon e)$, $t=1,\dots,\theta-1$, $\alpha\delta^{t+1}\underline{x}^{t+1} \leqq \delta^t(\underline{y}^t-\underline{s}^t)$, $\alpha\gamma^{t+1}\underline{u}^{t+1} \leqq \gamma^t(\underline{v}^t-{}^{*}s^t-\varepsilon e)$, $t=\theta,\theta+1,\dots$, and such that $(\mu^t(\underline{x}^t;\underline{y}^t))_1^\infty$, $(\underline{\wedge}\mu^t(\underline{u}^t;\underline{v}^t))_1^\infty \in L_\infty$; the existence is affirmed by 5.2-(4). Then, by 5.3-(1), -(2), a necessary condition for trajectory $(x^t,y^t)_1^\infty$, feasible with respect to $r^1 \geqq x^1$, $(s^t)_1^\infty \leqq (\underline{s}^t)_1^\infty$, to be optimal with respect to $({}^{*}s^t)_1^\infty \leqq ({}^{*}\underline{s}^t)_1^\infty$, is that for every $\nu \in R^1_{++}$, $h \in N$, $h > \theta$, there is a $T \in N$, $T > h$, such that: $-\nu-\xi_1\|(\lambda^{t,h}\gamma^t\delta^t)_1^T\|_1-\xi_2\|(\lambda^{t,h}\gamma^t\delta^t\,{}^{*}s^t)_1^T\|_1 \leqq \Sigma_{t=1}^T \lambda^{t,h}\gamma^t\delta^t(\mu^t(x^t;y^t)+{}^{*}s^t.y^t)$; $\{\lambda^{t,h}\}_{t=1}^\infty$ being defined in 5.3 for $\underline{\alpha}:=\alpha$, and $\xi_1:=\|(\mu^t(\underline{x}^t;\underline{y}^t))_1^\infty\|_\infty$, $\xi_2:=\|(\underline{y}^t)_1^\infty\|_\infty$. Putting, for every $h \in N$, $h > \theta:\nu:=(\alpha)^{-h}$, the above implies the existence of a sequence $\{T^h\}_{h=\theta+1}^\infty$ $T^h \in N$, $T^h > h$ such that

$$-(\alpha)^{-h}-\xi_1\|(\lambda^{t,h}\gamma^t\delta^t)_1^\infty\|_1-\xi_2\|(\lambda^{t,h}\gamma^t\delta^t\,{}^{*}s^t)_1^\infty\|_1 \leqq \Sigma_{t=1}^{T^h} \lambda^{t,h}\gamma^t\delta^t(\mu^t(x^t;y^t)+{}^{*}s^t.y^t),$$

h=θ+1,θ+2,.... With the suppositions $\delta^t \leqq (\rho)^t$, $\gamma^t \leqq (\pi)^t$, $t=1,2,\dots,\rho,\pi > 0$, $(\rho\pi) < 1$, $\alpha \in]1,(\rho\pi)^{-1}[$, $\beta_2:=\|(\rho\pi\alpha)^t\,{}^{*}s^t)_1^\infty\|_1 < +\infty$, the latter implies the existence of numbers ν_1,ν_2 (independently of $({}^{*}s^t)_1^\infty$), such that

(i) $-(\nu_1+\nu_2\beta_2)(\alpha)^{-h} \leqq \Sigma_{t=1}^{T^h} \lambda^{t,h}\gamma^t\delta^t(\mu^t(x^t;y^t)+{}^{*}s^t.y^t)$, $h=\theta+1,\theta+2,\dots$, is a necessary condition for $(x^t,y^t)_1^\infty$ to be optimal.

By virtue of 5.3-(3), the suppositions mentioned above, together with L_∞-boundedness of $(\underline{v}^t)_1^\infty$, $(\underline{\wedge}\mu^t(\underline{u}^t;\underline{v}^t))_1^\infty$, with $\beta_1:=\|(\rho\pi\alpha)^t s^t)_1^\infty\|_1 < +\infty$, $\beta_3:=\|((\rho\pi\alpha)^t\|s^t\|_1\|{}^{*}s^t\|_1)_1^\infty\|_1 < +\infty$, and together with non-negativity of all $x^t, (y^t - s^t)$, imply the existence of numbers ν_3 to ν_7 (independently of $(s^t)_1^\infty$ and $({}^*s^t)_1^\infty$) such that:

$$\text{(ii)} \begin{cases} \Sigma_{t=q}^{T} \lambda^{t,h} \gamma^t \delta^t (\mu^t(x^t;y^t) + {}^*s^t . y^t) \leqq \\ \leqq \nu_3 (\rho\pi\alpha)^q \| x^q \|_1 (\alpha)^{-h} - \lambda^{T,h} \gamma^T \delta^T (\underline{v}^T - {}^*s^T) . (y^T - s^T) + \\ + (\nu_4 + \nu_5 \beta_1 + \nu_6 \beta_3)(\alpha)^{-h} - \nu_7 \| ((\rho\pi\alpha)^t (y^t - s^t))_q^k \|_1 (\alpha)^{-h}, \end{cases}$$

for every $T,q,h \in N$, $h > \theta$, $T > q \geqq 1$, $q \leqq h+1$, $k := \min\{T-1, h+1\}$. Putting $q:=1$, $h \in \{\theta+1, \theta+2, \ldots\}$, $T:=T^h$, and taking in account that $0 \leqq x^1 \leqq r^1$ and that all $(y^t - s^t).(\underline{v}^t - {}^*s^t) \geqq 0$, the first part of statement (1) is an immediate consequence of (i) and (ii). In order to prove the second part of (1), we write (i) into the form $-(\nu_1 + \nu_2\beta_2)(\alpha)^{-h} \leqq \lambda^{p,h}\gamma^p\delta^p(\mu^p(x^p;y^p) + {}^*s^p.y^p) + \Sigma_{t=1}^{p-1} \lambda^{t,h}\gamma^t\delta^t(\mu^t(x^t;y^t) + {}^*s^t.y^t) + \Sigma_{t=p+1}^{T^h} \lambda^{t,h}\gamma^t\delta^t(\mu^t(x^t;y^t) + {}^*s^t.y^t)$, where the second term is dropped in case $p:=1$. With the help of (ii) where the terms $\lambda^{T,h}\gamma^T\delta^T(v^T - {}^*s^T).(y^T - s^T)$ and $\nu_7 \| ((\rho\pi\alpha)^t(y^t - s^t))_q^k \|_1 (\alpha)^{-h}$ can be dropped because of non-negativity, the second and third term in the right hand member can be eliminated, resulting into:

$$\text{(iii)} \begin{cases} -(\nu_1 + \nu_2\beta_2)(\alpha)^{-h} - 2(\nu_4 + \nu_5\beta_1 + \nu_6\beta_3)(\alpha)^{-h} - \nu_3((\rho\pi\alpha)\|x^1\|_1 - \\ -(\rho\pi\alpha)^{p+1}\|x^{p+1}\|_1)(\alpha)^{-h} \leqq \lambda^{p,h}\gamma^p\delta^p(\mu^p(x^p;y^p) + {}^*s^p.y^p), \end{cases}$$

$h = \theta+1, \theta+2, \ldots$, $p = 1, \ldots, h$, as a necessary condition for $(x^t, y^t)_1^\infty$ to be primal optimal. Further we have the inequalities:
$\lambda^{p,h}\gamma^p\delta^p(\mu^p(x^p;y^p) + {}^*s^p.y^p) \leqq \lambda^{p,h}\gamma^p\delta^p(\underline{\wedge\mu}^p(\underline{u}^p;\underline{v}^p) + \underline{u}^p.x^p - (\underline{v}^p - {}^*s^p).y^p)$,
$p = 1,2,\ldots$ $h = \theta+1, \theta+2, \ldots$. With non-negativity of $(\underline{v}^p - {}^*s^p).(y^p - s^p)$, $p = 1,2,\ldots$, with $\beta_3 := \| ((\rho\pi\alpha)^t \|s^t\|_1 \|{}^*s^t\|_1)_1^\infty \|_1 \geqq (\alpha)^p\gamma^p\delta^p\, {}^*s^p.s^p$, $p = 1,2,\ldots$, and with $0 < \gamma^t\delta^t \leqq (\rho\pi)^t < 1$, $t = 1,2,\ldots$ these inequalities imply:

$$\text{(iv)} \begin{cases} \lambda^{p,h}\gamma^p\delta^p(\mu^p(x^p;y^p) + {}^*s^p.y^p) \leqq (\alpha)^{-h}(\| (\underline{\wedge\mu}^t(\underline{u}^t;\underline{v}^t))_1^\infty \|_\infty + \\ + \| (\underline{u}^t)_1^\infty \|_\infty \| ((\rho\pi\alpha)^t x^t)_1^\infty \|_1 + \beta_3 + \| (v^t)_1^\infty \|_1 \| ((\rho\pi\alpha)^t y^t)_1^\infty \|_1), \end{cases}$$

$h = \theta+1, \theta+2, \ldots$, $p = 1, \ldots, h$. Now, multiplying (iii) and (iv) by $(\alpha)^h$, and taking in account that the first part of statement (1) is a necessary condition for optimality, it follows that the second part of (1) is a necessary condition for $(x^t,y^t)_1^\infty$ to be primal optimal. Finally, taking in account the term $\gamma^1\delta^1 r^1.u^1$ in the dual optimality criterion, statement (2) can be verified by elaborating the dual version of 5.3 in a similar manner. □

Under the hypotheses that $((\rho\pi\underline{\alpha})^t s^t)_1^\infty$, $((\rho\pi\underline{\alpha})^t\, {}^*s^t)_1^\infty$ and $((\rho\pi\underline{\alpha})^t \| s^t\|_1 \| {}^*s^t\|_1)_1^\infty$ are L_1-bounded for some $\underline{\alpha} > 1$, and that L_∞-bounded primal and dual strictly feasible solutions exist, the necessary conditions of 5.4 with $\alpha:=1$ are well-known and much easier to be verified. However, 5.4 presents a much stronger result. For the hypotheses mentioned above imply (cf. 5.2-(2)) primal and dual strict feasibility and strict feasibility at some radius $\alpha \in]1,(\rho\pi)^{-1}[$ (close enough to 1), which evidently generates a more restrictive optimality condition. As a consequence, convergency of the sequences $\{\Sigma_{t=1}^h \gamma^t\delta^t(\mu^t(x^t;y^t)+ {}^*s^t.y^t\}_{h=1}^\infty$ and $\{\Sigma_{t=1}^h \gamma^t\delta^t(\wedge\mu^t(u^t;v^t)-s^t.v^t)\}_{h=1}^\infty$ is a necessary condition for optimality. As a matter of fact, the latter will be the crucial point in our proof concerning the existence of primal and dual optimal trajectories, to be presented in 5.6.

First we shall deduce a stronger boundedness condition under the hypothesis that the system is strictly feasibile at a radius $\alpha:=(\rho\pi)^{-1}$. Then, by 5.2-(2) the system also is strictly feasible at radius $\underline{\alpha} > (\rho\pi)^{-1}$ (close enough to $(\rho\pi)^{-1}$). With the hypotheses $0 < \delta^t \leqq (\rho)^t$, $0 < \gamma^t \leqq (\pi)^t$, $t=1,2,\dots,(\rho\pi) < 1$, $\underline{\alpha} > (\rho\pi)^{-1}$ we have $\Sigma_{t=1}^T \lambda^{t,h}\gamma^t\delta^t \leqq \eta_0(\rho\pi)^h$, $T=1,2,\dots,h=1,2,\dots$, for some $\eta_0 > 0$; $\{\lambda^{t,h}\}_1^\infty$ being defined in 5.3. Consequently we have for every $(w^t)_1^\infty \in L_\infty$: $\| (\lambda^{t,h}\gamma^t\delta^t w^t)_1^\infty\|_1 \leqq \eta_0(\rho\pi)^h \| (w^t)_1^\infty\|_\infty$, $T=1,2,\dots,h=1,2,\dots$. Now, by similar methods as used in 5.4, one may verify:

5.5. <u>Theorem (L_∞-boundedness as a necessery condition for optimality)</u>.

Given $\underline{r}^1 \in R^{m^1}$, $(\underline{s}^t)_1^\infty, ({}^*\underline{s}^t)_1^\infty \in (R^{n^t})_{t=1}^\infty \cap L_\infty$, such that for $r^1:=\underline{r}^1$, $(s^t)_1^\infty:=(\underline{s}^t)_1^\infty$, $({}^*s^t)_1^\infty:=({}^*\underline{s}^t)_1^\infty$ the ∞-horizon system 5.1 is primal and dual strictly feasible and strictly feasible at a radius $\alpha:=(\rho\pi)^{-1}$. Then positive numbers κ_1 to κ_4 exist such that, for every $r^1 \in R^{m^1}$, $(s^t)_1^\infty, ({}^*s^t)_1^\infty \in (R^{n^t})_{t=1}^\infty$ with $r^1 \geqq \underline{r}^1$, $(s^t)_1^\infty \leqq (\underline{s}^t)_1^\infty$, $({}^*s^t)_1^\infty \leqq ({}^*\underline{s}^t)_1^\infty$, and $\beta_1:=\| (s^t)_1^\infty\|_\infty$, $\beta_2:=\| ({}^*s^t)_1^\infty\|_\infty$ finite, the following holds:

(1) $\| (x^t,y^t)_1^\infty\|_\infty \leqq \kappa_1(1+\beta_1+\beta_2+\beta_1\beta_2+\|r^1\|_1)$, and $\| ((\rho\pi)^{-t}\gamma^t\delta^t(\mu^t(x^t;y^t)+ {}^*s^t.y^t))_1^\infty\|_\infty \leqq \kappa_2(1+\beta_1+\beta_2+\beta_1\beta_2+\|r^1\|_1)$, are necessary conditions for

a trajectory $(x^t,y^t)_1^\infty \in (S^t)_1^\infty$, $x^1 \leqq r^1$, $\delta^{t+1}x^{t+1} \leqq \delta^t(y^t-s^t)$, $t=1,\ldots,$ to be primal optimal.

(2) $\|(u^t,v^t)_1^\infty\|_\infty \leqq \kappa_3(1+\beta_1+\beta_2+\beta_1\beta_2+\|r^1\|)$, and $\|((\rho\pi)^{-t}\gamma^t\delta^t(\underline{\wedge}\mu^t(u^t;v^t)-s^t.v^t))_1^\infty\|_\infty \leqq \kappa_4(1+\beta_1+\beta_2+\beta_1\beta_2+\|r^1\|_1)$, are necessary conditions for $(u^t,v^t)_1^\infty \in (\underline{\wedge}S^t)_1^\infty$, $\gamma^{t+1}u^{t+1} \leqq \gamma^t(v^t-{}^*s^t)$, $t=1,2,\ldots$ to be dual optimal.

Below we focus our attention to the existence of optimal trajectories. The starting point will be theorem 5.4. In the proof we shall use the concept of weak* convergency; with respect to the L_1-space, a sequence $\{(\xi_i^t)_{t=1}^\infty\}_{i=1}^\infty \subset L_1$ is called <u>weak* convergent</u>, if there is a $(\xi_0^t)_{t=1}^\infty \in L_1$ such that every $({}^*\xi^t)_1^\infty \in L_\infty$ with $\lim_{t\to\infty} {}^*\xi^t=0$: $\lim_{i\to\infty} \Sigma_{t=1}^\infty {}^*\xi^t\xi_i^t = \Sigma_{t=1}^\infty {}^*\xi^t\xi_0^t$. Obviously, a necessary condition for $\{(\xi_i^t)_{t=1}^\infty\}_{i=1}^\infty \subset L_1$ in order to converge weak* to $(\xi_0^t)_1^\infty \in L_1$, is that for every $t \in N$, $t > 0$ $\lim_{i\to\infty} \xi_i^t = \xi_0^t$. Further we shall use Alaoglu's theorem in the following specific form: every sequence $\{(\xi_i^t)_{t=1}^\infty\}_{i=1}^\infty$ with $\|(\xi_i^t)_{t=1}^\infty\|_1 \leqq 1$, $i=1,2,\ldots$ contains a subsequence $\{(\xi_{i(j)}^t)_{t=1}^\infty\}_{j=1}^\infty$ which converges weak* to a $(\xi_0^t)_1^\infty$, $\|(\xi_0^t)_{t=1}^\infty\|_1 \leqq 1$. In other words the closed unit sphere in L_1 is <u>weak* compact</u>. An immediate consequence of Alaoglu's theorem is that every bounded set in L_1 contains a weak* convergent sequence.

5.6. <u>Theorem (existence of optimal trajectories).</u>

If, concerning the ∞-horizon system 5.1, $((\rho\pi\underline{\alpha})^t s^t)_1^\infty$, $((\rho\pi\underline{\alpha})^t\, {}^*s^t)_1^\infty$ and $((\rho\pi\underline{\alpha})^t\|{}^*s^t\|_1\|s^t\|_1)_1^\infty$ are L_1-bounded for some $\underline{\alpha} > 1$, and if L_∞-bounded primal and dual strictly feasible trajectories exist, then there exist primal and dual optimal trajectories.

<u>Proof.</u> By virtue of 5.2-(2) the hypotheses imply that the system is strictly feasible at some radius $\alpha \in]1,\underline{\alpha}[$. Then, defining, for some $\xi \in R^1$ (large enough),:

(i) $$Z:=\{(x^t,y^t)_1^\infty \in (S^t)_1^\infty | x^1 \leqq r^1, \delta^{t+1}x^{t+1} \leqq \delta^t(y^t-s^t),\ t=1,2,\ldots,\ \|(\gamma^t\delta^t(\mu^t(x^t;y^t)+{}^*s^t.y^t),(\rho\pi)^t(x^t,y^t)_1^\infty)\|_1 \leqq \xi\},$$

theorem 5.4-(1) implies that the condition $(x^t,y^t)_1^\infty \in Z$ is necessary for primal optimality; ξ can be chosen so large that Z contains a primal strictly feasible trajectory, implying $Z \neq \emptyset$. In addition, the definition implies that the sequences $\{\Sigma_{t=1}^{h} \gamma^t \delta^t (\mu^t(x^t;y^t) + {}^{*}s^t . y^t)\}_{h=1}^{\infty}$ converge for all $(x^t,y^t)_1^{\infty} \in Z$; the limits are denoted $\varphi((x^t,y^t)_1^{\infty})$. Let

(ii) $\quad \bar{\varphi} := \sup \varphi((x^t,y^t)_1^{\infty})$, over $(x^t,y^t)_1^{\infty} \in Z, (x^t,y^t) \in R^{m^t} \times R^{n^t}, t=1,2,..,$

and let $\{(x_i^t,y_i^t)_{t=1}^{\infty}\}_{i=1}^{\infty} \subset Z$ be a sequence with:

(iii) $\quad \lim_{i\to\infty} \varphi((x_i^t,y_i^t)_{t=1}^{\infty}) = \bar{\varphi}$;

the existence is a consequence of $Z \neq \emptyset$ and $\bar{\varphi} < +\infty$. Since $\{(\gamma^t \delta^t (\mu^t(x_i^t;y_i^t) + {}^{*}s^t . y_i^t), (\rho\pi)^t (x_i^t,y_i^t))_{t=1}^{\infty}\}_{i=1}^{\infty}$ is situated in the weak* compact set

(iv) $\quad W := \{(\nu^t,p^t,q^t)_1^{\infty} \in (R^1 \times R^{m^t} \times R^{n^t})_{t=1}^{\infty} \mid \|(\nu^t,p^t,q^t)_1^{\infty}\|_1 \leqq \xi\}$,

there is a subsequence defined by an index set $I \subset N$, such that

(v) $\quad \{(\gamma^t \delta^t (\mu^t(x_i^t;y_i^t) + {}^{*}s^t . y_i^t), (\rho\pi)^t (x_i^t,y_i^t))_{t=1}^{\infty}\}, i \in I,$

for $i\to\infty$ converges weak* to a $(\gamma^t \delta^t \nu_0^t, (\rho\pi)^t (x_0^t,y_0^t))_1^{\infty} \in W$, where $(\nu_0^t,x_0^t,y_0^t)_1^{\infty} \in (R^1 \times R^{m^t} \times R^{n^t})_{t=1}^{\infty}$. We shall prove that the part $(x_0^t,y_0^t)_1^{\infty}$ is primal optimal. Firstly, weak* convergency implies:

(vi) $\quad \lim_{i\to\infty, i\in I} (x_i^t,y_i^t) = (x_0^t,y_0^t)$, $t=1,2,...$

(vii) $\quad \lim_{i\to\infty, i\in I} (\mu^t(x_i^t;y_i^t) + {}^{*}s^t . y_i^t) = \nu_0^t$, $t=1,2,....$

With the inequalities $x_i^1 \leqq r^1$, $\delta^{t+1} x_i^{t+1} \leqq \delta^t (y_i^t - s^t)$, $t=1,2,...,$ $i=1,2,..,$ relation (vi) implies:

(viii) $\quad x_0^1 \leqq r^1$, $\delta^{t+1} x_0^{t+1} \leqq \delta^t (y_0^t - s^t)$, $t=1,2,....$

With closed-concavity of each $\mu^t : S^t \to R^1$, (vi) and (vii) imply:

(ix) $\quad (x_0^t,y_0^t) \in S^t$, $t=1,2,...$

(x) $\quad \mu^t(x_0^t;y_0^t) + {}^{*}s^t . y_0^t = \nu_0^t$, $t=1,2,...$

With $(\gamma^t \delta^t \nu_0^t, (\rho\pi)^t (x_0^t;y_0^t))_1^{\infty} \in W$, the relations (iii),(iv),(viii),(ix), and (x) imply:

(xi) $\quad (x_0^t, y_0^t)_1^\infty \in Z,$

(xii) $\quad \Sigma_{t=1}^\infty \gamma^t \delta^t (\mu^t(x_0^t; y_0^t) + {}^*s^t . y_0^t) =$

$$= \sup \Sigma_{t=1}^\infty \gamma^t \delta^t (\mu^t(x^t; y^t) + {}^*s^t . y^t), \text{ over } (x^t, y^t)_1^\infty \in Z.$$

Since $(x^t, y^t)_1^\infty \in Z$ is a necessary condition for optimality, (xi) and (xii) imply that $(x_0^t, y_0^t)_1^\infty$ is primal optimal, indeed. The existence of dual optimal trajectories follows by symmetry. □

The proof that the open horizon system is normal in the generalized sense of 3.2-(5), implying that the sufficient conditions for optimalit 3.6 are necessary, as well, can be delivered with the help of the Hahn-Banach separation theorem on L_1 (cf. [2]). However, here we shall prese this result as a by-product of a finite horizon approximation procedure

5.7. Approximation by finite horizon I/O-systems.

We start from the ∞-horizon system 5.1, primal and dual strictly feasible at a radius $\alpha \in]1, (\rho\pi)^{-1}[$, and such that for this α the composed vectors $((\rho\pi\alpha)^t(s^t))_1^\infty$, $((\rho\pi\alpha)^t({}^*s^t))_1^\infty$ and $((\rho\pi\alpha)^t \| {}^*s^t \|_1 \| s^t \|_1)_1^\infty$ are L_1-bounded. Let $(\underline{x}^t, \underline{y}^t)_1^\infty$, $(\underline{u}^t, \underline{v}^t)_1^\infty$ be the trajectories as described in 5.2-(2). For every horizon h=2,3,..., we consider the problem:

$$(1) \quad \begin{cases} \bar{\varphi}^h := \sup \gamma^h \delta^h (\underline{v}^h - {}^*s^h) . y^h + \Sigma_{t=1}^h \gamma^t \delta^t (\mu^t(x^t; y^t) + {}^*s^t . y^t), \\ \text{over } (x^t, y^t)_1^h \in (S^t)_1^h, x^1 \leqq r^1, \delta^{t+1} x^{t+1} \leqq \delta^t (y^t - s^t), t=1,..,h- \end{cases}$$

together wit its dual (cf. 3.2-(4)):

$$(2) \quad \begin{cases} \bar{\Psi}^h := \inf \gamma^1 \delta^1 r^1 . u^1 + \Sigma_{t=1}^h \gamma^t \delta^t (\underline{\wedge} \mu^t (u^t; v^t) - s^t . v^t), \\ \text{over } (u^t, v^t)_1^h \in (\underline{\wedge} S^t)_1^h, \gamma^{t+1} u^{t+1} \leqq \gamma^t (v^t - {}^*s^t), t=1,..,h-1, v^h = \end{cases}$$

Because of the assumptions concerning $(\underline{u}^t, \underline{v}^t)_1^\infty$ and primal strict feasibility, the problems (1) and (2) are strictly feasible, and consequently primal and dual solutions exist; the supremum and infimum are rela ted by: $\bar{\varphi}^h = \bar{\Psi}^h + \gamma^h \delta^h \underline{v}^h . s^h + \Sigma_{t=1}^{h-1} \gamma^t \delta^t \, {}^*s^t . s^t$. Now let, for horizon h, $(\hat{u}^{t,h}, \hat{v}^{t,h})_{t=1}^h$ be a dual optimal solution. Then, on account of the assumption concerning $(\underline{u}^t,\underline{v}^t)_1^\infty$, it follows that $(u^t,v^t)_1^{h+1}$, defined $(u^t,v^t)_1^h := (\hat{u}^{t,h},\hat{v}^{t,h})_{t=1}^h$, $(u^{h+1},v^{h+1}):=(\underline{u}^{h+1},\underline{v}^{h+1})$ is dual feasible with respect to the horizon (h+1)-problem. Consequently we have $\bar{\Psi}^{h+1} \leqq \bar{\Psi}^h+\gamma^{h+1}\delta^{h+1}(\underline{\wedge}\mu^{h+1}(\underline{u}^{t+1};\underline{v}^{t+1})-s^{h+1}.\underline{v}^{h+1})$. Denoting the infimum of the dual ∞-horizon problem $\bar{\Psi}^\infty$ (i.e. the infimum of the limits of converging sequences $\{\gamma^1\delta^1r^1.u^1+\Sigma_{t=1}^T\ \gamma^t\delta^t(\underline{\wedge}\mu^t(u^t;v^t)-s^t.v^t)\}_{T=1}^\infty$, $(u^t,v^t)_1^\infty$ being dual feasible) the same arguments lead to the inequality $\bar{\Psi}^\infty \leqq \bar{\Psi}^h+\Sigma_{t=h+1}^\infty\ \gamma^t\delta^t(\underline{\wedge}\mu^t(\underline{u}^t;\underline{v}^t)-s^t.\underline{v}^t)$. Thus we arrive at a non-increasing sequence of upper bounds with respect to $\bar{\Psi}^\infty$.

In order to construct a sequence of lower bounds, we consider for every horizon h=2,3,... the problem:

$$(3)\quad \begin{cases} \underline{\varphi}^h := \sup \Sigma_{t=1}^h\ \gamma^t\delta^t(\mu^t(x^t;y^t)+{}^*s^t.y^t), \text{ over } (x^t,y^t)_1^h \in (S^t)_1^h, \\ x^1 \leqq r^1,\ \delta^{t+1}x^{t+1} \leqq \delta^t(y^t-s^t),\ t=1,\ldots,h-1,\ y^h = \underline{y}^h, \end{cases}$$

and its dual:

$$(4)\quad \begin{cases} \underline{\psi}^h := \inf \gamma^1\delta^1r^1.u^1-\gamma^h\delta^h(\underline{y}^h-s^h).v^h+\Sigma_{t=1}^h\gamma^t\delta^t(\underline{\wedge}\mu^t(u^t;v^t)-s^t.v^t), \\ \text{over } (u^t,v^t)_1^h \in (\underline{\wedge}S^t)_1^h,\ \gamma^{t+1}u^{t+1} \leqq \gamma^t(v^t-{}^*s^t),\ t=1,\ldots,h-1. \end{cases}$$

Similar arguments in the opposite orientation, lead to the inequalities $\underline{\varphi}^{h+1} \geqq \underline{\varphi}^h+\gamma^{h+1}\delta^{h+1}(\mu^{h+1}(\underline{x}^{h+1};\underline{y}^{h+1})+{}^*s^{h+1}.y^{h+1})$ and $\underline{\varphi}^\infty \geqq \underline{\varphi}^h+\Sigma_{t=h+1}^\infty\ \gamma^t\delta^t(\mu^t(\underline{x}^t;\underline{y}^t)-{}^*s^t.\underline{y}^t)$, $\underline{\varphi}^\infty$ being the supremum with respect to the primal infinite horizon problem.

Evidently, every feasible trajectory of (3) is feasible with respect to (1); consequently we have: $\bar{\varphi}^h \geqq \underline{\varphi}^h+\gamma^h\delta^h(\underline{v}^h-{}^*s^h).\underline{y}^h$. By symmetry we also have: $\bar{\Psi}^h-\gamma^h\delta^h(\underline{y}^h-s^h).\underline{v}^h \geqq \underline{\Psi}^h$. These relations wil be elaborated in the following theorem:

5.8. <u>Theorem.</u>

Consider the ∞-horizon system 5.1 under the hypotheses of 5.7. Let $\beta_0:=\Sigma_{t=1}^\infty\ \gamma^t\delta^t\ {}^*s^t.s^t$. Then, concerning the finite horizon systems

5.7-(1) to -(4), and concerning the supremum $\underline{\varphi}^{\infty}$ and the infimum $\bar{\Psi}^{\infty}$ of the primal and dual ∞-horizon system the folowing holds:

(1) For every $h \in N$, $h \geqq 2$:

$$\underline{\varphi}^{h}+\Sigma_{t=h+1}^{\infty}\ \gamma^{t}\delta^{t}(\mu^{t}(\underline{x}^{t};\underline{y}^{t})+{}^{*}s^{t}.\underline{y}^{t}) \leqq \underline{\varphi}^{\infty} \leqq$$
$$\leqq \bar{\Psi}^{\infty}+\beta_{0} \leqq \bar{\Psi}^{h}+\Sigma_{t=h+1}^{\infty}\ \gamma^{t}\delta^{t}(\wedge\mu^{t}(\underline{u}^{t};\underline{v}^{t})-s^{t}.\underline{v}^{t}).$$

(2) A number β_1 exists, so that for every $h \in N$; $h \geqq 2$:

$$|\underline{\varphi}^{h}+\Sigma_{t=h+1}^{\infty}\ \gamma^{t}\delta^{t}(\mu^{t}(\underline{x}^{t};\underline{y}^{t})+{}^{*}s^{t}.\underline{y}^{t})$$
$$-\bar{\Psi}^{h}-\beta_{0}-\Sigma_{t=h+1}^{\infty}\gamma^{t}\delta^{t}(\wedge\mu^{t}(\underline{u}^{t};\underline{v}^{t})-s^{t}.v^{t})| \leqq \beta_{1}(\alpha)^{-h}.$$

Proof. (1) The inequality $\underline{\varphi}^{\infty} \leqq \bar{\Psi}^{\infty}+\beta_0$ is an immediate consequence of 3.5-(1) and of non-negativity of all $(y^t-s^t).(v^t-{}^{*}s^t)$. The argumentation of the other inequalities is given in 5.7.

(2): Let us denote a primal optimal trajectory of an horizon-h problem 5.7-(1) by $(\hat{x}^{t,h},\hat{y}^{t,h})_{t=1}^{h}$, let $(\tilde{x}^{t,h},\tilde{y}^{t,h})_{t=1}^{h}$ be defined $(\tilde{x}^{t,h},\tilde{y}^{t,h}) := (1-\lambda^{t,h})(\hat{x}^{t,h},\hat{y}^{t,h})+\lambda^{t,h}(\underline{x}^{t},\underline{y}^{t})$, $t=1,\dots,h$, where $\{\lambda^{t,h}\}_{t=1}^{\infty}$, $h=\theta+1$, $\theta+2,\dots$ are sequences as defined in 5.3, and where $(\underline{x}^{t},\underline{y}^{t})_{1}^{\infty}$ is the trajectory as postulated in 5.7. Let $\kappa_1^h := \lambda^{h,h}\gamma^{h}\delta^{h}(\underline{v}^{h}-{}^{*}s^{h}).\hat{y}^{h,h}+ +\Sigma_{t=1}^{h}\lambda^{t,h}\gamma^{t}\delta^{t}(\mu^{t}(\hat{x}^{t,h};\hat{y}^{t,h})+{}^{*}s^{t},\hat{y}^{t,h})$, and let $\kappa_2^h := \lambda^{h,h}\gamma^{h}\delta^{h}(\underline{v}^{h}-{}^{*}s^{h}).\underline{y}^{h}+ +\Sigma_{r=1}^{h}\lambda^{t,h}\gamma^{t}\delta^{t}(\mu^{t}(\underline{x}^{t};\underline{y}^{t})+{}^{*}s^{t}.\underline{y}^{t})$. Then 5.3-(1) and optimality of $(\hat{x}^{t,h},\hat{y}^{t,h})_{t=1}^{h}$ implies:

$$\gamma^{h}\delta^{h}(\underline{v}^{h}-{}^{*}s^{h}).\tilde{y}^{h,h}+\Sigma_{t=1}^{h}\ \gamma^{t}\delta^{t}(\mu^{t}(\tilde{x}^{t,h};\tilde{y}^{t,h})+{}^{*}s^{t}.\tilde{y}^{t,h}) \geqq \bar{\varphi}^{h}-\kappa_1^h+\kappa_2^h.$$

Since $(\tilde{x}^{t,h},\tilde{y}^{t,h})_{1}^{h}$ is feasible with respect to 5.7-(3), and consequently feasible in 5.7-(1), we have: $\bar{\varphi}^{h} \geqq \gamma^{h}\delta^{h}(\underline{v}^{h}-{}^{*}s^{h}).\tilde{y}^{h,h}+\underline{\varphi}^{h} \geqq \bar{\varphi}^{h}-\kappa_1^h+\kappa_2^h$.

Reducing κ_1 with the help of 5.3-(3), it follows:

$$\bar{\varphi}^{h} \geqq \gamma^{h}\delta^{h}(\underline{v}^{h}-{}^{*}s^{h}).\tilde{y}^{h,h}+\underline{\varphi}^{h} \geqq$$
$$\geqq \bar{\varphi}^{h}+\kappa_2^h-\lambda^{1,h}\gamma^{1}\delta^{1}\underline{u}^{1}.x^{1}-\Sigma_{t=1}^{h}\ \lambda^{t,h}\gamma^{t}\delta^{t}\wedge\mu^{t}(\underline{u}^{t};\underline{v}^{t})+\Sigma_{t=1}^{h-1}\ \lambda^{t,h}\gamma^{t}\delta^{t}(\underline{v}^{t}-{}^{*}s^{t}).s^{t};$$

where $(\underline{u}^{t},\underline{v}^{t})_{1}^{\infty}$ is the dual trajectory as postulated in 5.7. With the assumptions concerning $(\underline{x}^{t},\underline{y}^{t})_{1}^{\infty}$, $(\underline{u}^{t},\underline{v}^{t})_{1}^{\infty}$, $(s^{t})_{1}^{\infty}$, $({}^{*}s^{t})_{1}^{\infty}$ and α, there exists a number κ_3 (independently of h or $(\hat{x}^{t,h},\hat{y}^{t,h})_{t=1}^{h}$) so that:

(i) $$\bar{\varphi}^{h} \geqq \gamma^{h}\delta^{h}(\underline{v}^{h}-{}^{*}s^{h}).\underline{y}^{h}+\underline{\varphi}^{h} \geqq \bar{\varphi}^{h}-\kappa_3(\alpha)^{-h}.$$

The supremum of 5.7-(3) and the infimum in 5.7-(4) are related:

(ii) $$\underline{\varphi}^{h} = \underline{\Psi}^{h}+\gamma^{h}\delta^{h}\ {}^{*}s^{t}.(\underline{y}^{h}-s^{h})+\Sigma_{t=1}^{h}\ \gamma^{t}\delta^{t}\ {}^{*}s^{t}.s^{t}.$$

Further $\mu^t(\underline{x}^t;\underline{y}^t) \leq {}_\wedge\mu^t(\underline{u}^t;\underline{v}^t)+\underline{u}^t.x^t-\underline{v}^t.y^t$, and $\gamma^t\delta^t\underline{u}^t.\underline{x}^t \leqq \gamma^{t-1}\delta^{t-1}(\underline{v}^t-{}^*s^t).(\underline{y}^t-s^t)$, t=1,... imply:

$$\text{(iii)}\qquad \Sigma_{t=h+1}^{\infty}\gamma^t\delta^t(\mu^t(\underline{x}^t;\underline{y}^t)+{}^*s^t.\underline{y}^t) \leqq \gamma^h\delta^h(\underline{v}^h-{}^*s^h).(\underline{y}^h-s^h)+ + \Sigma_{t=h+1}^{\infty}\gamma^t\delta^t({}_\wedge\mu^t(\underline{u}^t;\underline{v}^t)-s^t.\underline{v}^t)+\Sigma_{t=h+1}^{\infty}\gamma^t\delta^t\,{}^*s^t.s^t.$$

Combining (i),(ii) and (iii) with the assumptions concerning $(\underline{x}^t,\underline{y}^t)_1^h$, $(\underline{u}^t,\underline{y}^t)_1^\infty$, $(s^t)_1^\infty$, $({}^*s^t)_1^\infty$, it follows that there is a number κ_4 (independently of h), so that:

$$\text{(iv)}\qquad |\underline{\varphi}^h+\Sigma_{t=h+1}^{\infty}\gamma^t\delta^t(\mu^t(\underline{x}^t;\underline{y}^t)+{}^*s^t.\underline{y}^t)- -\bar{\Psi}^h-\beta_0-\Sigma_{t=h+1}^{\infty}\gamma^t\delta^t({}_\wedge\mu^t(\underline{u}^t;\underline{v}^t)-s^t.\underline{v}^t)| \leqq \kappa_4(\alpha)^{-h},$$

$h=\theta+1,\theta+2,\ldots$. Putting κ_4 large enough, (iv) is true for $h=1,\ldots,\theta$, as well. □

Obviously, the approximation procedure converges with a rate of $(1/\alpha)$. An important consequence of the theorem is that $\underline{\varphi}^\infty=\bar{\Psi}^\infty+\Sigma_{t=1}^{\infty}\gamma^t\delta^t\,{}^*s^t.s^t$. Then, as a consequence of 3.5-(1) (where $r^{t+1}:=0$, ${}^*r^t:=0$, t=1,2,...), the feasibility conditions $x^1 \leqq r^1, \delta^{t+1} \leqq y^t-s^t, \gamma^{t+1}u^{t+1} \leqq v^t-{}^*s^t$, t=1,2,... and of non-negativity of the inner products $(y^t-s^t).(v^t-{}^*s^t)$, we have the following optimality conditions:

5.9. <u>Theorem (necessary and sufficient conditions for optimality).</u> Suppose, concerning the ∞-horizon system 5.1, that for some $\alpha > 1$, $((\rho\pi\alpha)^t s^t)_1^\infty$, $((\rho\pi\alpha)^t\,{}^*s^t)_1^\infty$, $((\rho\pi\alpha)^t\|s^t\|_1\|{}^*s^t\|_1)_1^\infty$ are L_1-bounded, and suppose that the system is primal and dual strictly feasible. Then primal and dual feasible trajectories $(x^t,y^t)_1^\infty$, $(u^t,v^t)_1^\infty$ are optimal, if and only if simultaneously:

(i) $\mu^t(x^t;y^t)+v^t.y^t = {}_\wedge\mu^t(u^t;v^t)+u^t.x^t$, t=1,2,...

(ii) $u^1.(r^1-x^1) = 0$, $\gamma^{t+1}\delta^{t+1}u^{t+1}.x^{t+1} = \gamma^t\delta^t(v^t-{}^*s^t).(y^t-s^t)$, t=1,2,...

(iii) $\lim_{h\to\infty}\gamma^h\delta^t(v^h-{}^*s^h).(y^h-s^h) = 0$.

With respect to polyhedral I/O-processes similar results are presented by Evers [2]. Observe that the approximation theorem 5.8 and its consequence, theorem 5.9, are obtained without using the boundedness theorem 5.4 or theorem 5.6 concerning the existence of optimal trajectories. As a matter of fact one may prove the existence of optimal trajectories directly with the help of 5.8, by elaborating convergency aspects of the sequence of finite horizon optimal trajectories. In a less general context such an approach is proposed by Grinold.

6. Continuity and stability of ∞-horizon dynamic systems.

Under the hypothesis of strict feasibility at a radius $\alpha := (\rho\pi)^{-1}$ we shall study continuity and stability aspects of optimal trajectories conceived as multi-functions of the composed vectors $(r^1, (s^t)_1^\infty)$ and $({}^*s^t)_1^\infty$. First we shall discuss some general continuity properties of maximization problems in L_∞, and next these properties will be transferred to the ∞-horizon problem (cf. theorem 6.3). The results will be the bases of the global stability theorem 6.5 and the global convergency theorem 6.6, concerning invariant open horizon systems.

6.1. Continuity of maximization problems in L_∞.

Below continuity will be defined in terms of weak* convergency with respect to the L_∞-space: $(\xi_i^t)_{t=1}^\infty \in L_\infty$, $i=1,2,...$ is called weak* convergent if there is a $(\xi_0^t)_{t=1}^\infty \in L_\infty$ so that for every $({}^*\xi^t)_1^\infty \in L_1$: $\lim_{i\to\infty} \Sigma_{t=1}^\infty \; {}^*\xi^t \xi_i^t = \Sigma_{t=1}^\infty \; {}^*\xi^t \xi_0^t$. A necessary condition for $\{(\xi_i^t)_{t=1}^\infty\}_{i=1}^\infty \subset L_\infty$ in order to convergence weak* to $(\xi_0^t)_{t=1}^\infty \in L_\infty$ is that for every $t=1,2,$: $\lim_{i\to\infty} \xi_i^t = \xi_0^t$; a sufficient condition is convergency with respect to the L_∞-norm, i.e. $\lim_{i\to\infty} \| (\xi_i^t)_{t=1}^\infty - (\xi_0^t)_{t=1}^\infty \|_\infty = 0$. A set $S \subset L_\infty$ is called weak* compact, if every sequence in S contains a subsequence which converges weak* to a point of S. A set $S \subset L_\infty$ is called compact, if every sequence in S contains a subsequence which converges (with respect to the L_∞-norm) to a point of S. We shall use the following properties:

- (Alaoglu's theorem in L_∞) the closed unit sphere in L_∞ (i.e.: $\Omega_\infty := \{(\xi^t)_1^\infty \subset L_\infty | \| (\xi^t)_1^\infty \|_\infty \leqq 1\}$) is weak* compact,
- weak* convergency of a sequence in a compact set in L_∞ implies convergency with respect to the L_∞-norm.

Below a vector $(z^t)_1^\infty$ in L_∞ (or L_1) will be denoted briefly z.

Given, $\Gamma: P \to \mathbb{P}(Q)$, (note: $\mathbb{P}(Q)$ is the power set of Q) with P compact in L_∞, $Q \subset L_\infty$, $\Gamma(p) \neq \emptyset$ for every $p \in P$, $\mathrm{grf}(P;\Gamma) := \{(p,q) \in P\times Q | q \in \Gamma(p)\}$ weak* compact, and given $\nu: P\times Q \to R^1$ with $\mathrm{hypo}(P\times Q;\nu) := \{(p,q,\lambda) \in P\times Q\times R^1 | \lambda \leqq$

$\leq \nu(p;q)\}$ weak* closed (i.e. for every $\{(p_i,q_i,\lambda_i)\}_1^\infty \subset \text{hypo}(P\times Q;\nu)$ so that $\lim_{i\to\infty}\|\lambda_i-\lambda_0\|_\infty = 0$ for some $\lambda_0 \in L_\infty$, and so that $\{p_i\}_1^\infty,\{q_i\}_1^\infty$ converge weak* to some $p_0,q_0 \in L_\infty$, it holds $(p_0,q_0,\lambda_0) \in \text{hypo}(P\times Q;\nu))$, our open horizon problem will be fitted in the scheme $\varphi:P\to]-\infty,+\infty]$, $\hat{\Gamma}:P\to \mathbb{P}(Q)$, defined:

$$(1)\begin{cases} \varphi(p) := \sup \nu(p;q), \text{ over } q \in \Gamma(p), \\ \hat{\Gamma}(p) := \{q \in \Gamma(p) \mid \nu(p;q) = \varphi(p)\}. \end{cases}$$

As straightforward generalisations of well-known results in finite dimensions, one may verify that under the hypotheses mentioned above: (i) $\varphi(P) \subset R^1$, (ii) $\forall p \in P:\hat{\Gamma}(p) \neq \emptyset$. In the case that $\varphi:P\to R^1$ is continuous (representing the open horizon problem it will be shown that $\varphi:P\to R^1$ is continuous, or even Lipschitz continuous) we have, in addition: (iii) $\text{grf}(P;\hat{\Gamma})$ is weak* compact. Namely, let $\{(p_i,q_i)_1^\infty \subset \text{grf}(P;\hat{\Gamma})$. Then weak* compactness of $\text{grf}(P;\Gamma)$ implies the existence of a subsequence $\{(p_i,q_i)\}_{i\in I}$, which converges weak* to a $(p_0,q_0) \in \text{grf}(P;\Gamma)$. Weak* convergency $\{p_i\}_{i\in I}$ implies (by compactness of P) convergency of $\{p_i\}_{i\in I}$, and next (by continuity of $\varphi:P\to R^1$) convergence of $\{\varphi(p_i)\}_{i\in I}$ to $\varphi(p_0)$. With $\nu(p_i;q_i) = \varphi(p_i)$, i=1,2,... and with weak* closedness of $\text{hypo}(P\times Q;\nu)$ it follows $\nu(p_0;q_0) \geq \varphi(p_0)$, and consequently $(p_0,q_0)\in\text{grf}(P;\hat{\Gamma})$.

An important consequence of (iii) is the following continuity property: (iv) for every $p \in P$, $\varepsilon > 0$, there is a $\delta > 0$ so that $\tilde{p} \in P, \|\tilde{p}-p\|_\infty \leq \delta$ implies $\hat{\Gamma}(\tilde{p}) \subset \hat{\Gamma}(p)+\varepsilon\mathring{\Omega}_\infty$; where $\mathring{\Omega}_\infty := \{z \in L_\infty \mid \|z\|_\infty < 1\}$. In order to prove this statement by contradiction, suppose that for some $p_0 \in P$, $\varepsilon > 0$, there is a sequence $\{p_i\}_1^\infty \subset P$, $\lim_{i\to 0}\|p_i-p_0\|_\infty = 0$, $\hat{\Gamma}(p_i) \not\subset \hat{\Gamma}(p_0)+\varepsilon\mathring{\Omega}_\infty$. Let $\{q_i\}_1^\infty$ be a corresponding sequence $q_i \in \hat{\Gamma}(p_i)$, $q_i \not\in \hat{\Gamma}(p_0)+\varepsilon\Omega_\infty$, i=1,2,.... Then weak* compactness of $\text{grf}(P;\hat{\Gamma})$ implies the existence of a subsequence $\{(p_i,q_i)\}_{i\in I}$ which converges weak* to a point $(\bar{p},\bar{q}) \in \text{grf}(P;\hat{\Gamma})$; in addition weak* closedness of the complement of $\Gamma(p_0)+\varepsilon\mathring{\Omega}_\infty$ implies $\bar{q} \not\in \hat{\Gamma}(p_0)+\varepsilon\mathring{\Omega}_\infty$. Since $\bar{p} = p_0$ and consequently $\bar{q}\in\hat{\Gamma}(p_0)$, the assumptions lead to contradiction. It is interesting to compair this result with Berge's maximum theorem.

6.2. Continuity of the open horizon system.

We consider the open horizon system in relation to convex sets $Z \subset R^{m^1} \times ((R^{n^t})_1^\infty \cap L_\infty)$, $W \subset (R^{n^t})_1^\infty \cap L_\infty$, compact with respect to the L_∞-norm and such that, for every $(r^1,(s^t)_1^\infty) \in Z$, $({}^*s^t)_1^\infty \in W$, the open horizon system of 5.1 is primal and dual strictly feasible and strictly feasible at a radius $(\rho\pi)^{-1}$; the corresponding sets of primal and dual optimal trajectories are represented by multi-functions $\hat{\Gamma}:Z\times W\to P((S^t)_1^\infty)$, ${}^*\hat{\Gamma}:Z\times W\to \mathbb{P}((\underline{\wedge}S^t)_1^\infty)$ respectively. For convenience sake we sometimes shall denote $(s^t)_1^\infty$, $({}^*s^t)_1^\infty$ briefly by s and ${}^*s$.

Under the hypotheses concerning Z and W, theorem 5.5 implies for every $(r^1,s) \in Z$, ${}^*s \in W$ the existence of an open neigbourhood $\sigma(r^1,s,{}^*s)$ (with respect to the L_∞-norm) and numbers τ_1,τ_2 so that $\|(x^t,y^t)_1^\infty\|_\infty \leqq \tau_1$, $\|(\mu^t(x^t;y^t))_1^\infty\|_\infty \leqq \tau_2$ for all $(x^t,y^t)_1^\infty \in \hat{\Gamma}(\sigma(r^1,s,{}^*s))$
Since Z and W are supposed to be compact, there exists a finite covering with respect to these neighbourhoods; consequently numbers β_1,β_2 exist so that $\|(x^t,y^t)_1^\infty\|_\infty \leqq \beta_1$, $\|(\mu^t(x^t;y^t))_1^\infty\|_\infty \leqq \beta_2$ for every $(x^t,y^t)_1^\infty \in \hat{\Gamma}(Z,W)$. Of course the same is true for the dual optimal trajectories. Thus we have:

$$(1)\quad \begin{cases} \forall (x^t,y^t)_1^\infty \in \hat{\Gamma}(Z\times W): \|(x^t,y^t)_1^\infty\|_\infty \leqq \beta_1, \|(\mu^t(x^t;y^t))_1^\infty\|_\infty \leqq \beta_2, \\ \forall (u^t,v^t)_1^\infty \in {}^*\hat{\Gamma}(Z\times W): \|(u^t,v^t)_1^\infty\|_\infty \leqq \beta_3, \|(\underline{\wedge}\mu^t(u^t;v^t))_1^\infty\|_\infty \leqq \beta_4, \end{cases}$$

where β_1 to β_4 are taken large enough. Defining $(\bar{\mu}^t:\bar{S}\to R^1, m^t\times n^t)$ and $({}^*\bar{\mu}^t:{}^*\bar{S}^t\to R^1, m^t\times n^t)$, $t=1,2,\ldots$:

$$(2)\quad \begin{cases} \bar{S}^t:=\{(x,y) \in S^t \mid \mu^t(x;y) \geqq \beta_2, \|y\|_\infty \leqq \beta_1\},\ \bar{\mu}^t(x;y) := \min\{\beta_2,\mu^t(x;y)\}, \\ {}^*\bar{S}^t:=\{(u,v) \in \underline{\wedge}S^t \mid \underline{\wedge}\mu^t(u;v) \leqq \beta_4, \|v\|_\infty \leqq \beta_3\},\ {}^*\bar{\mu}^t(u;v):=\max\{\beta_4,\underline{\wedge}\mu^t(u;v)\}, \end{cases}$$

implying convergency of $\{\Sigma_{t=1}^h \gamma^t\delta^t(\bar{\mu}^t(x^t;y^t)+{}^*s^t.y^t)\}_{h=1}^\infty$ and of $\{\Sigma_{t=1}^h \gamma^t\delta^t({}^*\bar{\mu}^t(u^t;v^t)-s^t.v^t)\}_{h=1}^\infty$ for every $(x^t,y^t)_1^\infty \in (\bar{S}^t)_1^\infty$, $(u^t,v^t)_1^\infty \in ({}^*\bar{S}^t)_1^\infty, (s^t)_1^\infty, ({}^*s^t)_1^\infty \in L_\infty$, it follows that the functions $\bar{\varphi}:Z\times W\to R^1$, $\bar{\Psi}:Z\times W\to R^1$,

$$(3)\quad\begin{cases}\bar{\varphi}((r^1,s);{}^*s) := \sup \Sigma_{t=1}^{\infty} \gamma^t\delta^t(\bar{\mu}^t(x^t;y^t)+{}^*s^t.y^t),\ \text{over}\ (x^t,y^t)_1^{\infty} \in (\bar{S}^t)_1^{\infty} \\ \qquad \text{subject to}\ x^1 \leqq r^1,\ \delta^{t+1}x^{t+1} \leqq \delta^t(y^t-s^t),\ t=1,2,\ldots, \\ \bar{\Psi}((r^1,s);{}^*s) := \inf \gamma^1\delta^1 r^1.u^1 + \Sigma_{t=1}^{\infty} \gamma^t\delta^t({}^*\bar{\mu}^t(u^t;v^t)-s^t.v^t), \\ \qquad \text{over}\ (u^t,v^t)_1^{\infty} \in ({}^*\bar{S}^t)_1^{\infty},\ \text{subject to}\ \gamma^{t+1}u^{t+1} \leqq \gamma^t(v^t-{}^*s^t), \\ \qquad t=1,\ldots,\end{cases}$$

are well defined. In addition, the problems in (3) are equivalent to the original primal and dual open horizon problems in the sense that the sets of optimal trajectories are equivalent.

As straightforward generalisations of well-known properties in finite dimensions, one may verify: (i) $\forall {}^*s \in W: \bar{\varphi}(.;{}^*s): Z \to R^1$ is concave, (ii) $\forall (r^1,s) \in Z: \bar{\varphi}((r^1,s);.): W \to R^1$ is convex, (iii) $\bar{\varphi}: Z \times W \to R^1$ is Lipschitz continuous; i.e. a number τ exists so that for every $(r^1,s),(\bar{r}^1,\bar{s}) \in Z$, ${}^*s, {}^*\bar{s} \in W$: $|\bar{\varphi}((r^1,s);{}^*s) - \bar{\varphi}((\bar{r}^1,\bar{s});{}^*\bar{s})| \leqq \tau \| (r^1,s,{}^*s) - (\bar{r}^1,\bar{s},{}^*\bar{s}) \|_{\infty}$. Since the primal and dual functions are related by $\bar{\varphi}((r^1,s);{}^*s) = \bar{\Psi}((r^1,s^1);{}^*s) + \Sigma_{t=1}^{\infty} \gamma^t\delta^t\, {}^*s^t.s^t$ (cf. 5.8), the same is true with respect to the dual function.

The primal system in (3) can be fitted in the abstract scheme 6.1-(1) by
$P := Z \times W$, $Q := (R^{m^t} \times R^{n^t})_1^{\infty} \cap L_{\infty}$,
$\Gamma(r^1,s,{}^*s) := \{(x^t,y^t)_1^{\infty} \in (\bar{S}^t)_1^{\infty} \mid x^1 \leqq r^1, \delta^{t+1}x^{t+1} \leqq \delta^t(y^t-s^t),\ t=1,\ldots\}$
$\nu(r^1,s,{}^*s;(x^t,y^t)_1^{\infty}) := \Sigma_{t=1}^{\infty} \gamma^t\delta^t(\bar{\mu}^t(x^t;y^t)+{}^*s^t.y^t)$.
It is easy to verify that under closedness of all $\text{hypo}(S^t;\mu^t)$ and under the hypothesis of $S^t \subset R_+^{m^t} \times R^{n^t}$, $t=1,2,\ldots$, the conditions of 6.1 are satisfied, and consequently the continuity property (iv) of 6.1 applies to the primal system. Changing the orientation of 6.1-(1), the similar can be done concerning the dual system. Summarizing we have:

6.3. <u>Theorem (continuity).</u>

Let Z,W be the sets as postulated in 6.2. Let $\hat{\Gamma}: Z \times W \to \mathbb{P}((S^t)_1^{\infty})$ and ${}^*\hat{\Gamma}: Z \times W \to \mathbb{P}((\underline{\wedge}S^t)_1^{\infty})$ represent the primal and dual optimal trajectories concerning the open horizon problem 5.1. Then the following holds:

(1) Numbers β_1 to β_4 exist so that:

$\forall (x^t,y^t)_1^{\infty} \in \hat{\Gamma}(Z \times W): \| (x^t,y^t)_1^{\infty} \|_{\infty} \leqq \beta_1,\ \| (\mu^t(x^t;y^t))_1^{\infty} \|_{\infty} \leqq \beta_2,$

$\forall (u^t,v^t)_1^{\infty} \in {}^*\hat{\Gamma}(Z \times W): \| (u^t,v^t)_1^{\infty} \|_{\infty} \leqq \beta_3,\ \| (\underline{\wedge}\mu^t(u^t;v^t))_1^{\infty} \|_{\infty} \leqq \beta_4.$

(2) The function: $\bar{\varphi}: Z\times W \to R^1$, $\bar{\varphi}((r^1,(s^t)_1^\infty);(^*s^t)_1^\infty) :=$
$:= \Sigma_{t=1}^\infty \gamma^t \delta^t (\mu^t(x^t;y^t) + {}^*s^t.y^t)$, with $(x^t,y^t)_1^\infty \in \hat{\Gamma}((r^1,(s^t)_1^\infty);(^*s^t)_1^\infty)$ is concave in the first argument and convex in the second. In addition the function is Lipschitz continuous on $Z\times W$.

(3) For every $(r^1,s) \in Z$, ${}^*s \in W$ and every $\varepsilon > 0$ there is a $\delta > 0$ so that, for every $(\tilde{r}^1,\tilde{s}) \in Z$, ${}^*\tilde{s} \subset W$ with $\|(\tilde{r}^1,\tilde{s})-(r^1,s)\|_\infty \leqq \delta$, $\|{}^*\tilde{s}-{}^*s\|_\infty \leqq \delta$: $\hat{\Gamma}((\tilde{r}^1,\tilde{s});{}^*\tilde{s}) \subset \hat{\Gamma}((r^1,s);{}^*s)+\varepsilon\Omega_\infty$, ${}^*\hat{\Gamma}((\tilde{r}^1,\tilde{s});{}^*\tilde{s}) \subset {}^*\hat{\Gamma}((r^1,s);{}^*s)+\varepsilon\Omega_\infty$.

As an interesting application of the latter, we shall deduce a particular stability property. We start with introducing some concepts.

6.4. Local and global stability.

Let $Z \subset R^{m^1}\times((R^{n^t})_1^\infty \cap L_\infty)$, $W \subset (R^{n^t})_1^\infty \cap L_\infty$ be the sets of composed vectors $(r^1,(s^t)_1^\infty)$ and $(^*s^t)_1^\infty$ respectively, so that the open horizon system 5.1 is primal and dual strictly feasible and strictly feasible at a radius $(\rho\pi)^{-1}$. Let $\hat{\Gamma}: Z\times W \to \mathbb{P}((S^t)_1^\infty)$, ${}^*\hat{\Gamma}: Z\times W \to \mathbb{P}((\underline{\wedge}S^t)_1^\infty)$ represent the primal and dual optimal trajectories. Given $(r^1,s) \in Z$, ${}^*s \in W$, we call a pair of optimal trajectories $(x^t,y^t)_1^\infty \in \hat{\Gamma}((r^1,s);{}^*s)$, $(u^t,v^t)_1^\infty \in {}^*\hat{\Gamma}((r^1,s);{}^*s)$ <u>local stable</u> if there is an $\varepsilon > 0$ such that every $(\tilde{x}^t,\tilde{y}^t)_1^\infty \in \hat{\Gamma}((\tilde{r}^1,\tilde{s});{}^*\tilde{s})$, $(\tilde{u}^t,\tilde{v}^t)_1^\infty \in {}^*\hat{\Gamma}((\tilde{r}^1,\tilde{s});{}^*\tilde{s})$ with $(\tilde{r}^1,\tilde{s}) \in Z$, ${}^*\tilde{s} \in W$, $\|(\tilde{r}^1,\tilde{s})-(r^1,s)\|_\infty \leqq \varepsilon$, $\|{}^*\tilde{s}-{}^*s\|_\infty \leqq \varepsilon$, $\lim_{t\to\infty}\|(\tilde{s}^t,{}^*\tilde{s}^t)-(s^t,{}^*s^t)\|_\infty = 0$, converges with respect to $(x^t,y^t)_1^\infty$, $(u^t,v^t)_1^\infty$ in the sense of $\lim_{t\to\infty}\|(\tilde{x}^t,\tilde{y}^t)-(x^t,y^t)\|_\infty = 0$, $\lim_{t\to\infty}\|(\tilde{u}^t,\tilde{v}^t)-(u^t,v^t)\|_\infty = 0$; the pair $(x^t,y^t)_1^\infty$, $(u^t,v^t)_1^\infty$ is called <u>global stable</u> if the convergency property holds with respect to every $(\tilde{x}^t,\tilde{y}^t)_1^\infty \in \hat{\Gamma}((\tilde{r}^1,\tilde{s});{}^*\tilde{s})$, $(\tilde{u}^t,\tilde{v}^t)_1^\infty \in {}^*\hat{\Gamma}(\tilde{r}^1,\tilde{s});{}^*\tilde{s}^t)$, provided $(\tilde{r}^1,\tilde{s}) \in Z$, ${}^*\tilde{s} \in W$, $\lim_{t\to\infty}\|(\tilde{s}^t,{}^*\tilde{s}^t)-(s^t,{}^*s^t)\|_\infty = 0$.

6.5. Theorem (global stability).

If, concerning $r^1 \in R^{m^1}$, $(s^t)_1^\infty,(^*s^t)_1^\infty \in (R^{n^t})_1^\infty \cap L_\infty$ such that the open horizon 5.1 is primal and dual strictly feasible and strictly feasible at a radius $(\rho\pi)^{-1}$, a corresponding pair of primal and dual optimal trajectories is local stable, then these trajectories are global stable, as well.

Proof. Let Z,W be the sets as postulated in 6.4, and let $\hat{\Gamma}:Z\times W\to\mathbb{P}((S^t)_1^\infty)$, ${}^*\hat{\Gamma}:Z\times W\to\mathbb{P}((\underline{\wedge}S^t)_1^\infty)$ represent the primal and dual optimal trajectories. Given $(r^1,(s^t)_1^\infty)\in Z$, $({}^*s^t)_1^\infty\in W$, let $(x^t,y^t)_1^\infty$, $(u^t,v^t)_1^\infty$ be a local stable pair of optimal trajectories and let $\varepsilon>0$ the number as postulated in the definition. In order to prove the convergency property concerning an $(\tilde{x}^t,\tilde{y}^t)_1^\infty\in\hat{\Gamma}((\tilde{r}^1,(\tilde{s}^t)_1^\infty;({}^*\tilde{s}^t)_1^\infty)$, $(\tilde{u}^t,\tilde{v}^t)_1^\infty\in{}^*\hat{\Gamma}((\tilde{r}^1,(\tilde{s}^t)_1^\infty);({}^*s^t)_1^\infty)$, with $(\tilde{r}^1,(\tilde{s}^t)_1^\infty)\in Z$, $({}^*\tilde{s}^t)_1^\infty\in W$, $\lim_{t\to\infty}\|(\tilde{s}^t,{}^*\tilde{s}^t)-(s^t,{}^*s^t)\|_\infty=0$, we consider the intervals $\bar{Z}:=\{\lambda(r^1,(s^t)_1^\infty)+(1-\lambda)(\tilde{r}^1,(\tilde{s}^t)_1^\infty|\lambda\in[0,1]\}$, $\bar{W}:=\{\lambda({}^*s^t)_1^\infty+(1-\lambda)({}^*\tilde{s}^t)_1^\infty|\lambda\in[0,1]\}$. Clearly, $\bar{Z}$ and $\bar{W}$ are convex and compact, $\bar{Z}\subset Z$, $\bar{W}\subset Z$, and in addition $(\bar{r}^1,\bar{s})\in\bar{Z}$, ${}^*\bar{s}\in\bar{W}$ satisfies the provisio of 6.4. Then, by virtue of 6.3-(3) it follows that for every $(\bar{r}^1,\bar{s})\in\bar{Z}$, ${}^*\bar{s}\in\bar{W}$ there is a neighbourhood $(\bar{\eta}\times{}^*\bar{\eta})\subset\bar{Z}\times\bar{W}$ so that $\hat{\Gamma}(\bar{\eta}\times{}^*\bar{\eta})\subset\hat{\Gamma}((\bar{r}^1,\bar{s});{}^*\bar{s})+\varepsilon/3$, ${}^*\hat{\Gamma}(\bar{\eta}\times{}^*\bar{\eta})\subset{}^*\hat{\Gamma}((\bar{r}^1,\bar{s});{}^*\bar{s})+\varepsilon/3$. Consequently, compactness of $\bar{Z}\times\bar{W}$ implies the existence of a finite covering $\{\eta_i\times{}^*\eta_i\}_{i=1}^k$ of such neighbourhoods, being arranged in such a manner that $\hat{\Gamma}(\eta_i\times{}^*\eta_i)\subset\hat{\Gamma}(\eta_{i+1}\times{}^*\eta_{i+1})+\varepsilon/3$, ${}^*\hat{\Gamma}(\eta_i\times{}^*\eta_i)\subset{}^*\hat{\Gamma}(\eta_{i+1}\times{}^*\eta_{i+1})+\varepsilon/3$, $i=1,\ldots,k-1$, $(r^1,(s^t)_1^\infty)\in\eta_k$, $({}^*s^t)_1^\infty\in{}^*\eta_k$, $(\tilde{r}^1,(\tilde{s}^t)_1^\infty)\in\eta_1$, $({}^*\tilde{s}^t)_1^\infty\in\eta_1$. Then, with the hypothesis concerning ε, we may conclude: local stability of $(x^t,y^t)_1^\infty$, $(u^t,v^t)_1^\infty$ in succession implies that all optimal trajectories of $\hat{\Gamma}(\eta_i\times{}^*\eta_i)$, ${}^*\hat{\Gamma}(\eta_i\times{}^*\eta_i)$ $i=k,k-1,\ldots,1$ possess the convergency property with respect to $(x^t,y^t)_1^\infty,(u^t,v^t)_1^\infty$; consequently we have: $\lim_{t\to\infty}\|(\tilde{x}^t,\tilde{y}^t)-(x^t,y^t)\|_\infty=0$, $\lim_{t\to\infty}\|(\tilde{u}^t,\tilde{v}^t)-(u^t,v^t)\|_\infty=0$. □

As a straightforward consequence of 6.5 and the result of section 4, we have the following global convergency theorem concerning invariant open horizon systems:

6.6. Theorem (global convergency).

Suppose concerning the invariant version of the open horizon problem 5.1 defined by I/O-process $(\mu:S\to R^1,m\times m)$, $\gamma^t:=(\pi)^t$, $\delta^t:=(\rho)^t$, $t=1,2,\ldots$, $\rho,\pi>0$, $(\rho\pi)<1$, that, for $s,{}^*s\in R^m$, the systems $(1/\pi)x<y-s$, $(x,y)\in S$ and $(1/\rho)u<v-{}^*s$, $(u,v)\in\underline{\wedge}S$, are solvable (cf. theorem 4.5 and its dual version). Suppose that for these $s,{}^*s$, that $(\hat{x},\hat{y})\in S$,

$(\hat{u},\hat{v}) \in \underline{\wedge}S$ is a stationary optimal solution (cf. 4.6 and 4.9) with the properties that for $r^1:=\hat{x}$, $s^t:=s$, ${}^*s^t:={}^*s$, $t=1,2,...$ the open horizon system is primal strictly feasible and that the stationary optimal trajectories $(x^t,y^t)_1^\infty$, $(u^t,v^t)_1^\infty$, $(x^t,y^t):=(\hat{x},\hat{y})$, $(u^t,v^t):=(\hat{u},\hat{v})$, $t=1,2,...$ are local stable. Then every primal and dual optimal $(\tilde{x}^t,\tilde{y}^t)_1^\infty$, $(\tilde{u}^t,\tilde{v}^t)$ belonging to an $(r^1,(s^t)_1^\infty)$, $({}^*s^t)_1^\infty$ so that $\lim_{t\to\infty} s^t=s$, $\lim_{t\to\infty} {}^*s^t={}^*s$, and so that the system is primal and dual strictly feasible and strictl feasible at a radius $(\rho\pi)^{-1}$, converges in the sense of $\lim_{t\to\infty}(\tilde{x}^t,\tilde{y}^t) = (\hat{x},\hat{y})$, $\lim_{t\to\infty}(\tilde{u}^t,\tilde{v}^t)=(\hat{u},\hat{v})$.

In the case of a polyhedral I/O-process, local stability of stationary optimal trajectories can be proved by eigenvalue methods (cf. [2]).

The author is indepted to professor J. Kriens for his critical remarks.

REFERENCES.

[1] D. Cass, "Duality: A Symmetric Approach from the Economist's Vantage Point", Journal of Economic Theory, 7 (1974), 272-295.

[2] J.J.M. Evers, "Linear Programming over an Infinite Horizon", Tilburg University Press, Academic Book Services, Holland (1973).

[3] ———————— "Linear ∞-Horizon Programming and Lemke's complementarity", Economic Institute Tilburg Research Memorandum (1973).

[4] ———————— "A Duality Theory for Convex ∞-horizon Programming", cowles Foundation Discussion Paper No. 392 (1975).

[5] ———————— "More with the Lemke Complementarity Algorithm", Mathematical Programming, 15 (1978), 214-219.

[6] D. Gale, "On optimal Development in a Multi-Sector Economy", Review of Economic studies, 34 (1967), 1-18.

[7] R.C. Grinold, "Finite Horizon Approximations of Infinite Horizon Linear Programs", Mathematical Programming 12 (1977), 1-17.

[8] M. Halkin, "Necessary Conditions for Optimal Control Problems with Infinite Horizons", Econometrica, 42, (1974), 267-272.

[9] T. Hansen and T.C. Koopmans, "On the definition and Computation of a Capital Stock Invariant under Optimization", Journal of Economic Theory, 5 (1973), 487-523.

[10] T.C. Koopmans, in "Decision and Organization" (McGuire and Rodner, editors; North-Holland, 1972).

[11] A.S. Manne, "Sufficiency Conditions for Optimality in an Infinite Horizon Development Plan", Econometrica, 38 (1970), 18-38.

[12] R.T. Rockafellar, "Convex Analysis", Princeton University Press, 1970.

[13] W.R. Sutherland, "On Optimal Development in a Multi-Sectorial Economy: The Discounted Case", Review of Economic Studies, 37 (1970), 585-589.

[14] M.L. Weitzman, "Duality Theory for Infinite Horizon Convex Models", Management Science, 19 (1973), 783-789.

Department of Applied Mathematics,
Twente University of Technology,
Box 217, Enschede, Netherlands.

III. CONVEX PROCESSES AND HAMILTONIAN DYNAMICAL SYSTEMS

R.T. Rockafellar*

UNIVERSITY OF WASHINGTON, U.S.A.

Many economists have studied optimal growth models of the form

$$\text{(1)} \qquad \begin{aligned} &\text{maximize} \quad \int_0^\infty e^{-\rho t}\, U(k(t),\, z(t))dt \\ &\text{subject to} \;\; k(0) = k_0,\; \dot{k}(t) = z(t) - \gamma k(t), \end{aligned}$$

where k is a vector of capital goods, γ is the rate of depreciation, ρ is the discount rate, and U is a continuous concave utility function defined on a closed convex set D in which the pair (k,z) is constrained to lie. The theory of such problems is plagued by technical difficulties caused by the infinite time interval. The optimality conditions are still not well understood, and there are serious questions about the existence of solutions and even the meaningfulness, in certain cases, of the expression being maximized.

One thing is clear, however. Any trajectory $\bar{k}(t)$ which is worthy of consideration as optimal in (1) would in particular have to have the property that for every finite time interval $[t_0, t_1] \subset [0, \infty)$ one has

$$\text{(2)} \qquad \int_{t_0}^{t_1} e^{-\rho t}\, U(k(t), \dot{k}(t) + \gamma k(t))dt \leqq \int_{t_0}^{t_1} e^{-\rho t}\, U(\bar{k}(t), \dot{\bar{k}}(t) + \gamma \bar{k}(t))dt.$$

(For otherwise, the portion of $\bar{k}$ over $[t_0, t_1]$ could be replaced by k, and this would constitute a definite improvement.) This condition severely limits candidates for optimal paths and allows us to study them in terms of Hamiltonian dynamical systems involving subgradients.

Hamiltonian dynamical systems arise in the optimality conditions for variational problems of the form

---

* Research sponsored in part by the Air Force Office of Scientific Research, Air Force Systems Command, USAF, under AFOSR grant number 77-0546 at the University of Washington, Seattle.

$$(3)\quad \begin{aligned} &\text{minimize} \quad \int_{t_0}^{t_1} L(t,x(t),\dot{x}(t))dt \\ &\text{subject to} \quad x(t_0) \in D_0,\ x(t_1) \in D_1. \end{aligned}$$

Classically, one always supposed L to a finite, differentiable function, but for the purpose of applications to economic models it is essential that one be able to treat the case where $L(t,.,.)$ is for each t a closed, proper, convex function on $R^n \times R^n$. The theory of problem (3) has been extended in this direction by Rockafellar [1], [2], [3]. The model (1) corresponds with the change of notation $x(t) = e^{\gamma t}k(t)$ to

$$(4)\qquad L(t,x,v) = -e^{-\rho t}\, U(e^{-\gamma t}x, e^{-\gamma t}v),$$

where U is interpreted as $-\infty$ outside of D.

Of course something must be assumed about the way that L depends on t. The correct condition in general is that L should be a "normal integrand" [1], [4]. This technical property of measurability will not be discussed here, but it is certainly satisfied when L is of the form (4) (under the assumptions already stated) and also when L is independent of t. Concerning the trajectory $x(t)$, one does not have to assume differentiability, but merely absolute continuity; the time derivative $\dot{x}(t)$ then exists for almost every t.

The Hamiltonian associated with L is the function

$$(5)\qquad H(t,x,p) := \sup_{v \in R^n}\{p.v - L(t,x,v)\}.$$

Thus $H(t,x,.)$ is the convex function conjugate to $L(t,x,.)$, so that L is in turn determined uniquely by H:

$$L(t,x,v) = \sup_{p \in R^n}\{p.v - H(t,x,p)\}.$$

Since $L(t,x,v)$ is not just convex in v but in (x,v), it turns out that $H(t,x,p)$ is not just convex in p but concave in x. The subgradient sets $\partial_x H(t,x,p)$ (concave sense) and $\partial_p H(t,x,p)$ (convex sense) are therefore welldefined [5]. The relation

$$(6)\qquad \dot{\bar{x}}(t) \in \partial_p H(t,\bar{x}(t),\bar{p}(t)),\ -\dot{\bar{p}}(t) \in \partial_x H(t,\bar{x}(t),\bar{p}(t))$$

is the generalized Hamilton condition. If H were differentiable as in classical mathematics, it would reduce to the equations

$$\dot{\bar{x}}(t) = \nabla_p H(t,\bar{x}(t),\bar{p}(t)), \quad -\dot{\bar{p}}(t) = \nabla_x H(t,\bar{x}(t),\bar{p}(t)).$$

An absolutely continuous trajectory $\bar{x}(t)$ is said to be an extremal for L over an interval I if there is an absolutely continuous $\bar{p}(t)$ (called a co-extremal for $\bar{x}$) such that the Hamiltonian condition (6) holds (for almost every t in I). On the other hand, $\bar{x}$ is said to be piecewise optimal for L over I if for every finite subinterval $[t_0,t_1] \subset I$ one has

$$(7) \qquad \int_{t_0}^{t_1} L(t,x(t),\dot{x}(t))dt \geqq \int_{t_0}^{t_1} L(t,\bar{x}(t),\dot{\bar{x}}(t))dt$$

for all (absolutely continuous) x(t) over $[t_0,t_1]$ such that $x(t_0) = \bar{x}(t_0)$ $x(t_1) = \bar{x}(t_1)$. The main result about these concepts in the present setting is the following.

THEOREM 1[1],[2],[3]. *If x is an extremal for L, then x is piecewise optimal for L. If x is piecewise optimal for L and certain "constraint qualifications" are fulfilled, then x is an extremal for L.*

The exact nature of the "constraint qualifications" will not be discussed here; see [2], [3]. Basically one needs to know that the pair $(\bar{x}(t_0), \bar{x}(t_1))$ always belongs to the relative interior of the (convex) set of all pairs $(x(t_0),x(t_1))$ corresponding to trajectories for which the integral on the left of (7) is finite, and also that $\bar{x}(t)$ does not touch the boundary of the natural "state constraint set"

$$\{x \in R^n \mid v \in R^n \text{ with } L(t,x,v) < \infty\}.$$

(If the second condition fails, a more general theory must be invoked in which p(t) is not absolutely continuous and may have jumps. The corresponding version of the Hamiltonian equation has been developed in [3]. This is indeed the situation that must be dealt with in economic applications where x(t) is a nonnegative vector of goods, some component of which may well vanish from time to time.)

In economics, the variables p(t) usually have an interpretation as prices of some kind. It is of great interest, therefore, that they have optimality properties relative to a function M dual to L, namely

$$M(t,p,w) := \sup_{(x,v)\in R^{2n}} \{p.v+x.w-L(t,x,v)\},$$

$$L(t,x,v) := \sup_{(p,w)\in R^{2n}} \{p.v+x.w-M(t,p,w)\}.$$

THEOREM 2[1]. <u>If</u> x <u>is an extremal for</u> L <u>with co-extremal</u> p, <u>then</u> p <u>is an extremal for</u> M <u>with co-extremal</u> x, <u>and hence in particular</u> p <u>is piecewise optimal for</u> M.

For the case of the economic model (4), one obtains

(8) $$H(t,x,p) = \sup_{v\in R^n} \{e^{-\rho t}U(e^{-\gamma t}x,e^{-\gamma t}v) + p.v\}$$

$$= e^{-\rho t}\, h(e^{-\gamma t}x,e^{\delta t}p)$$

where δ is the interest rate defined by

(9) $$\delta = \rho + \gamma,$$

and h is the concave-convex function defined by

(10) $$h(k,q) := \sup_{z\in R^n} \{q.z+U(k,z)\}.$$

The Hamiltonian condition (7) has a rather complicated expression in terms of $\bar{x}(t)$ and $\bar{p}(t)$, but in terms of

(11) $$\bar{k}(t) := e^{-\gamma t}\bar{x}(t),\ \bar{q}(t) := e^{\delta t}\bar{p}(t),$$

it takes the autonomous form

(12) $$\begin{aligned} \dot{\bar{k}}(t) &\in \partial_q h(\bar{k}(t),\bar{q}(t))-\gamma\bar{k}(t), \\ -\dot{\bar{q}}(t) &\in \partial_k h(\bar{k}(t),\bar{q}(t))-\delta\bar{q}(t). \end{aligned}$$

It follows from Theorem 1 that <u>every trajectory</u> k(t) <u>satisfying</u> (12) <u>has the piecewise optimality property in</u> (2) (and the converse is "almost" true).

The function dual to L in this model is

$$(13) \qquad M(t,p,w) = \sup_{(x,v)\in R^{2n}} \{p.v+x.w+e^{-\rho t}U(e^{-\gamma t}x,e^{-\gamma t}v)\}$$

$$= e^{-\rho t}V\,(e^{\delta t}p,e^{\delta t}w)$$

where

$$(14) \qquad V(q,s) := \sup_{(k,z)\in D} \{q.z+s.k+U(k,z)\}.$$

According to Theorem 2, the trajectories q(t) appearing in (12) have the piecewise optimality property that for every finite subinterval $[t_0,t_1]$ one has

$$(15) \qquad \int_{t_0}^{t_1} e^{-\rho t}V(q(t),\dot{q}(t)-\delta q(t))dt \geqq \int_{t_0}^{t_1} e^{-\rho t}V(\bar{q}(t),\dot{\bar{q}}(t)-\delta\bar{q}(t))dt$$

for all trajectories q(t) over $[t_0,t_1]$ with $q(t_0) = \bar{q}(t_0)$, $q(t_1) = \bar{q}(t$

Here q can be interpreted as a vector of dated prices and r = -s as a vector of rents: $\dot{q} = \delta q-r$. Thus V(q,s) represents the maximum rate at which "value" can be created in the economy.

A big advantage in the study of (12) (and more generally (6)) is that this condition is an "ordinary differential equation with multivalued right side". It is known, for example, that a solution (k(t),q(t)) exists over an interval $[t_0,t_0+\varepsilon)$ starting from any point $(k(t_0),q(t_0))$ (k_0,q_0) interior to the region where h is finite (cf. [6],[7]). For th most part, the solutions turn out to be unique despite the multivalued ness, although branching can sometimes occur.

In the context of the infinite horizon problem (1), a critical questio is how to single out, from among the trajectories k(t) with $k(0) = k_0$ that satisfy (12) for some q(t) (and there seems more or less to be on such for each choice of q_0), a trajectory worthy of being deemed "opti mal" (or at least "extremal") over the whole interval $[0,\infty)$. No limita tions are imposed a priori on the behavior of k(t) as $t\to\infty$ (free end-point problem). Heuristic considerations lead one to believe that ther should "usually" be just one trajectory k(t) of the desired type for each k_0 (in a reasonable region) and this seems to suggest a correspon dence between k_0 and q_0 whose graph forms a sort of n-dimensional mani fold in R^{2n}. The corresponding special trajectories (k(t),q(t)) would trace out this manifold.

If so, then in looking at examples of dynamical systems of the form (12) we should readily be able to detect a special n-dimensional manifold that is the natural candidate for expressing "optimality" over $[0,\infty)$. One approach to this question is to try to analyze behavior about a rest point (constant solution) to the system.

A rest point (k^*,q^*) of (12) is characterized by the relations

$$0 \in \partial_q h(k^*,q^*)-\gamma k^*,$$

(16)

$$0 \in \partial_k h(k^*,q^*)-\delta q^*.$$

These are equivalent to the condition that

(17) $$0 \in \partial_q \bar{h}(k^*,q^*), \quad 0 \in \partial_k \bar{h}(k^*,q^*),$$

where

$$\bar{h}(k,q) = h(k,q)-\gamma k^*.q-\delta k.q^*,$$

and (17) means that (k^*,q^*) is a minimax saddle point of the function $\bar{h}$ (which, like h, is concave-convex). What might this imply for the behavior of Hamiltonian system (12) around (k^*,q^*)?

If h were actually twice differentiable, it would be possible to write the system in the form $(\dot{k},\dot{q}) = F(k,q)$ and analyze the behavior in terms of the matrix of derivatives of F at (k^*,q^*) in the classical manner of the theory of ordinary differential equations. If h were in fact strongly concave in k and strongly convex in q, the Jacobian of F with respect to k would be negative definite at k^*, while the Jacobian with respect to q would be positive definite. Thus the matrix in question would have n negative and n positive eigenvalues, so that system would have a dynamic saddle point at (k^*,q^*). This means that there would exist (locally) an n-dimensional manifold traced by the solutions $(k(t),q(t))$ that coverage to (k^*,q^*) as $t\to\infty$, as well as another n-dimensional manifold traced by the solutions that diverge form (k^*,q^*) at $t = -\infty$, the two manifolds intersecting only in the point (k^*,q^*) itself.

Karl Shell focused on this idea in his study of economic growth models and was led to conjecture that the picture of dynamic saddle point behavior should generalize somehow to the case where h is not differentiable. Moreover, <u>the trajectories that are "optimal" over</u> $[0,\infty)$ <u>should be the ones converging to</u> (k^*,q^*) <u>as</u> $t\to\infty$. For the economic background, see the articles [8] and [9] of Cass and Shell.

This conjecture was verified by Rockafellar in [10] for the case $\rho = 0$ $(\delta = \gamma)$ with h strictly concave-convex and in [11] for $\rho > 0$ $(\delta > \gamma)$ with h strongly concave-convex. (There is a mistake in the proof of Proposition 2' of [11] which invalidates the assertions made in the article about the complementary manifold of Hamiltonian trajectories <u>diverging</u> from (k^*,q^*) at $t = -\infty$ when $\rho > 0$, but this does not affect the main results, which concern the trajectories converging to (k^*,q^*).) In the case of $\rho = 0$, "optimality" must be interpreted in a certain relative sense. For $\rho > 0$, it is necessary to limit attention in (1) to trajectories k(t) which do not grow at a rate faster than ρ. It must also be supposed that ρ is not too large.

The complications involved in establishing "true" optimality of some sort, and the serious restrictions on the nature of h and ρ that are entailed, bring one to the view that "optimality" over $[0,\infty)$ may not be the natural concept to be aiming at in models like (1). The justification usually given for the infinite horizon is that it enables one to avoid the selection of a particular terminal time τ and the awkward decision about what the levels of goods or prices should be at that time. However, there are other ways of avoiding this dilemma.

For example, one could consider for each time τ the trajectories k(t) that would solve (1) with ∞ replaced by τ (no constraint being imposed on $k(\tau)$) and then see what trajectories these converge to as $\tau\to\infty$. Such limit trajectories would be a natural object of study. They would again be "piecewise optimal", but not necessarily optimal in any sense with respect to the integral (1) over $[0,\infty)$ (which anyway might not be well defined). There is reason to believe that this is the desired class of trajectories that exhibits the dynamic saddle point behavior (approach a rest point as $t\to\infty$) in the many cases where the Hamiltonian system has such behavior and yet "optimality over $[0,\infty)$" cannot be established.

<u>Convex Processes.</u> The subject of discussion is related more closely than might be supposed to the theory of economic models in which the evolution of the state X(t) (a vector of goods, resources, labor, etc.) is governed by $(X(t),\dot{X}(t)) \in T$, where T is a nonempty closed convex set in $R^N \times R^N$. In such a setting there is no real loss of generality (and

considerable advantage) in taking T to be a cone and writing the dynamics in the form

(18) $\dot{X}(t) \in A(X(t))$.

Since the graph of the multifunction A is a closed convex cone containing the origin, A is called a closed convex process. The general theory of convex processes has been developed in [5, §39]; for the special "monotone" and "polyhedral" cases, see [12] and [13], respectively. Convex processes play a large role in the 1973 book of Makarov and Rubinov on economic dynamics (translated 1977 by Springer-Verlag [14]).

If we associate with A the convex function

(19) $$L(X,V) := \begin{cases} 0 \text{ if } V \in A(X), \\ +\infty \text{ if } V \notin A(X), \end{cases}$$

the problem (3) appears rather degenerate. Indeed, one has

(20) $$\int_{t_0}^{t_1} L(X(t),\dot{X}(t))dt = \begin{cases} 0 \text{ if } X \text{ satisfies (18)} \\ +\infty \text{ otherwise} \end{cases} .$$

Nevertheless, the corresponding Hamiltonian system is very interesting. The Hamiltonian function is

(21) $$H(X,P) := \sup_{V \in A(X)} P.V .$$

This is not only concave in X and convex in P but positively homogeneous in each of these variables separately. For each $P \in R^N$, let

(22) $$A^*(P) := \{W | W.X \geq P.V, \forall X, V \in A(X)\}.$$

(The multifunction A^* is the closed convex process adjoint to A.) The Hamiltonian condition

(23) $$\dot{\bar{X}}(t) \in \partial_P H(\bar{X}(t),\bar{P}(t)), \quad -\dot{\bar{P}}(t) \in \partial_X H(\bar{X}(t),\bar{P}(t)),$$

is then equivalent to

$$\sup\{\bar{P}(t).V \mid V \in A(\bar{X}(t))\} \text{ attained at } \dot{\bar{X}}(t),$$

(24)

$$\inf\{W.X(t) \mid W \in A^*(\bar{P}(t))\} \text{ attained at } -\dot{\bar{P}}(t).$$

It can also be written simply as

$$\text{(25)} \qquad \dot{\bar{X}}(t) \in A(\bar{X}(t)),\ -\dot{\bar{P}}(t) \in A^*(\bar{P}(t)),$$

$$\bar{P}(t).\dot{\bar{X}}(t) \equiv -\dot{\bar{P}}(t).\bar{X}(t).$$

Observe that the last relation is equivalent to

$$\text{(26)} \qquad \bar{X}(t).\bar{P}(t) \equiv \text{const.}$$

Trajectories $\bar{X}(t)$ which satisfy (25) for some $\bar{P}(t) \not\equiv 0$ are said to be price-supported or competitive. It is remarkable that such trajectories and their "supports" can be generated by solving the ordinary differential "equation" (23) from arbitrary initial points (X_0,P_0) inside the region where H is finite, just as with the Hamiltonian systems discussed earlier [6],[7].

The origin (0,0) is always a rest point of (23), but it usually lies on the boundary of the region where H is finite. A more promising class of points for study is obtained through change of variables. Setting

$$\text{(27)} \qquad \bar{K}(t) := e^{-\gamma t}\bar{X}(t),\ \bar{Q}(t) := e^{\delta t}\,\bar{P}(t),$$

for arbitrary real numbers γ and δ, one can express the Hamiltonian condition in the form

$$\dot{\bar{K}}(t) \in \partial_P H(\bar{K}(t),\bar{Q}(t))-\gamma\bar{K}(t),$$

(28)

$$-\dot{\bar{Q}}(t) \in \partial_X H(\bar{K}(t),\bar{Q}(t))-\delta\bar{Q}(t),$$

or equivalently

$$\dot{\bar{K}}(t)+\gamma\bar{K}(t) \in A(\bar{K}(t)),\ -\dot{\bar{Q}}(t)+\delta\bar{Q}(t) \in A^*(\bar{Q}(t)),$$

(29)

$$\bar{Q}(t).(\dot{\bar{K}}(t)+\gamma\bar{K}(t)) = (-\dot{\bar{Q}}(t)+\delta\bar{Q}(t)).\bar{K}(t).$$

(This transformation makes use of the homogeneity of H.) A rest point

(K^*, Q^*) of the transformed system is characterized by the relations

$$\gamma K^* \in A(K^*),\ \delta Q^* \in A^*(Q^*),$$

(30)

$$0 = (\delta-\gamma)K^*.Q^* = \rho K^*.Q^*$$

(where (9) is used now as the definition of ρ).
The study of the vectors K^* and Q^* satisfying (3) for various choices of γ and δ amounts to the generalized eigenvalue theory for the process A and its adjoint. In the case of A "monotone", it is closely related to the theory of growth and interest rates for the Gale-Von Neumann model (cf. [12], [13], [14]). Presumably the dynamic system (28) should exhibit a kind of "turnpike" behavior around rest points (K^*,Q^*) in (30) for which $K^*.Q^* \neq 0$ (implying $\delta = \gamma$), or in other words, such that (K^*,Q^*) is a "nondegenerate" minimax saddle point for the concave-convex function

$$\phi_\lambda(K,Q) := H(K,Q) - \lambda K.Q \quad (\lambda = \delta = \gamma).$$

It would be interesting to see this worked out in detail, which has not yet been done. The "turnpike" behavior should correspond to the geometric picture of a dynamic saddle point.

In fact, the theory of the inhomogeneous Hamiltonian system (12) can be recast to fit the mold of a homogeneous system associated with a closed convex process A. Consider a decomposition $R^N = R \times R^n \times R$ with corresponding notation

(31) $$X = (x_\ell, x, x_c),\ P = (p_\ell, p, p_c).$$

Let the graph of A be the closure of the set of all pairs

$$(X,V) = (x_\ell, x, x_c, v_\ell, v, v_c)$$

such that

(32) $$x_\ell > 0,\ v_c \leqq x_\ell U(x/x_\ell, v/x_\ell) + \delta x_c,\ \ v_\ell = \gamma x_\ell.$$

The graph of the adjoint A^* is then the closure of the set of all pairs

$$(P,S) = (p_\ell, p, p_c, s_\ell, s, s_c)$$

such that

(33) $$p_c > 0,\ s_\ell \geqq p_c V(p/p_c, -s/p_c) + \gamma p_\ell,\ s_c = \delta p_c,$$

where V is the convex function in (14). The corresponding Hamiltonian is

(34) $$H(X,P) = x_\ell p_c h(x/x_\ell, p/p_c) + \gamma x_\ell p_\ell + \delta x_c p_c$$

$$\text{for } x_\ell > 0,\ p_\ell > 0,$$

where h is given by (10). (For $x_\ell = 0$ or $p_\ell = 0$, the values of H are obtained from (34) by a limit process; for $x_\ell < 0$ or $p_\ell < 0$, the values of H are infinite.)

The dynamical relation $\dot{X} \in A(X)$ reduces under (32) to

(35)
$$x_\ell(t) = \alpha e^{\gamma t} \quad (\alpha > 0)$$
$$\dot{x}_c(t) \leqq \alpha e^{\gamma t} U(e^{-\gamma t} x(t)/\alpha, e^{-\gamma t}\dot{x}(t)/\alpha) + \delta x_c(t).$$

The interpretation is that x_ℓ represents a basic factor that grows at a constant rate γ (positive, negative or zero!); the parameter α merely sets the scale and can just as well be chosen as 1. The variable x_c measures "utility satisfaction" and is typically negative; it would grow (more negative) at the rate δ if this tendency were not counteracted by continual inputs of utility dependent on the vectors x/x_ℓ and $\dot{x}/x_\ell$ (quantities of goods per unit of the basic factor). Similarly, the dual dynamical relation $-\dot{P} \in A^*(P)$ reduces under (33) to

(36)
$$p_c(t) = \beta e^{-\delta t} \quad (\beta > 0)$$
$$-\dot{p}_\ell(t) \geqq \beta e^{-\delta t} V(e^{\delta t} p(t)/\beta, e^{\delta t}\dot{p}(t)/\beta) + \gamma p_\ell(t).$$

Again β is just a scale parameter that can be taken as 1.

The Hamiltonian system (23) for the function (34) takes on a particularly simple form when expressed equivalently as in (28) in terms of

$$(\bar{k}_\ell(t), \bar{k}(t), \bar{k}_c(t)) = e^{-\gamma t}(\bar{x}_\ell(t), \bar{x}(t), \bar{x}_c(t)),$$

$$(\bar{q}_\ell(t), \bar{q}(t), \bar{q}_c(t)) = e^{\delta t}(\bar{p}_\ell(t), \bar{p}(t), \bar{p}_c(t)),$$

namely:

$$\bar{k}_\ell(t) \equiv \alpha, \quad \bar{q}_c(t) \equiv \beta,$$

$$\dot{\bar{k}}(t) \in \alpha\partial_q h(\bar{k}(t)/\alpha, \bar{q}(t)/\beta) - \gamma\bar{k}(t)$$

(37) $$-\dot{\bar{q}}(t) \in \beta\partial_k h(\bar{k}(t)/\alpha, \bar{q}(t)/\beta) - \delta\bar{q}(t)$$

$$\dot{\bar{k}}_c(t) = \alpha U(\bar{k}(t)/\alpha, [\dot{\bar{k}}(t) + \gamma\bar{k}(t)]/\alpha) + \rho\bar{k}_c(t)$$

$$-\dot{\bar{q}}_\ell(t) = \beta V(\bar{q}(t)/\beta, [\dot{\bar{q}}(t) - \delta\bar{q}(t)]/\beta) - \rho\bar{q}_\ell(t).$$

Taking $\alpha = 1 = \beta$, one can write this as the previous system (12) for h, augmented by the equations (for all $\tau > 0$):

(38) $$\bar{k}_c(\tau) = e^{\rho\tau}[\bar{k}_c(0) + \int_0^\tau e^{-\rho t}\, U(\bar{k}(t), \dot{\bar{k}}(t) + \gamma\bar{k}(t))dt],$$
$$\bar{q}_\ell(\tau) = e^{\rho\tau}[\bar{q}_\ell(0) - \int_0^\tau e^{-\rho t}\, V(\bar{q}(t), \dot{\bar{q}}(t) - \delta\bar{q}(t))dt].$$

This demonstrates that the inhomogeneous system (12) can indeed be treated in terms of a special case of the homogeneous system (28). The analysis of rest points carries over at the same time. As a matter of fact, for the convex process A in question, a vector pair

(39) $$K^* = (1, k^*, k_c^*), \quad Q^* = (q_\ell^*, q^*, 1),$$

is a rest point for (28) (i.e. satisfies (30)) if and only if (k^*, q^*) is a rest point for (12) and (from (37))

(40) $$\rho k_c^* = -U(k^*, \gamma k^*), \quad \rho q_\ell^* = V(q^*, -\delta q^*).$$

Of course, due to the special way the numbers γ and δ enter the definition of A, they are then unique values for which (30) has a solution $K^* \neq 0$, $Q^* \neq 0$.

It is interesting to note that the rest points (K^*, Q^*) just described necessarily have $K^*.Q^* = 0$, however. Despite this, the analysis of the homogeneous system around (K^*,Q^*) is important, because it corresponds to the inhomogeneous system. Thus one apparently should not, in the general study of (28), limit attention to rest points (30) such that $K^*.Q^* \neq 0$.

REFERENCES

[1] R.T. Rockafellar, "Conjugate, convex functions in optimal control and the calculus of variations", Journal of Mathematical Analysis and Applications, 32 (1970), 174-222.

[2] ——————, "Existence and duality theorems for convex problems of Bolza", Transactions American Mathematical Society, 159 (1971), 1-40.

[3] ——————, "Dual problems of Lagrange for arcs of bounded variation", in Calculus of Variations and Control Theory (Academic Press, 1976), 155-192.

[4] ——————, "Integral functionals, normal integrands and measurable selections", in Nonlinear Operators and the Calculus of Variations, Bruxelles 1975 (Springer-Verlag Lecture Notes in Math., no. 543, 1976), 157-207.

[5] ——————, Convex Analysis, Princeton University Press, 1970.

[6] C. Castaing, "Sur les équations différentielles multivoques", Comptes Rendus de l'Académie de Science, Paris 263 (1966), 63-66.

[7] R.T. Rockafellar, "Generalized Hamiltonian equations for convex problems of Lagrange", Pacific Journal of Mathematics, 33 (1970), 411-427.

[8] D. Cass and K. Shell, "Introduction to Hamiltonian dynamics in economics", Journal of Economic Theory, 12 (1976), 1-10.

[9] D. Cass and K. Shell, "The structure and stability of competitive dynamical systems", Journal of Economic Theory, 12 (1976), 31-70.

[10] R.T. Rockafellar, "Saddle points of Hamiltonian systems in convex problems of Lagrange", Journal of Optimization Theory and Applications, 12 (1973), 367-390)

[11] ————————, "Saddle points of Hamiltonian systems in convex Lagrange problems having a nonzero discount rate", Journal of Economic Theory 12 (1976), 71-113.

[12] ————————, Monotone Processes of Convex and Concave Type, Memoir No. 77 of the American Mathematical Society (1967).

[13] ————————, "Convex algebra and duality in dynamic models of production", in Mathematical Models in Economics (J. Łoś and M.W. Łoś, editors; Noth-Holland, 1974), 351-778.

[14] V.L. Makarov and A.M. Rubinov, Mathematical Theory of Economic Dynamics and Equilibria, Springer Verlag, 1977.

DEPARTMENT OF MATHEMATICS
UNIVERSITY OF WASHINGTON
SEATTLE, WA 98195, U.S.A.

. 59: J. A. Hanson, Growth in Open Economies. V, 128 pages. 71.

. 60: H. Hauptmann, Schätz- und Kontrolltheorie in stetigen namischen Wirtschaftsmodellen. V, 104 Seiten. 1971.

. 61: K. H. F. Meyer, Wartesysteme mit variabler Bearbeitungse. VII, 314 Seiten. 1971.

. 62: W. Krelle u. G. Gabisch unter Mitarbeit von J. Burgerister, Wachstumstheorie. VII, 223 Seiten. 1972.

l. 63: J. Kohlas, Monte Carlo Simulation im Operations Rearch. VI, 162 Seiten. 1972.

l. 64: P. Gessner u. K. Spremann, Optimierung in Funktionenmen. IV, 120 Seiten. 1972.

l. 65: W. Everling, Exercises in Computer Systems Analysis. I, 184 pages. 1972.

l. 66: F. Bauer, P. Garabedian and D. Korn, Supercritical Wing ctions. V, 211 pages. 1972.

l. 67: I. V. Girsanov, Lectures on Mathematical Theory of tremum Problems. V, 136 pages. 1972.

l. 68: J. Loeckx, Computability and Decidability. An Introduction Students of Computer Science. VI, 76 pages. 1972.

l. 69: S. Ashour, Sequencing Theory. V, 133 pages. 1972.

l. 70: J. P. Brown, The Economic Effects of Floods. Investigans of a Stochastic Model of Rational Investment. Behavior in the ce of Floods. V, 87 pages. 1972.

l. 71: R. Henn und O. Opitz, Konsum- und Produktionstheorie II. 134 Seiten. 1972.

l. 72: T. P. Bagchi and J. G. C. Templeton, Numerical Methods in arkov Chains and Bulk Queues. XI, 89 pages. 1972.

l. 73: H. Kiendl, Suboptimale Regler mit abschnittweise linearer ruktur. VI, 146 Seiten. 1972.

l. 74: F. Pokropp, Aggregation von Produktionsfunktionen. VI, 7 Seiten. 1972.

l. 75: GI-Gesellschaft für Informatik e.V. Bericht Nr. 3. 1. Fachgung über Programmiersprachen · München, 9.–11. März 1971. erausgegeben im Auftrag der Gesellschaft für Informatik von H. ngmaack und M. Paul. VII, 280 Seiten. 1972.

l. 76: G. Fandel, Optimale Entscheidung bei mehrfacher Zieltzung. II, 121 Seiten. 1972.

ol. 77: A. Auslender, Problèmes de Minimax via l'Analyse Conexe et les Inégalités Variationelles: Théorie et Algorithmes. VII, 32 pages. 1972.

ol. 78: GI-Gesellschaft für Informatik e.V. 2. Jahrestagung, Karlshe, 2.–4. Oktober 1972. Herausgegeben im Auftrag der Gesellhaft für Informatik von P. Deussen. XI, 576 Seiten. 1973.

l. 79: A. Berman, Cones, Matrices and Mathematical Programng. V, 96 pages. 1973.

l. 80: International Seminar on Trends in Mathematical Modelg, Venice, 13–18 December 1971. Edited by N. Hawkes. VI, 8 pages. 1973.

l. 81: Advanced Course on Software Engineering. Edited by L. Bauer. XII, 545 pages. 1973.

l. 82: R. Saeks, Resolution Space, Operators and Systems. X, 7 pages. 1973.

l. 83: NTG/GI-Gesellschaft für Informatik, Nachrichtentechsche Gesellschaft. Fachtagung „Cognitive Verfahren und Syeme", Hamburg, 11.–13. April 1973. Herausgegeben im Auftrag r NTG/GI von Th. Einsele, W. Giloi und H.-H. Nagel. VIII, 373 iten. 1973.

l. 84: A. V. Balakrishnan, Stochastic Differential Systems I. tering and Control. A Function Space Approach. V, 252 pages. 73.

l. 85: T. Page, Economics of Involuntary Transfers: A Unified proach to Pollution and Congestion Externalities. XI, 159 pages. 73.

Vol. 86: Symposium on the Theory of Scheduling and its Applications. Edited by S. E. Elmaghraby. VIII, 437 pages. 1973.

Vol. 87: G. F. Newell, Approximate Stochastic Behavior of n-Server Service Systems with Large n. VII, 118 pages. 1973.

Vol. 88: H. Steckhan, Güterströme in Netzen. VII, 134 Seiten. 1973.

Vol. 89: J. P. Wallace and A. Sherret, Estimation of Product. Attributes and Their Importances. V, 94 pages. 1973.

Vol. 90: J.-F. Richard, Posterior and Predictive Densities for Simultaneous Equation Models. VI, 226 pages. 1973.

Vol. 91: Th. Marschak and R. Selten, General Equilibrium with Price-Making Firms. XI, 246 pages. 1974.

Vol. 92: E. Dierker, Topological Methods in Walrasian Economics. IV, 130 pages. 1974.

Vol. 93: 4th IFAC/IFIP International Conference on Digital Computer Applications to Process Control, Part I. Zürich/Switzerland, March 19–22, 1974. Edited by M. Mansour and W. Schaufelberger. XVIII, 544 pages. 1974.

Vol. 94: 4th IFAC/IFIP International Conference on Digital Computer Applications to Process Control, Part II. Zürich/Switzerland, March 19–22, 1974. Edited by M. Mansour and W. Schaufelberger. XVIII, 546 pages. 1974.

Vol. 95: M. Zeleny, Linear Multiobjective Programming. X, 220 pages. 1974.

Vol. 96: O. Moeschlin, Zur Theorie von Neumannscher Wachstumsmodelle. XI, 115 Seiten. 1974.

Vol. 97: G. Schmidt, Über die Stabilität des einfachen Bedienungskanals. VII, 147 Seiten. 1974.

Vol. 98: Mathematical Methods in Queueing Theory. Proceedings 1973. Edited by A. B. Clarke. VII, 374 pages. 1974.

Vol. 99: Production Theory. Edited by W. Eichhorn, R. Henn, O. Opitz, and R. W. Shephard. VIII, 386 pages. 1974.

Vol. 100: B. S. Duran and P. L. Odell, Cluster Analysis. A Survey. VI, 137 pages. 1974.

Vol. 101: W. M. Wonham, Linear Multivariable Control. A Geometric Approach. X, 344 pages. 1974.

Vol. 102: Analyse Convexe et Ses Applications. Comptes Rendus, Janvier 1974. Edited by J.-P. Aubin. IV, 244 pages. 1974.

Vol. 103: D. E. Boyce, A. Farhi, R. Weischedel, Optimal Subset Selection. Multiple Regression, Interdependence and Optimal Network Algorithms. XIII, 187 pages. 1974.

Vol. 104: S. Fujino, A Neo-Keynesian Theory of Inflation and Economic Growth. V, 96 pages. 1974.

Vol. 105: Optimal Control Theory and its Applications. Part I. Proceedings 1973. Edited by B. J. Kirby. VI, 425 pages. 1974.

Vol. 106: Optimal Control Theory and its Applications. Part II. Proceedings 1973. Edited by B. J. Kirby. VI, 403 pages. 1974.

Vol. 107: Control Theory, Numerical Methods and Computer Systems Modeling. International Symposium, Rocquencourt, June 17–21, 1974. Edited by A. Bensoussan and J. L. Lions. VIII, 757 pages. 1975.

Vol. 108: F. Bauer et al., Supercritical Wing Sections II. A Handbook. V, 296 pages. 1975.

Vol. 109: R. von Randow, Introduction to the Theory of Matroids. IX, 102 pages. 1975.

Vol. 110: C. Striebel, Optimal Control of Discrete Time Stochastic Systems. III. 208 pages. 1975.

Vol. 111: Variable Structure Systems with Application to Economics and Biology. Proceedings 1974. Edited by A. Ruberti and R. R. Mohler. VI, 321 pages. 1975.

Vol. 112: J. Wilhelm, Objectives and Multi-Objective Decision Making Under Uncertainty. IV, 111 pages. 1975.

Vol. 113: G. A. Aschinger, Stabilitätsaussagen über Klassen von Matrizen mit verschwindenden Zeilensummen. V, 102 Seiten. 1975.

Vol. 114: G. Uebe, Produktionstheorie. XVII, 301 Seiten. 1976.

Vol. 115: Anderson et al., Foundations of System Theory: Finitary and Infinitary Conditions. VII, 93 pages. 1976

Vol. 116: K. Miyazawa, Input-Output Analysis and the Structure of Income Distribution. IX, 135 pages. 1976.

Vol. 117: Optimization and Operations Research. Proceedings 1975. Edited by W. Oettli and K. Ritter. IV, 316 pages. 1976.

Vol. 118: Traffic Equilibrium Methods, Proceedings 1974. Edited by M. A. Florian. XXIII, 432 pages. 1976.

Vol. 119: Inflation in Small Countries. Proceedings 1974. Edited by H. Frisch. VI, 356 pages. 1976.

Vol. 120: G. Hasenkamp, Specification and Estimation of Multiple-Output Production Functions. VII, 151 pages. 1976.

Vol. 121: J. W. Cohen, On Regenerative Processes in Queueing Theory. IX, 93 pages. 1976.

Vol. 122: M. S. Bazaraa, and C. M. Shetty,Foundations of Optimization VI. 193 pages. 1976

Vol. 123: Multiple Criteria Decision Making. Kyoto 1975. Edited by M. Zeleny. XXVII, 345 pages. 1976.

Vol. 124: M. J. Todd. The Computation of Fixed Points and Applications. VII, 129 pages. 1976.

Vol. 125: Karl C. Mosler. Optimale Transportnetze. Zur Bestimmung ihres kostengünstigsten Standorts bei gegebener Nachfrage. VI, 142 Seiten. 1976.

Vol. 126: Energy, Regional Science and Public Policy. Energy and Environment I. Proceedings 1975. Edited by M. Chatterji and P. Van Rompuy. VIII, 316 pages. 1976.

Vol. 127: Environment, Regional Science and Interregional Modeling. Energy and Environment II. Proceedings 1975. Edited by M. Chatterji and P. Van Rompuy. IX, 211 pages. 1976.

Vol. 128: Integer Programming and Related Areas. A Classified Bibliography. Edited by C. Kastning. XII, 495 pages. 1976.

Vol. 129: H.-J. Lüthi, Komplementaritäts- und Fixpunktalgorithmen in der mathematischen Programmierung. Spieltheorie und Ökonomie. VII, 145 Seiten. 1976.

Vol. 130: Multiple Criteria Decision Making, Jouy-en-Josas, France. Proceedings 1975. Edited by H. Thiriez and S. Zionts. VI, 409 pages. 1976.

Vol. 131: Mathematical Systems Theory. Proceedings 1975. Edited by G. Marchesini and S. K. Mitter. X, 408 pages. 1976.

Vol. 132: U. H. Funke, Mathematical Models in Marketing. A Collection of Abstracts. XX, 514 pages. 1976.

Vol. 133: Warsaw Fall Seminars in Mathematical Economics 1975. Edited by M. W. Loś, J. Loś, and A. Wieczorek. V. 159 pages. 1976.

Vol. 134: Computing Methods in Applied Sciences and Engineering. Proceedings 1975. VIII, 390 pages. 1976.

Vol. 135: H. Haga, A Disequilibrium – Equilibrium Model with Money and Bonds. A Keynesian – Walrasian Synthesis. VI, 119 pages. 1976.

Vol. 136: E. Kofler und G. Menges, Entscheidungen bei unvollständiger Information. XII, 357 Seiten. 1976.

Vol. 137: R. Wets, Grundlagen Konvexer Optimierung. VI, 146 Seiten. 1976.

Vol. 138: K. Okuguchi, Expectations and Stability in Oligopoly Models. VI, 103 pages. 1976.

Vol. 139: Production Theory and Its Applications. Proceedings. Edited by H. Albach and G. Bergendahl. VIII, 193 pages. 1977.

Vol. 140: W. Eichhorn and J. Voeller, Theory of the Price Index. Fisher's Test Approach and Generalizations. VII, 95 pages. 1976.

Vol. 141: Mathematical Economics and Game Theory. Essays in Honor of Oskar Morgenstern. Edited by R. Henn and O. Moeschlin. XIV, 703 pages. 1977.

Vol. 142: J. S. Lane, On Optimal Population Paths. V, 123 pages. 1977.

Vol. 143: B. Näslund, An Analysis of Economic Size Distributions. XV, 100 pages. 1977.

Vol. 144: Convex Analysis and Its Applications. Proceedings 1976. Edited by A. Auslender. VI, 219 pages. 1977.

Vol. 145: J. Rosenmüller, Extreme Games and Their Solutions 126 pages. 1977.

Vol. 146: In Search of Economic Indicators. Edited by W. H. Str XVI, 198 pages. 1977.

Vol. 147: Resource Allocation and Division of Space. Proceedi Edited by T. Fujii and R. Sato. VIII, 184 pages. 1977.

Vol. 148: C. E. Mandl, Simulationstechnik und Simulationsmod in den Sozial- und Wirtschaftswissenschaften. IX, 173 Seiten. 19

Vol. 149: Stationäre und schrumpfende Bevölkerungen: Demo phisches Null- und Negativwachstum in Österreich. Herausgege von G. Feichtinger. VI, 262 Seiten. 1977.

Vol. 150: Bauer et al., Supercritical Wing Sections III. VI, 179 pa 1977.

Vol. 151: C. A. Schneeweiß, Inventory-Production Theory. VI, 116 pa 1977.

Vol. 152: Kirsch et al., Notwendige Optimalitätsbedingungen ihre Anwendung. VI, 157 Seiten. 1978.

Vol. 153: Kombinatorische Entscheidungsprobleme: Methoden Anwendungen. Herausgegeben von T. M. Liebling und M. Röss VIII, 206 Seiten. 1978.

Vol. 154: Problems and Instruments of Business Cycle Analy Proceedings 1977. Edited by W. H. Strigel. VI, 442 pages. 19

Vol. 155: Multiple Criteria Problem Solving. Proceedings 1977. Ed by S. Zionts. VIII, 567 pages. 1978.

Vol. 156: B. Näslund and B. Sellstedt, Neo-Ricardian Theory. W Applications to Some Current Economic Problems. VI, 165 pa 1978.

Vol. 157: Optimization and Operations Research. Proceedings 19 Edited by R. Henn, B. Korte, and W. Oettli. VI, 270 pages. 19

Vol. 158: L. J. Cherene, Set Valued Dynamical Systems and Econ Flow. VIII, 83 pages. 1978.

Vol. 159: Some Aspects of the Foundations of General Equilibr Theory: The Posthumous Papers of Peter J. Kalman. Edited by J. Gr VI, 167 pages. 1978.

Vol. 160: Integer Programming and Related Areas. A Classi Bibliography. Edited by D. Hausmann. XIV, 314 pages. 1978.

Vol. 161: M. J. Beckmann, Rank in Organizations. VIII, 164 pages. 19

Vol. 162: Recent Developments in Variable Structure Systems, E nomics and Biology. Proceedings 1977. Edited by R. R. Mohler A. Ruberti. VI, 326 pages. 1978.

Vol. 163: G. Fandel, Optimale Entscheidungen in Organisatio VI, 143 Seiten. 1979.

Vol. 164: C. L. Hwang and A. S. M. Masud, Multiple Objective cision Making – Methods and Applications. A State-of-the-Art Sur XII, 351 pages. 1979.

Vol. 165: A. Maravall, Identification in Dynamic Shock-Error Mod VIII, 158 pages. 1979.

Vol. 166: R. Cuninghame-Green, Minimax Algebra. XI, 258 pa 1979.

Vol. 167: M. Faber, Introduction to Modern Austrian Capital The X, 196 pages. 1979.

Vol. 168: Convex Analysis and Mathematical Economics. Proceed 1978. Edited by J. Kriens. V, 136 pages. 1979.